THE MAKING OF M(
CHILDREN'S LITERATUR

Lucy Pearson's lively and engaging book examines British children's literature during the period widely regarded as a 'second golden age'. Drawing extensively on archival material, Pearson investigates the practical and ideological factors that shaped ideas of 'good' children's literature in Britain, with particular attention to children's book publishing. Pearson begins with a critical overview of the discourse surrounding children's literature during the 1960s and 1970s, summarizing the main critical debates in the context of the broader social conversation that took place around children and childhood. The contributions of publishing houses, large and small, to changing ideas about children's literature become apparent as Pearson explores the careers of two enormously influential children's editors: Kaye Webb of Puffin Books and Aidan Chambers of Topliner Macmillan. Brilliant as an innovator of highly successful marketing strategies, Webb played a key role in defining what were, in her words, 'the best in children's books', while Chambers' work as an editor and critic illustrates the pioneering nature of children's publishing during this period. Pearson shows that social investment was a central factor in the formation of this golden age, and identifies its legacies in the modern publishing industry, both positive and negative.

Ashgate Studies in Childhood, 1700 to the Present

Series Editor: Claudia Nelson, Texas A&M University, USA

This series recognizes and supports innovative work on the child and on literature for children and adolescents that informs teaching and engages with current and emerging debates in the field. Proposals are welcome for interdisciplinary and comparative studies by humanities scholars working in a variety of fields, including literature; book history, periodicals history, and print culture and the sociology of texts; theater, film, musicology, and performance studies; history, including the history of education; gender studies; art history and visual culture; cultural studies; and religion.

Topics might include, among other possibilities, how concepts and representations of the child have changed in response to adult concerns; postcolonial and transnational perspectives; "domestic imperialism" and the acculturation of the young within and across class and ethnic lines; the commercialization of childhood and children's bodies; views of young people as consumers and/or originators of culture; the child and religious discourse; children's and adolescents' self-representations; and adults' recollections of childhood.

Also in the series

Representations of China in British Children's Fiction, 1851–1911
Shih-Wen Chen

Contemporary Adolescent Literature and Culture
The Emergent Adult
Edited by Mary Hilton and Maria Nikolajeva

Constructing Girlhood through the Periodical Press, 1850–1915
Kristine Moruzi

The Idea of Nature in Disney Animation
From Snow White *to* WALL-E
David Whitley

Genre, Reception, and Adaptation in the "Twilight" Series
Edited by Anne Morey

The Making of Modern Children's Literature in Britain

Publishing and Criticism in the 1960s and 1970s

LUCY PEARSON

University of Newcastle, UK

Routledge
Taylor & Francis Group

LONDON AND NEW YORK

First published 2013 by Ashgate Publisher

2 Park Square, Milton Park, Abingdon, Oxon OX14 4RN
711 Third Avenue, New York, NY 10017, USA

Routledge is an imprint of the Taylor & Francis Group, an informa business

First issued in paperback 2016

British Library Cataloguing in Publication Data
Pearson, Lucy (Lucy R.)
    The making of modern children's literature in Britain: publishing and criticism in the 1960s and 1970s. – (Ashgate studies in childhood, 1700 to the present)
    1. Children's literature – Publishing – Great Britain – History – 20th century. 2. Children's literature, English – Appreciation – Great Britain – History – 20th century. 3. Webb, Kaye – Influence. 4. Chambers, Aidan – Influence.
    I. Title II. Series
    070.5'083'0941–dc23

The Library of Congress has cataloged the printed edition as follows:
Pearson, Lucy, 1980–
    The making of modern children's literature in Britain: publishing and criticism in the 1960s and 1970s / by Lucy Pearson.
        pages cm.—(Ashgate studies in childhood, 1700 to the present)
    Includes index.
    ISBN 978-1-4094-4341-4 (hardcover: alk. paper)
    1. Children's literature, English—History and criticism. 2. Children's literature, English—Publishing—History—20th century. 3. Publishers and publishing—Great Britain—History—20th century. 4. Webb, Kaye—Chriticism and interpretation. 5. Chambers, Aidan—Criticism and interpretation. 6. Children—Books and reading—Great Britain—History—20th century. 7. Children—Books and reading.
    I. Title.
    PR990.P43 2013
    820.9'92820933—dc22

                                                                          2013003629

ISBN 978-1-4094-4341-4 (hbk)
ISBN 978-1-138-25218-9 (pbk)

For my family.

Contents

Acknowledgements   *ix*

Introduction: Golden Ages   1

1   The Children's Literature Scene   15

2   Kaye Webb and Puffin Books   73

3   Aidan Chambers and Topliner   119

Conclusion: The Making of Modern Children's Literature   169

Appendix: Interview with Aidan Chambers   179

Bibliography   *187*
Index   *211*

Acknowledgements

With thanks to Aidan Chambers, for his encouragement and generous support of the project, and to Seven Stories: the National Centre for Children's Books.

Introduction:
Golden Ages

The second golden age is now.
> —John Rowe Townsend, *Written for Children: An Outline of English Children's Literature* (London: Garnet Miller, 1965), p. 151.

It was the Kaye Webb 'fluence, permeating the whole field, that was so liberating and encouraging. Whatever the Scene is today, most probably you set it.
> —Nicholas Fisk to Kaye Webb, editor of Puffin Books, 12th November 1979

The period 1950 to 1979 is widely regarded as a 'second golden age' of children's literature.[1] A brief survey of the books published during this period is enough to confirm John Rowe Townsend's 1965 claim that 'by the end of the [twentieth] century the great names of the 1950s and 1960s will stand out for all to see': titles such C.S. Lewis's *Chronicles of Narnia* (1950–1956), Roald Dahl's *Charlie and the Chocolate Factory* (1964), Shirley Hughes's *Dogger* (1977) and Richard Adams' *Watership Down* (1972) have been both critically acclaimed and enduringly popular.[2] The influential status of the authors and illustrators who emerged during this period is widely recognised, yet the contributions of the individuals who published these 'modern classics' has been largely overlooked. As Nicholas Fisk's comment on the influence of Puffin editor Kaye Webb makes clear, however, the editors and publishers of this period were integral to the creation of this second golden age. The energy and vision of figures such as Kaye Webb (Puffin), Marni Hodgkin (Macmillan) and Judy Taylor (The Bodley Head) fostered the emergence of new and exciting books for children and established children's publishing as a vibrant and central part of the British publishing industry. While the groundwork for this transformation was laid in the 1950s, it is from 1960 onwards that the most dramatic changes took place in children's publishing. The radical expansion and diversification of children's publishing which took place during the 1960s and 1970s is such that it should be considered a golden age of children's publishing.

The 1960s and 1970s saw a strong political, social and educational focus on childhood and children's literature which created a propitious environment for

---

[1]   See for example Peter Hollindale and Zena Sutherland, 'Internationalism, Fantasy and Realism: 1945–1970' in *Children's Literature: An Illustrated History*, ed. by Peter Hunt (Oxford: Oxford University Press, 1995), 252–88; Peter Hunt, *Children's Literature* (Oxford: Blackwell, 2001), p. 157; Fred Inglis, *The Promise of Happiness: Value and Meaning in Children's Fiction* (Cambridge: Cambridge University Press, 1981), p. 129.

[2]   John Rowe Townsend, *Written for Children: An Outline of English Children's Literature* (London: Garnet Miller, 1965). p. 151.

children's publishing. High levels of social funding helped to provide a buoyant market for children's books in schools and libraries; at the same time, changing ideas about childhood and education brought the concept of a 'good' book for children under increasing scrutiny. Consequently, children's editors were engaged not only in establishing the commercial importance of children's books to the British publishing industry, but also in shaping contemporary debates about what children's literature could or should do. The perception of this period as a second golden age of children's literature means that these debates have had a lasting impact on children's literature in Britain. The editors who engaged in these debates – and who expanded the range and diversity of children's publishing in response – should be considered makers of modern children's literature. Despite their influential contributions, however, children's editors and publishers have been largely overlooked not only by children's literature scholarship, but also in histories of publishing. This book begins to address this neglect with case studies of two very different figures in children's publishing: Kaye Webb, editor of Puffin Books, and Aidan Chambers, a writer and critic who also founded and edited teenage imprint Macmillan Topliner.

Kaye Webb was one of the most prominent and influential figures of the children's literature scene in the 1960s and 1970s. Puffin Books is perhaps the most well-known of all British children's publishing imprints, a fact which owes much to Webb's editorial success. Her tenure at Puffin spans the entirety of this period: she arrived at the imprint in 1961, at a moment when the sense of new possibilities in children's literature had created a desire within Penguin for a more innovative editor. By the time she departed in 1979, not only Puffin but the whole British children's publishing industry had undergone a radical transformation, which she had helped to effect. Her career therefore provides a useful starting point from which to assess the changes which took place during this period. Her prominence within British children's publishing is indicated by the fact that she is one of the few children's editors who is consistently mentioned by name in histories of publishing; it is also borne out by the interviews with publishing figures conducted by Kimberley Reynolds and Nicholas Tucker during the 1990s, in which respondents frequently cite Webb as a leading figure. Furthermore, as Nicholas Fisk's comment indicates, her influence permeated not only the publishing industry, but children's literature scene as a whole: as founder of the Puffin Club for child readers, her name was familiar to thousands of children across Britain and beyond. Although as editor of a paperback list Webb was rarely responsible for commissioning new titles, her energy and enthusiasm for connecting child readers with books shaped some of the essential spirit of the second golden age. At the same time, her success in establishing children's paperback publishing as both lucrative and exciting helped to precipitate a significant shift away from the dominance of the hardback in the children's market, with lasting consequences for the publishing industry.

Kaye Webb's work at Puffin established many key trends in mainstream children's publishing. One important feature of children's publishing in this period, however, was the emergence of smaller imprints which sought to serve particular groups or provide particular types of literature. Macmillan Topliner, which sought to cater to the 'reluctant' teenage reader, exemplifies this trend. Editor Aidan

Chambers was an influential critic, educationalist and author: his work at Topliner provides a particularly clear example of the way in which educational and critical debates were manifested in publishing endeavours. Although Topliner was a small and relatively short-lived imprint, Chambers' critical work and the rich research resources afforded by archival material relating to Macmillan Topliner make it possible to assemble a vivid picture of the connections between children's publishing and the changing critical discourse. Aidan Chambers himself also exemplifies the changing demographic of children's publishing itself: as a young man in the 1960s, he was part of a generation who were bringing new perspectives to the world of children's books.

In focusing on these two editors, this book necessarily passes lightly over the contributions of other key publishing figures, such as Grace Hogarth of Constable, Marni Hogkin at Macmillan and Judy Taylor at the Bodley Head. Nevertheless, Kaye Webb and Aidan Chambers typify many characteristic elements of British children's publishing during the 1960s and 1970s. By situating the publishing practices of these two contrasting editors and imprints within the broader context of the period, it is possible to identify some key contributions to the making of modern children's literature.

A Golden Age of Children's Publishing

John Rowe Townsend's 1965 assertion 'The second golden age is now' reflects the fact that this period was characterised by a new sense of excitement and possibility. This perception was partly fuelled by a dramatic expansion in children's publishing following a period of quiescence. Prior to the 1960s, British children's publishing was relatively limited in scope. The publishing industry had suffered a severe loss of expertise and materials as a consequence of two world wars, dramatically limiting the number of titles which could be produced, and children's publishing had been particularly severely affected. As a consequence, children's imprints were few: Kimberley Reynolds is mistaken when she states that 'there was not a single specialist publisher for children' by the end of the Second World War, but Brockhampton Press, established in 1940, is the only identifiable exception.[3] Moreover, the children's imprints then in existence were moderate in their output: Puffin Books, the only children's paperback imprint of note from its establishment in 1940 until the beginning of the 1960s, published on average only 12 new titles per year.[4]

From 1960 onwards, this situation was dramatically reversed, as children's publishing began to benefit from the social and economic trends emerging out

---

[3]   Kimberley Reynolds, 'Publishing Practices and the Practicalities of Publishing', in *Children's Book Publishing in Britain Since 1945*, ed. by Kimberley Reynolds and Nicholas Tucker (Aldershot: Scolar Press, 1998), 20–41, p. 22. Brockhampton Press had been acquired as part of Matthew Hodder Ltd. by 1970, but the firm retained a discrete identity.

[4]   Sally Gritten, *The Story of Puffin Books* (Harmondsworth: Penguin, 1991), p. 14.

of the post-war era. High levels of social funding for public libraries and schools created a supportive commercial environment for children's publishers as librarians sought to build large and diverse children's collections.[5] Individual consumer power also increased in the post-war years, broadening the potential demographic of book ownership: David Childs notes that despite economic difficulties in the 1960s and 1970s, 'in terms of income, working-class wages [in Britain] had gone up more between 1938 and 1976 than those of many professional people', so that more money was available for luxuries such as books.[6] The influence of earlier educational reforms was also beginning to make itself felt: the grammar system introduced in the 1944 Education Act had broadened access to education, producing a generation 'educated out' of the working class and more focused on the education of their children than their own parents had been. In this buoyant economic context children's publishing flourished: by the mid-1970s almost every mainstream publisher had established a children's list, and Puffin alone was publishing more than a hundred new titles a year.[7] If the 1950s heralded the beginning of a golden age of children's literature, then the 1960s marked the beginning of a golden age of children's publishing.

The increase in the number of books published for children was accompanied by an increase in the quality and variety of children's literature available. The practical exigencies of the two world wars had limited not only the volume of publishing for children, but also its scope. Nicholas Tucker argues that the conservatism and parochialism of the war years was reflected in children's literature: a public appetite for the safe and familiar, combined with publishers' cautious use of limited paper stocks, tended to privilege a small number of popular authors.[8] Although recent studies have begun to rehabilitate some of the titles which date from this period, the perception that the first half of the twentieth century was characterised by unadventurous publishing is evident in much of the critical work written during the 1960s and 1970s.[9] Children's author and critic John Rowe Townsend avers that 'The decade after the [first] war was the dreariest since at least the middle of the nineteenth century', while Frank Eyre, editor of the

---

[5]   Kimberley Reynolds, 'Publishing Practices and the Practicalities of Publishing', p. 27.

[6]   David Childs, *Britain Since 1945: A Political History*, 5th edition (London & New York: Routledge, 2001), p. 206.

[7]   Peter Hunt, *An Introduction to Children's Literature* (Oxford: Oxford University Press, 1994), p. 127; Penguin Books, *Complete Catalogue of the Publications of Penguin Books* (Harmondsworth: Penguin, 1970).

[8]   Nicholas Tucker, 'Setting the Scene' in *Children's Book Publishing in Britain Since 1945*, 1–19, pp. 1–2.

[9]   Some recent studies reassessing British children's literature from the 1920s to the 1940s include Dennis Butts, *Children's Literature and Social Change: Some Case Studies from Barbara Hofland to Philip Pullman* (Cambridge: Lutterworth Press, 2010) and Kimberley Reynolds' Leverhulme funded-research project on 'Modernism, the Left and Progressive Writing for Children 1910–1949', scheduled for publication in 2015.

children's list at the Oxford University Press from 1945 to 1949, states that the period beginning with the Second World War was one of 'intense disappointment to all who are seriously interested in children's reading'.[10] In contrast, the 1960s heralded an intense period of creativity and diversity in children's books which was fostered by children's publishers and editors. At the Oxford University Press, Mabel George recognised the possibilities inherent in photo-lithography and championed innovative picture books such as Brian Wildsmith's *A.B.C.* (1962).[11] Judy Taylor at the Bodley Head was also responsible for innovations in picture book publishing, bringing Maurice Sendak's *Where the Wild Things Are* (1964, UK edition 1967) to Britain, despite the misgivings of some of her colleagues over the controversy it had aroused in the United States.[12] The Bodley Head's 'Books for New Adults', launched in 1969, also drew upon the United States for new material: the list included challenging titles by writers such as Paul Zindel. These patterns were repeated across the industry; as the 1960s progressed, the expansion of children's publishing made it not only possible for publishers to take a chance on new authors and more experimental titles, but also commercially necessary.

New directions for children's books in the 1960s were also precipitated by a changing social context: as the conservatism of the post-war years gave way to radical social, political and cultural change, a demand arose for books which reflected the new realities of British life. The growing popularity of television presented children's literature with new challenges – a situation which has resonance in today's internet era – as both patterns of media consumption and conceptions of childhood shifted. Far from being detrimental, however, this context produced a diverse and exciting children's literature, and the 1960s and 1970s saw the emergence of a host of authors and illustrators now considered to be 'modern classics'. Alan Garner, Susan Cooper, Philippa Pearce and Diana Wynne Jones were among those producing exciting works of fantasy; innovative illustrators such as Brian Wildsmith and Charles Keeping took advantage of the increased scope offered by new printing techniques and high-quality publishing values to produce striking and colourful books; and writers like Bernard Ashley, Gene Kemp and Jan Mark rose to the challenge posed by a changing society and explored the possibilities of realism in children's fiction.[13] The influence of radio

---

[10] John Rowe Townsend, *Written For Children: An Outline of English-language Children's Literature*, 2nd rev. edn (Harmondsworth: Penguin, 1983), p. 163; Frank Eyre, *British Children's Books in the Twentieth Century* (London: Longman, 1971), p. 25.

[11] Judith Graham, 'Picture Books', in *Children's Book Publishing in Britain Since 1945*, 60–85, pp. 65–70.

[12] J.W. Lambert and Michael Ratcliffe, *The Bodley Head: 1887–1987* (London: The Bodley Head, 1987), p. 321.

[13] Charles Butler, *Four British Fantasists: Place and Culture in the Children's Fantasies of Penelope Lively, Alan Garner, Susan Cooper, and Diana Wynne Jones* (Oxford: Children's Literature Association and Scarecrow Press, 2006); Lucy Pearson and Kimberley Reynolds, 'Realism' in *The Routledge Companion to Children's Literature* (London: Routledge, 2010), pp. 63–74.

and television encouraged stylistic innovations: Alan Garner's complex young adult novel *Red Shift* (1973) is a notable example of a text in which the narrative modes of television are employed to striking effect. The parochialism of British children's literature also became less pronounced, as publishers added a wealth of overseas titles to their lists, notably works from America which was enjoying a similar golden age.[14] Faced with changing social mores and competition from a new media environment, children's literature redefined itself in terms which were relevant and exciting.

Developments in the field of children's literature were not confined to the books themselves, but were part of a wider cultural phenomenon. Children's books began to receive critical attention both in the media and in the fields of academia and education. The Federation of Children's Book Groups, founded in 1965 by Anne Wood, aimed to promote enthusiasm for children's literature among parents and other interested lay people, linking book groups across the United Kingdom.[15] A host of new awards appeared, notably the Guardian Award (1967), the Other Award (1975) and the children's book category for the Whitbread Literary Awards (1972).[16] The Whitbread at least nominally placed children's books on an equal footing with literature for adults, although a children's author was not to win the overall prize until Philip Pullman in 2001.

It is notable that children's publishers played an active role in this wider cultural activity. Many children's editors gave speeches and wrote articles on children's literature, contributing actively to public debates. OUP editor Frank Eyre published one of the first major works of criticism, *20th Century Children's Books* (1952), a substantially revised and expanded edition of which subsequently appeared as *British Children's Books in the Twentieth Century* (1971). The founding in 1962 of the Children's Book Circle (CBC), an association of children's editors, illustrates the degree to which those working in the publishing industry saw their roles as extending beyond the boundaries of their own particular lists.[17] The CBC was initiated by Constable editor Grace Hogarth, who had received formal training as a specialist children's editor in the United States and was keen to foster expertise in the British children's publishing industry as a whole. The CBC not only facilitated the exchange of expertise between editors, but concerned itself with the wider world of children's literature; in 1965 the group founded the Eleanor Farjeon

---

[14]   Virginia Haviland, 'A Second Golden Age? In a Time of Flood'. in *Children and Literature: Views and Reviews*, ed. by Virginia Haviland (London: Bodley Head, 1974), 88–97.

[15]   The Federation of Children's Book Groups, 'General Information', *The Federation of Children's Book Groups*, <http://www.fcbg.org.uk/general-information/> [accessed 01/07/09].

[16]   Keith Barker, 'Prize Fighting' in *Children's Book Publishing in Britain Since 1945*, 42–59.

[17]   Kimberley Reynolds, 'Publishing Practices and the Practicalities of Publishing', pp. 29–30; Sue Bradley (ed.), *The British Book Trade: An Oral History* (London: The British Library, 2008), p. 97.

Award, which aimed to recognise 'an outstanding contribution to the world of children's books', celebrating the work of librarians, critics and authors as well as of editors.[18] The work of Kaye Webb at Puffin Books and Aidan Chambers at Topliner – both recipients of the Eleanor Farjeon Award – was characteristic of this trend for editors to be concerned with the broader cultural and social aspects of children's literature. In examining their ideas and ideologies, therefore, this book will map not only their direct influence on the books they published, but also their contributions to children's literature as a broader cultural endeavour.

The Second Golden Age: Defining a Quality Ideal

The characterisation of the 1960s and 1970s as a golden age position it as a benchmark for children's literature. Claims for the existence of a 'third golden age' at the beginning of the new millennium often referred back to the second: publisher Barry Cunningham, whose 'discovery' of J.K. Rowling places him at the centre of some of the most prominent contemporary developments in children's literature, made the connection explicit, arguing, 'This is the real thing … I worked for Puffin in the 70s, which was also considered to be a time full of talent, but there is a much broader span of achievement now.'[19] The tendency to regard the second golden age as a measure of quality is reinforced by the perception that children's literature suffered a decline in the 1980s and early 1990s: recent critics have characterised this period as one in which ideals of 'quality' were subsumed by more commercial motives. Editor Tom Engelhardt argued in 1991 that the decline in funding for libraries towards the end of the 1970s created a vacuum which the fast-growing chain bookstore quickly filled. Access to children's books was no longer primarily mediated by the librarian or teacher. As a consequence, Engelhardt suggested, 'a quite different form of children's book was born – the book designed for the consumer child'.[20] Jack Zipes reiterates Engelhardt's claims, arguing that

> To attract children and adults as consumers of literature, the very nature of the book – its design and contents – began to change. Gradually, books began to be produced basically to sell and resell themselves and to make readers into consumers of brand names.[21]

---

[18]   Children's Book Circle, 'Eleanor Farjeon Award', *Children's Book Circle*, <http://www.childrensbookcircle.org.uk/farjeon.asp> [accessed 03/07/09].

[19]   Barry Cunningham, founder of children's publishing company The Chicken House, quoted in Dina Rabinovitch, 'The greatest stories ever told', *The Guardian*, 31 March 2005, <http://books.guardian.co.uk/news/articles/0,6109,1448965,00.html> [accessed 29/04/07].

[20]   Tom Engelhardt, 'Reading May Be Harmful To Your Kids: In the Nadirland of Today's Children's Books', *Harper's Magazine*, June 1991, pp. 55–62, p. 57.

[21]   Jack Zipes, 'The Cultural Homogenization of American Children' in *Sticks and Stones: The Troublesome Success of Children's Literature from Slovenly Peter to Harry Potter* (London: Routledge, 2000), 1–23, p. 6.

Although Zipes' and Engelhardt's analyses are focused on the American market, similar trends were at work in Britain. It is telling that while the commercial success of children's publishing in the United Kingdom extended well into the 1980s – Sally Gritten notes that by 1983 Puffin accounted for a third of Penguin's overall market share – this period is widely seen as a break with what had gone before.[22]

By contrast with the 1980s and 1990s, the relative lack of commercialism in the children's publishing industry of the 1960s and 1970s is held up as a 'purer' model for children's literature. According to Nadia Crandall, in the 1960s, 'Making a profit was almost secondary to a stated intention to produce well-written, high-quality books that reflected the middle-class mores of their authors, editors and readers'.[23] A commitment to 'quality' rather than profit is certainly a central theme in publishers' own definitions of their aims during this period. Kaye Webb's avowed adherence to the slogan 'Puffins for the best in children's reading' is characteristic of the accounts given by editors interviewed by Kimberley Reynolds and Nicholas Tucker in 1995, all of whom reiterated their desire to publish the 'best' rather than the 'best-selling' children's books.[24] While it is hard to imagine a publisher *dis*avowing a commitment to quality, it is clear that those working during this period perceived themselves as not only willing but also able to adhere to an objective standard of 'quality' literature which was not based simply on profit margins.[25] Given the characterisation of the 1960s and 1970s as a golden age which (implicitly) offers a benchmark for children's literature, it is important to evaluate the standards established for 'quality' literature and the basis on which such standards were established.

The concept of the golden age as a period in which publishers were committed to 'the best' in children's books suggests an objective and universally agreed upon standard of quality. In reality, however, the 1960s and 1970s saw a variety of different and often contradictory discourses around children's literature. This discourse reflects a broader social focus on childhood as a whole. Hugh Cunningham argues that the post-war era saw a shift from a focus on the needs and priorities of the adult to those of the child, as parents increasingly began to believe that their children could have better lives than those of previous generations and

---

[22]   Sally Gritten, *The Story of Puffin Books*, p. 27.

[23]   Nadia Crandall, 'The UK Children's Book Business 1995–2004: A Strategic Analysis', *New Review of Children's Literature and Librarianship*, 12:1 (April 2006), 1–18, p. 9.

[24]   Kimberley Reynolds and Nicholas Tucker, 'Interview with Paul Binding (Oxford University Press), 10 March 1997', in *Oral Archives: A Collection of Informal Conversations with Individuals Involved in Creating or Producing Children's Literature since 1945*, compiled by Kimberley Reynolds and Nicholas Tucker (London: Roehampton University, 1998), 57–68; Kimberley Reynolds and Nicholas Tucker, 'Interview with Judy Taylor (The Bodley Head), 21 February 1995', in *Oral Archives*, 332–47.

[25]   Kimberley Reynolds, 'Publishing Practices and the Practicalities of Publishing', p. 30.

so worked to achieve this.[26] This sense of childhood as an important and formative period of life was reflected and reinforced by new ideas about child development, notably the work of British psychiatrists Donald Winnicott and John Bowlby, and of American paediatrician Benjamin Spock, who followed his bestseller *The Pocket Book of Baby and Child-Care* (1946) with a host of other childcare manuals, attaining a dominance in the field of child development which has never been matched.[27] In the United Kingdom, social and political concern with childhood was reflected in successive Education Acts, which sought to improve both the duration and quality of education, legislatively extending the duration of childhood by retaining a large proportion of the adolescent population in school, bringing the new teenage demographic to the attention of those concerned with children's literature.[28] The growing interest in children's literature and the rise in the number of books published for children and young people during the 1960s directly reflect this sense that childhood was a special and important time. Margery Fisher, a critic and reviewer whose survey of children's literature, *Intent upon Reading* (1961), was one of the first major works of criticism in the 1960s, is characteristic in basing her argument for the existence of a separate children's literature on the special nature of the child. Adults have a responsibility to provide children with the 'right' reading material, she argues, because the child's reading is 'so much more thorough, so much more definite in its impact, than the reading of an adult'.[29] This perception that children's literature had an important role to play in a formative period of life is a recurring theme in the critical texts explored in Chapter 1.

Discussions about children's literature in the 1960s and 1970s took place in the context of rapidly changing perceptions of childhood. Despite the lengthening of childhood in the education system, there is evidence of a growing anxiety about the *shortening* of childhood. Educational initiatives served to focus more attention on childhoods which did not fit the idyllic model of the affluent middle-class childhood which had previously dominated public rhetoric, particularly within the world of children's literature. The growing popularity of new media visibly impinged upon the presumed protected space of childhood; when commercial television was proposed in 1954, the Archbishop of York urged in vain for the new initiative to be resisted 'for the sake of our children'.[30] The sense that television and other trends

---

[26] Hugh Cunningham, *The Invention of Childhood* (London: BBC Books, 2006), pp. 214–15.

[27] Henry Jenkins, 'The Sensuous Child: Dr. Benjamin Spock and the Sexual Revolution' in *The Children's Culture Reader*, ed. by Henry Jenkins (New York: New York University Press, 1998), 209–30; Kenneth C. Davis, *Two-Bit Culture: The Paperbacking of America* (Boston: Houghton Mifflin, 1984), pp. 3–11.

[28] David Childs, *Britain Since 1945: A Political History*, pp. 107–89; Marcus Crouch, *Treasure Seekers and Borrowers: Children's Books in Britain 1900–1960* (London: The Library Association, 1962), p. 96.

[29] Margery Fisher, *Intent upon Reading: A Critical Appraisal of Modern Children's Fiction* (Leicester: Brockhampton Press, 1961), p. 10.

[30] Quoted in David Childs, *Britain Since 1945: A Political History*, p. 61.

of the modern age were resulting in children 'growing up faster' frequently recurs in commentary and criticism of this period; indeed, by 1982, the American cultural theorist Neil Postman was gloomily asserting that the impact of new media was responsible for the disappearance of childhood in Western culture.[31] Challenges to the established cultural construction of childhood were also posed by a dramatic rise in immigration precipitated by the 1962 Commonwealth Immigration Act and by an increasing focus on the needs of working-class children: the 'white, middle-class, educationally successful' child who was typically the assumed reader in children's literature until the 1960s was replaced by an ethnically, socially and culturally diverse body of child readers.[32] Children's publishers concerned with providing their readers with the 'best' children's books, therefore, were perforce engaged in a broader cultural debate about the nature of childhood.

Ideology and the Children's Book

As Nadia Crandall's characterisation of 1960s publishing as focused on 'well-written, high-quality books that reflected the middle-class mores of their authors, editors and readers' implies, concepts of 'quality' children's literature were closely connected to constructions of the child reader. As the 1960s progressed, such books were increasingly criticised for their unexamined ideologies, amidst calls for a more inclusive children's literature which reflected a much broader demographic. The central role of schools and libraries in funding the growth of children's publishing during the 1960s and 1970s ensured that the utilitarian value of children's literature as an educational and socialising tool received considerable attention. Simultaneously, however, critics such as bibliographer and reviewer Brian Alderson were keen to emphasise the literary and aesthetic qualities of children's literature. John Rowe Townsend in 1968 characterised the two sides of the debate as 'child people' and 'book people', a division which Peter Hollindale argues dominated critical debate during the 1960s and 1970s, with a lasting influence upon children's literature criticism as a whole:

> The result is a crude but damaging conjunction of attitudes on each side, not as it necessarily is but as it is perceived by the other. A concern for the literary quality of children's books as works of imagination has become linked in a caricatured manifesto with indifference to the child reader and with tolerance or approval of obsolete, or traditional, or reactionary political values. A concern with the child reader has become linked with indifference to high standards of literary achievement and with populist ardour on behalf of the three political missions

---

[31]   Neil Postman, *The Disappearance of Childhood* (New York: Vintage, 1994) [first published 1982].

[32]   Kimberley Reynolds, 'Publishing Practices and the Practicalities of Publishing', p. 30; David Childs, *Britain Since 1945: A Political History*, pp. 147–9; Ian R.G. Spencer, *British Immigration Policy Since 1939: The Making of Multi-racial Britain* (London & New York: Routledge, 1997).

which are seen as most urgent in contemporary society: anti-racism, anti-sexism and anti-classism.[33]

As Hollindale's analysis implies, in reality the division between the 'child people' and the 'book people' was less distinct than it appeared; nevertheless, the perception of conflict between the two ideologies is an important characteristic of the 1960s and 1970s. Editors seeking to publish the 'best' in children's literature had perforce to position themselves in relation to these differing constructions of literary quality and, as the work of Kaye Webb and Aidan Chambers shows, the tension between the two was present in the work of individual editors and publishers.

As Peter Hollindale's comments on the concerns of the 'child people' indicate, explicit ideological concerns became increasingly prominent in the changing social context of the 1960s and 1970s. The increasing ideological consciousness in relation to gender, sexuality, ethnicity, class and morality which accompanied social and political change in Britain during this period had a direct impact upon children's literature.[34] Responses to these ideological issues during the 1960s and 1970s had a significant impact in shaping modern attitudes towards children's literature, in many cases forming the basis for new passive ideologies; for example, it is now taken for granted that a 'good' children's book ought not to perpetuate racist values, although in practice passive racist ideologies frequently endure.[35] Identifying the ideologies at work in this period – both overt and implicit – therefore constitutes an important opportunity to expose some of the ideological assumptions that have persisted to the modern era. Children's editors were not merely reacting to these discourses, but were actively engaged in shaping them: as Chapter 3 demonstrates, figures such as Aidan Chambers were concerned with children's publishing as an agent of social change. As publishers of books still regarded as setting a standard for quality children's literature, they were therefore responsible for shaping the ideological basis of contemporary children's literature.

---

[33]   John Rowe Townsend, 'Standards of Criticism in Children's Literature' in *Children's Literature: The Development of Criticism*, ed. by Peter Hunt (London: Routledge, 1990), 57–70, p. 63; Peter Hollindale, *Ideology and the Children's Book* (Stroud: Signal, 1988), p. 5.

[34]   David Childs cites a number of Acts of Parliament which reflect the radical changes to British society during this period, including the Murder (Abolition of the Death Penalty) Act (1965); the Sexual Offences Act (1967), which legalised homosexual practices in private; the Abortion Act (1967); the Domicile and Matrimonial Proceedings Act (1973), which allowed a married woman living apart from her husband to have a legal domicile of her own; and the Sex Discrimination Act (1975). (David Childs, *Britain Since 1945: A Political History*, pp. 155–87.)

[35]   Witness the recent controversy over the jacket artwork for Justine Larbalestier's young adult novel *Liar* in the United States, which depicted the protagonist – described in the book as 'black with nappy hair' – as a white girl with long, straight hair. Following a wave of criticism, the publisher, Bloomsbury, rejacketed the book with more representative artwork. (Justine Larbalestier, 'Ain't That a Shame (Updated)', *Justine Larbalestier: Writing, Reading, Eating, Drinking, Sport*, 23 July 2009, <http://justinelarbalestier.com/blog/2009/07/23/aint-that-a-shame/> [accessed 12/01/10].

Publisher Power

Children's imprints in the 1960s and 1970s were typically small and often overlooked by their parent publishing houses. As a result, editors were able to exert a strong individual influence over the lists for which they were responsible: to a large degree, the aims and beliefs of figures such as Kaye Webb and Aidan Chambers can be seen as synonymous with those of the imprints they edited. Despite the influential role of children's publishing in shaping children's literature, however, it has received little attention in children's literature scholarship. Publishing history as a whole has also tended to neglect the role of children's publishing houses and editors: although children's literature frequently has a high degree of financial importance within publishing houses, this is not reflected in these publishers' own histories, which frequently include no more than a passing mention of their children's divisions.[36] This picture has begun to shift in recent years: the 70th anniversary of Puffin Books in 2010 prompted parent company Penguin to revisit Puffin's history, commissioning a biography of editor Kaye Webb and collaborating on an exhibition on Puffin with Seven Stories, the National Centre for Children's Books, while in 2008 the University of Bristol, which holds the business archive of Penguin Books, launched a major research project on the history of Penguin which encompasses the work of Puffin.[37] Despite such recent initiatives, however, the dearth of material on the subject has in itself inhibited scholarship. While it is possible to draw conclusions about editorial ethos from the publishing output of a particular list, more detailed explorations of the role of children's editors and publishers are often challenging. Even basic facts such as dates, publishing statistics and even the existence of entire publishing divisions can be difficult to establish given the lack of any formal attempts to preserve such information; the work of Kimberley Reynolds and Nicholas Tucker – based heavily on interviews with key publishing figures – constitutes the only sustained attempt to address the children's publishing of this period.[38] As editors and practitioners of children's literature from the period reach the end of their careers, however, and space and infrastructure has been made available by archives and special collections, more and more material has become available, chiefly in the form of personal and professional archival collections. Access to material held by Seven Stories, the National Centre for Children's Books, the Penguin Archive, Bristol University and the Chambers Archive, Aberystwyth University, has been invaluable in constructing a much fuller picture of the motives and ideologies of editors who

---

[36]   Kimberley Reynolds, 'Publishing Practices and the Practicalities of Publishing', p. 23.

[37]   Valerie Grove, *So Much To Tell* (Harmondsworth: Viking, 2010); University of Bristol, 'Penguin Archive Project', University of Bristol, <http://www.bristol.ac.uk/penguinarchiveproject/> [accessed 20/12/09].

[38]   Kimberley Reynolds and Nicholas Tucker, eds, *Children's Book Publishing in Britain Since 1945*.

were active during the 'second golden age', and so to identify and understand the factors that shaped the children's literature industry as we know it today.

The personal archive of Kaye Webb, acquired in 2005 by Seven Stories, the National Centre for Children's Books, is of particular significance to the history of children's publishing in the 1960s and 1970s. Webb's work as Puffin editor is important both because of the cultural and commercial dominance of Puffin during the 1960s and 1970s, and because of her personal contribution to the firm and to children's literature as a whole. The Kaye Webb Collection, which spans almost the entirety of Webb's life, comprises correspondence, diaries, professional documents and material relating to her work at Puffin which offers an unparalleled insight into her ethos as editor. This personal archive is complemented by material in the Penguin Archive at the University of Bristol, which documents Webb's business activities. Editorial files for many of the books edited by Webb provide information about decisions made about specific titles and demonstrate some of the practical pressures at work in Puffin during this period. Since Webb's death in 1996, archive material has constituted the only evidence of Kaye Webb 'in her own words'. Although neither archive is comprehensive – much material relating to Kaye Webb's work at Puffin appears to have been discarded – this material offers a valuable picture of the ways in which Kaye Webb shaped children's literature during the 1960s and 1970s.

Macmillan Topliner, an imprint for the reluctant adolescent reader, was one of a number of more specialist imprints which emerged during the 1960s and 1970s. Macmillan Education, who published Topliner, owned several other specialist imprints, notably Club 75, another series for 'reluctant' readers, and Nippers, a reading scheme for younger children. Topliner is notable both because of the degree to which it represents some of the key trends in children's literature during the 1960s and 1970s, and because of the broad scope of editor Aidan Chambers' involvement in British children's literature. Chambers, who is best known for his novels for young adults, has published a substantial body of material in his capacities as critic and educationalist, including some pieces which directly address his aims as editor of Topliner. He continues to be an active participant in the world of children's literature, and has been generous in granting interviews for this book. A full picture of Chambers' editorial work at Topliner and his changing perceptions of children's and young adult literature would not, however, have been possible without access to archive materials. Correspondence, sales details and other planning materials relating to Topliner are included in the archive recently donated to Aberystwyth University by Aidan Chambers and his wife Nancy, whose work as an editor and critic is also of major significance to British children's literature. This extensive body of material evidences the development of Chambers' work as editor of Topliner much more directly than other available sources and provides a context for Chambers' later published work. The wealth of material relating to Topliner, and Chambers' clear statements about the purpose and intentions of the imprint, make it an ideal case study for the kind of smaller-scale children's publishing which emerged during the 1960s and 1970s.

Chapter 1
The Children's Literature Scene

The world of children's literature in the 1960s and 1970s clearly enjoyed the sense of a new golden age in the making. This was generated not only by the appearance of exciting new writing and the increased social and educational interest in children's reading outlined in the Introduction, but also in the degree to which these factors coalesced to form a coherent cultural phenomenon. The first half of the twentieth century had seen some important developments in British children's literature, including the appearance of landmark titles such as Noel Streatfeild's *Ballet Shoes* (1936) and J.R.R. Tolkien's *The Hobbit* (1937), the establishment of the Carnegie Medal (1936), and the launch of Puffin, the first major children's paperback imprint (1939).[1] A lack of serious critical attention for children's literature, however, meant that such developments happened in isolation: Geoffrey Trease, who started his career as a children's writer in 1934, recollects, 'I myself knew nothing of *Emil [and the Detectives]*. Nor did I know that in 1930 a man named Arthur Ransome had blazed a new trail with a book called *Swallows and Amazons*'.[2] By contrast, the 1960s saw an onslaught of new initiatives which served to fuel progression in a whole range of areas. Some of these developments were interdependent for practical reasons – the social and economic factors explored in the Introduction funded the expansion of children's publishing – but the sense of interconnection extended beyond these practical exigencies. In the rapidly changing social context of the 1960s and 1970s, childhood became a central focus of British culture, garnering attention both in academia and in popular culture. Due to this broader discourse about children and childhood, developments in separate fields such as education, librarianship and publishing did not take place in isolation but in direct response to one another. Many practitioners in the field of children's literature operated in several different spheres, carrying ideas and expertise from one to another. Librarians such as Sheila Ray and Elaine Moss became active and influential critics and reviewers, drawing on their experiences with child readers to develop new ideologies about the purpose and nature of children's literature. Geoffrey Trease and Jill Paton Walsh were among the many children's authors who also contributed to the field as critics and reviewers; John Rowe Townsend

---

[1]   Keith Barker, 'Prize-fighting' in *Children's Book Publishing in Britain Since 1945*, ed. by Kimberley Reynolds and Nicholas Tucker (Aldershot: Scolar Press, 1998), 42–59, p. 43; Sally Gritten, *The Story of Puffin Books* (Harmondsworth: Penguin, 1991), p. 6.

[2]   Geoffrey Trease, 'The Revolution in Children's Literature' in *The Thorny Paradise: Writers on Writing For Children*, ed. by Edward Blishen (Harmondsworth: Kestrel, 1975), 13–24, p. 16. Trease's article gives a good account of developments in British children's literature between the 1920s and the 1960s.

was children's book editor for the *Guardian* and published several influential works of criticism in addition to his prolific output of fiction for children and young adults. The activities of children's editors also extended beyond the world of publishing, and several wrote as well as published children's books; for example, Philippa Pearce, most famous for her fiction – notably Carnegie Medal winner *Tom's Midnight Garden* (1958) – also edited the children's list at Andre Deutsch.[3] Many authors and critics emerged from the world of education: authors Bernard Ashley, Farrukh Dhondy and Jan Mark, and critic Margaret Meek all began their careers as teachers, and in many cases were motivated by a desire for children's literature which would serve the kind of children they were teaching. Aidan Chambers, who is explored in depth in Chapter 3, is the epitome of this trend for inter-disciplinarity: his career spanned almost every aspect of children's literature. The endeavour of defining and producing 'quality' children's literature, therefore, was not fragmented or confined to a single discipline, but was part of the dominant social discourse. In order to understand the context within which children's publishers positioned their books as the 'best' in children's reading, therefore, it is essential to examine the contributions of practitioners from across a range of disciplines. This chapter explores the ways in which writers, critics, librarians and other children's literature practitioners defined the qualities of this 'golden age' of children's literature.

There is scope for a much more comprehensive survey of the field; however, this chapter examines some of the most significant themes which emerged in the children's literature and criticism of the 1960s and 1970s. Scholarly attention has hitherto focused upon the children's books themselves – John Rowe Townsend and Peter Hunt, among others, have published overviews of the children's literature of the period – and for this reason this chapter does not attempt to represent the full scope of fiction written for children.[4] Instead, it highlights a few key texts and their relationship to contemporary ideas about the nature and purpose of children's literature. Particular attention will be paid to books which won awards and therefore were formally identified as meeting some definition of quality; although literary awards are not unproblematic as a barometer of cultural standards, the criteria used to judge such awards and the changing ways in which these were applied do demonstrate changing perceptions of quality children's literature. Conversely, the critical output of the period has received little attention as a whole: this chapter addresses this neglect, highlighting and considering some of the most prominent debates in children's literature criticism.

---

[3]   Stephanie   Nettell,   'Obituary: Philippa   Pearce',   *The   Guardian*, 2   January   2007,   <http://www.guardian.co.uk/news/2007/jan/02/guardianobituaries. booksforchildrenandteenagers> [accessed 23/07/09].

[4]   Peter Hunt, *An Introduction to Children's Literature* (Oxford: Oxford University Press, 1994); John Rowe Townsend, *Written For Children: An Outline of English-Language Children's Literature*, 2nd rev edn (Harmondsworth: Kestrel, 1983). Townsend's survey was first published 1965; revised editions appeared 1974, 1983, 1987, 1990 and 1995.

The multi-disciplinary nature of the children's literature field means that very little of the critical work produced can be classed as 'pure' literary criticism, since the majority of those who wrote on children's literature brought the skills and concerns of other disciplines to their work; for brevity's sake, however, the terms 'critic' and 'criticism' are used throughout.

The Bigger Picture: Historical and International Trends in Children's Literature

The concentrated activity across a range of disciplines relating to children's literature helped to give the 1960s and 1970s a cohesive sense of being a golden age. The seeds of this flowering of children's literature can be found in the 1950s, supported by the socio-economic circumstances of the post-war years. Indeed, the impact of the two world wars is clearly evident in many of the trends which emerged during the 1960s and 1970s. Alan Sinfield contends that 'the post-1945 understanding of culture, the arts and education was formed in the same ideological framework as the other main welfare institutions'; the 1960s and 1970s can be seen as the culmination of several decades of change governed by these ideologies, and some post-war initiatives – notably the extension of compulsory education – were not enacted until this period.[5] It is important to acknowledge, therefore, that the confluence of social policy, creativity and economic prosperity which produced a new and distinctive children's literature during the 1960s and 1970s did not represent a complete break with the preceding decades. Conversely, the period was more fragmented than the term 'golden age' implies. The distinctive character of the 1960s and 1970s partly derived from the rapid and significant change in almost all aspects of British life, which had significant implications for the world of children's literature. Economic shifts in particular had a direct impact upon children's books: libraries, schools and publishers were all directly affected by the swing from a buoyant economic climate in the early 1960s to a period of severe recession in the 1970s. The continuity across these two decades, therefore, should not be conflated with stability – on the contrary, in many ways it was the rapidity of social change which helped to create the sense of new possibilities and challenges in children's literature.

The impact of the war years on children's literature is particularly evident when the international context is considered. The establishment of the International Board on Books for Young People (IBBY) in 1952 and the International Research Society for Children's Literature (IRSCL) in 1972 indicate a desire in Britain and elsewhere to forge bonds between nations which had so recently experienced

---

5   Alan Sinfield, *Literature, Politics and Culture in Postwar Britain* (London, New York: Continuum, 2004), p. 65.

The 1944 Education Act proposed the extension of the school leaving age to 16; this proposal was enacted in 1972. David Childs, *Britain Since 1945: A Political History*, 5th edn (London & New York: Routledge, 2001), pp. 107–89.

conflict: IBBY's stated aim was 'to promote international understanding through children's books'.[6] In the field of criticism, the seminal text by French scholar of comparative literature Paul Hazard, *Les Livres, les Enfants et les Hommes* (1932) – which appeared in English in 1944 as *Books, Children and Men* – remained an influential text on children's literature throughout the 1960s.[7] Hazard emphasised the distinctive qualities of childhood, arguing that the commonalities between children effaced national differences, creating a 'republic of childhood'. Internationally popular books such as Carlo Collodi's *Pinocchio* (1883), Hazard argued, 'bear the fruit of peace and scatter seeds of hope'.[8] A similar ethos is evident in the work of historian Mary Thwaite, who argued that

> [...] children everywhere play on a universal stage, and their domain knows nothing of the boundaries made by governments. And so their true literary inheritance will never be found within any one nation or period. It spans nothing less than this great globe itself since books began.[9]

These analyses are indicative of the way in which children's literature was enlisted in attempts to build a post-war world free of the conflict which had characterised the first half of the twentieth century. In pursuit of this aim, IBBY established the Hans Christian Andersen Award, intended to be an 'outstanding international award' in recognition of a writer or illustrator who has made a 'lasting contribution to children's literature'.[10] The degree to which this aim is predicated on an idea of quality children's literature as transcending cultural boundaries is illustrated by Virginia Haviland's assertion that 'One of the happiest privileges of serving on the jury is the gaining of an awareness that whatever one's own country of origin or profession within the children's book world, we speak a common language in regard to the literary and artistic qualities in children's books and the child's understanding'.[11] Combined with this belief in the universal qualities both of literature and of childhood was an emphasis on the potential for literature to broaden children's experience and offer insight into and understanding of other cultures and nations. Translator Patricia Crampton, writing in 1975, argued that one of the primary reasons for selecting a book for translation was that 'the book

---

[6]   IBBY publication, quoted in Patricia Crampton, 'Will It Travel Well?', *Signal*, 17 (May 1975), 75–80, p. 75.

[7]   Paul Hazard, *Books, Children and Men*, trans. Marguerite Mitchell (Boston: The Horn Book, 1965).

[8]   Paul Hazard, *Books, Children and Men*, p. 151.

[9]   M.F. Thwaite, *From Primer to Pleasure: An Introduction to the History of Children's Books in England, from the Invention of Printing to 1900* (London: The Library Association, 1963), p. 81.

[10]   Eva Glistrup, *The Hans Christian Andersen Awards 1956–2002* (Copenhagen: Gyldendal, 2002), p. 16.

[11]   Virginia Haviland, 'A New Internationalism' in *Children and Literature: Views and Reviews*, ed. by Virginia Haviland (London: Bodley Head, 1974), 328–34, p. 330.

provides an interesting, and truthful, picture of some aspect of its country of origin'.[12] The founding of the Bologna children's books fair in 1963 helped to support a more international outlook for children's publishing, providing publishers with an opportunity to acquire titles from overseas and to produce international co-editions, a particularly lucrative strategy in the case of picture books. Books from other English-speaking nations became a familiar feature on British children's lists – in 1971 Australian author Ivan Southall was awarded the Carnegie Medal for his book *Josh* (1971), one of the few non-British authors ever to receive this award – along with increasing numbers of books in translation. Writers who were awarded the Hans Christian Andersen Award – notably Erich Kästner, Tove Jansson and Astrid Lindgren – were particularly successful, but the increasing willingness of British publishers to accept works in translation was also reflected in the publication of less high-profile authors. From the Netherlands came Jan Terlouw, Jaap der Haar and An Rutgers van der Loeff, who found considerable success with her books *Children on the Oregon Trail* (1949; translated 1961) and *Avalanche* (1954; translated 1957). Sweden and Germany were an important source of fiction for adolescents, reflecting the fact that – in Patricia Crampton's words – they were 'doing something which, at a particular time, our own literature [was] not': this is particularly evident in Aidan Chambers' Topliner list, discussed in Chapter 3.[13]

The humanist ideals which characterise international approaches to children's literature are clearly present in many of the books published during the 'second golden age'. In Susan Cooper's Dark is Rising series (1965–1977), the benevolent Old Ones are drawn from all nations and all periods of time in order to fight against the evil forces of the Dark; when they assemble at the climax of the second book in the series, *The Dark is Rising* (1973), the hero Will sees 'an endless variety of faces – gay, sombre, old, young, paper-white, jet black, and every shade and graduation of pink and brown between, vaguely recognizable, or totally strange', and thinks 'Every one of us is linked, for the greatest purpose in the world'.[14] By contrast, Rosemary Sutcliff's *The Lantern Bearers* (1959), which was awarded the Carnegie Medal, foregrounds the question of national conflict in its depiction of Britain at the end of Roman occupation and under threat of a Saxon invasion. Despite the image of encroaching darkness with which Sutcliff ends the book, she continually reminds readers of the connections as well as the conflicts between different peoples. The assimilation of her Roman hero, Aquila, into Britain, where he chooses to remain after the rest of his regiment leaves, is followed in turn by the assimilation of Aquila's sister into the ranks of the Saxon enemy. When at the

---

[12]   Patricia Crampton, 'Will It Travel Well?', p. 75. Crampton asserts that in practice, this was not the reason that most frequently operated; unfortunately she fails to identify which criteria *were* the most commonly applied, although the title of her article indicates a likely consideration.

[13]   Patricia Crampton, 'Will It Travel Well?', p. 76; Peter Graves, 'Swedish Children's Books in Britain', *Signal* 18 (September 1975), 137–41.

[14]   Susan Cooper, *The Dark is Rising* (Harmondsworth: Puffin, 1976), p. 255. It should be noted, however, that the series is ultimately Anglocentric, drawing heavily upon Arthurian legend.

climax of the book he recognises one of the marauding Saxons as his sister's son, Aquila chooses to protect the wounded warrior. He sends a message to his sister along with her son: 'Say to her – as though it were I who spoke through you, "Look. I've a dolphin on my shoulder. I'm your long-lost brother"'.[15] This scene, in which Aquila recognises the legitimacy of their familial bonds along with the essential humanity of the Saxons by literally identifying himself with his sister's son, is a powerful assertion of the idea that there are universal human values which transcend conflict. It is significant that Sutcliff links this theme to the power of story: Aquila is referencing the tale of Odysseus, which recurs throughout the novel as a point of connection, first between Aquila and his sister, then between Aquila and his Saxon captors and finally in this scene of reconciliation. Sutcliff's novel presents the same thesis which underpinned the efforts of IBBY to champion books in translation: it suggests that stories are valuable for the bonds they forge between people.

The most significant foreign influence on children's literature in Britain during the 1960s and 1970s was the United States. Children's literature in the United States was subject to social influences similar to those in the United Kingdom, including broadening access to education, a buoyant economy and high levels of social funding, but had not been so severely affected by the exigencies of two world wars. The efforts of children's librarians such as Anne Carroll Moore helped to produce greater status and visibility for children's books at the turn of the century: Marcus Crouch argues that by the 1920s 'interest in Britain lagged at least ten years behind America'.[16] This retardation is evident when key dates are compared, for example, in the 15-year gap between the establishment of the Newbery Medal (1922), the United States' literary award for children's books, and the institution of the equivalent Carnegie Medal (1936) in Britain. By 1960, criticism and reviewing of children's literature were also well advanced in the United States, fostered by *The Horn Book Magazine* (founded 1924), which sought 'to herald the best in children's literature', and its associated publishing houses.[17] Those seeking to develop theory and practice in Britain were able to draw upon this existing tradition. The influence of the American scene was further intensified by the activities of a number of Americans working in Britain from the 1950s onwards, notably Grace Hogarth and Marni Hodgkin, both trained as specialist children's editors, and Kathleen Lines, who had trained as a children's librarian. As Britain developed its own scholarship and journalism on children's literature, the influence of American critical works became less pronounced, but close ties between the two countries remained, and the United States continued to lead the way in some key areas. Increased awareness of race and culture in children's literature owed much to the example set in the United States, where this

---

[15]   Rosemary Sutcliff, *The Lantern Bearers* (Oxford: Oxford University Press, 2007), p. 292.

[16]   Marcus Crouch, *Treasure Seekers and Borrowers: Children's Books in Britain, 1900–1960* (London: The Library Association, 1962), p. 39.

[17]   The Horn Book, 'About Us', *The Horn Book*, <http://www.hbook.com/aboutus/> (2009) [accessed 27/07/09].

issue had been brought into prominence through the struggle for African-American civil rights, while the United States also led the way with the developing genre of fiction for adolescents. The parallels between Britain and America are not exact, and a detailed treatment of the relationship between the two would constitute a study in itself: nevertheless, while this book discusses American material only where particularly relevant, it is important to remember that much of the criticism and literature originating in Britain drew upon developments in the United States.

Increased interest in children's literature internationally helped to sustain the sense of a golden age in Britain. The desire to include more books from other cultures in the British canon is consonant with a move towards a more inclusive British literature which reflected a diverse range of different childhoods. The Hans Christian Andersen Award, however, exemplifies the degree to which international cooperation was predicated upon an assumption of a universal childhood and – by extension – universal human values. The dialogue between these two positions is a key theme in children's literature and criticism of the 1960s and 1970s.

The Publishing Context

Part of the special character of the golden age during the 1960s lay in the flourishing nature of the publishing industry. The buoyant economy helped to ensure that there were not just a handful of high-quality books for children, as had been the case in the 1950s, but a much more wide-ranging selection of literature. The rapid expansion of Puffin Books, the subject of Chapter 2, demonstrates the speed and scale with which children's publishing began to change. Other paperback imprints were beginning to emerge: Pan Piccolo took a more market-oriented approach, publishing adventure anthologies and joke books as well as children's fiction, while popular authors such as Enid Blyton and W.E. Johns appeared in paperback on the Armada list, launched in 1962.[18] In 1967 Brockhampton took on Puffin on its own terms with a new paperback imprint, Knights, which offered books in several different categories. Black and Red Knights featured what Brockhampton termed 'top-quality' titles by authors such as Rosemary Sutcliff, Geoffrey Trease and Noel Streatfeild, while Green Knights provided 'stories by the most popular authors of all', including Helen Dore Boylston – author of the popular Nurse Sue Barton series – and the ubiquitous Enid Blyton.[19] Towards the end of the 1960s and into the 1970s, children's publishing began to diversify further: a growing

---

[18]   Lesley Croome, 'A million a month', *T.L.S Children's Books*, 15 June 1973, pp. 1–2, p. 1. It is difficult to ascertain an exact date for the launch of Pan Piccolo, but despite Lesley Croome's assertion that Armada were the first competitor to Puffin, Pan appear to have entered the market at the same time, if not before.

[19]   Brockhampton Press, 'Knight Books', promotional leaflet, 1967, Aberystwyth University, Chambers archive, Box 110/111 02, Folder: Series Publicity.

Note: At the time of access, the Chambers archive held at the University of Aberrystwyth was uncatalogued. Citations therefore provide as many details of location as possible in order to facilitate further access to this material.

belief in the need for books which catered to particular groups of child readers led to the establishment of imprints such as Nippers (1968), Bodley Head's Books for New Adults (1969) and Topliner (1969). Hardback publishing was also flourishing, thanks to the unprecedented demand from well-funded schools and libraries. Oxford University Press editor Paul Binding recollects that 75–80 per cent of sales were made to public libraries, and the expectation of guaranteed sales allowed children's lists to expand rapidly: 'the influence of children's librarians on the financial success of children's publishing during the formative years of the 1960s cannot be overestimated'.[20] The increasingly diverse nature of the market, and the existence of vocal stakeholders such as the public libraries, inevitably raised new questions about the nature of good children's literature. Thanks to the activity of reviewers, children's librarians and the publishers themselves, children's publishing was no longer a small and largely overlooked area, but was involved with a broader cultural debate.

The high levels of social funding which supported the boom of the 1960s did not survive into the 1970s. Schools and libraries faced massive budget cuts, and the dramatically increased publishing output of children's lists was suddenly deprived of its guaranteed markets. In 1974 librarian Elaine Moss voiced the fear that 'a cutback in the numbers of books published, combined with the acute cash flow problem, will force upon some children's publishers the choice between the quick safe sell or financial insecurity'.[21] Moss's assumption that the harsh economic climate would lead publishers to cut down on the scope of their lists proved unfounded: on the contrary, the trend was towards a greater range of titles closely targeted at particular types of reader. Until the end of the 1960s, imprints such as Puffin had built up variety in their lists by keeping titles in print for long periods of time. The effects of recession and the rising costs of warehousing made this strategy more difficult, and by 1976 it was becoming apparent that publishers were sacrificing longevity rather than variety, 'driven inexorably towards shorter printing runs, fast selling lines or both'.[22] Nevertheless, children's publishing continued to grow. In 1971, Collins seized the opportunity to launch a new paperback list, Armada Lions, when Puffin's paperback rights for popular authors such as Michael Bond and Alan Garner expired.[23] Two years later, Tandem Books established a children's department with a different slant: its Target Books enjoyed

---

[20]   Kimberley Reynolds and Nicholas Tucker, 'Interview with Paul Binding (Oxford University Press), 10 March 1997', in *Oral Archives: A Collection of Informal Conversations with Individuals Involved in Creating or Producing Children's Literature since 1945*, compiled by Kimberley Reynolds and Nicholas Tucker (London: Roehampton University, 1998), 57–68, p. 60; Kimberley Reynolds, 'Publishing Practices and the Practicalities of Publishing' in *Children's Book Publishing in Britain Since 1945*, ed. by Kimberley Reynolds and Nicholas Tucker (Aldershot: Scolar Press, 1998), 20–41, p. 27.

[21]   Elaine Moss, *Children's Books of the Year 1974*, ed. by Elaine Moss (London: Hamish Hamilton, 1975), p. 7.

[22]   Noel Hughes, article in the *Times Educational Supplement*, 28 January 1977, quoted in Elaine Moss, 'Introduction', *Children's Books of the Year 1976*, 5–10, p. 5.

[23]   Lesley Croome, 'A million a month', p. 1.

some of the highest sales of the 1970s with its novelisations of the popular television series *Doctor Who*.[24] The TV tie-in became increasingly important to children's publishers during the late 1970s and early 1980s: many of the key paperback originals produced by Magnet Books, founded by Jane Nissen in 1979, were tie-ins for popular children's programmes such as *Rainbow* and *Button Moon*.[25] In a more competitive market, vertical publishing became more important: by the end of the 1970s Kestrel/Puffin, Collins/Fontana Lions, Methuen/Magnet and Abelard Schulman/Grasshopper were all producing both hardback and paperback titles, thus guaranteeing that they would have quality titles to launch on the more lucrative paperback market.[26] Recession and budget cuts, therefore, did not halt the expansion of children's publishing in the 1970s, but they radically changed the nature of the market. Although it is discussed in only a limited way in the present work, therefore, it is important to recognise that the commercial viability of titles became an increasingly important factor in publishers' negotiations of the idea of 'good' children's books in the mid- to late 1970s.

Critical Voices: An Expanding Field

The increase in publishing for children encouraged a concomitant increase in publishing *about* children's literature. Librarians, teachers and parents faced with the task of selecting from an ever-growing range of children's books were in need of reviews and critical material to guide their choices. The publication in 1961 of Margery Fisher's critical survey of children's books, *Intent upon Reading*, marks the start of a new wave of critical interest in children's literature.[27] The following year, Fisher launched her review magazine *Growing Point*, and two more review magazines appeared soon after: *Children's Book News* was launched in 1965, and *Books For Your Children* in 1966. The latter, published by the Federation of Children's Books Groups, was explicitly aimed at non-professionals: founder Anne Wood stated that 'The society was formed because we *didn't* know [about children's books]'.[28] Mainstream journalism was also beginning to pay more attention to children's literature: by 1968, most of the major broadsheets had appointed specialist children's book editors. Margery Fisher held the position

---

[24] Mark Gatiss, *On the Outside it Looked Like an Old Fashioned Police Box*, BBC Radio 4 broadcast, 23 June 2009.

[25] Mary Hoffman, 'Children's paperbacks in a state of change', *The Bookseller*, No. 4132, 2 March 1985, pp. 855–9.

[26] Elaine Moss, 'The Seventies in Children's Books', in *Part of the Pattern: A Personal Journey Through the World of Children's Books, 1960–1985* (London: The Bodley Head, 1986), 136–60, p. 143.

[27] Margery Fisher, *Intent upon Reading: A Critical Appraisal of Modern Children's Fiction* (Leicester: Brockhampton Press, 1961).

[28] Anne Wood, '"Books For Your Children" – The First Ten Years', *Children's Literature in Education*, 6:1 (1975), 31–8, p. 31.

at the *Sunday Times*, Naomi Lewis at the *Observer* and Brian Alderson at the *Times*. At the *Guardian*, John Rowe Townsend started as a journalist but quickly brought children's literature into prominence, launching the Guardian Award for children's literature in 1967.[29] Many of these editors were active critics as well as reviewers, publishing extensively in the field of children's literature. Margery Fisher was not the only reviewer to attempt a more comprehensive survey of children's books. *Treasure Seekers and Borrowers* by Marcus Crouch, a critic and librarian who was one of the judges for the Carnegie Medal, was published in the same year as Fisher's *Intent upon Reading*, and in 1965 the first edition of John Rowe Townsend's important monograph *Written for Children* appeared. During the 1970s, more guides intended to assist the general public in choosing children's books were produced, including Gladys Williams' *Children and Their Books* (1970), Peter Hollindale's *Choosing Books for Children* (1974), the National Book League's *Children's Books of the Year*, which began publication in 1970, and the *Reading for Enjoyment* series published by Children's Book News (1970–1975). In addition to these new texts, there was a resurgence of interest in earlier works, notably Geoffrey Trease's *Tales Out of School* (1949) and Roger Lancelyn Green's *Tellers of Tales* (1946), both of which appeared in revised and expanded editions during the 1960s. The first edition of *Tellers of Tales* had been written for 'young readers' in their early 'teens'; it is symptomatic of the changed status of children's literature that the revised edition, published in 1969, was aimed at adults.[30] Children's literature had become not just a pastime, but a significant adult concern.

Increased interest in children's literature was part of broader social interest in children and childhood during the 1960s and 1970s. The first major British work on children's literature, Harvey Darton's *Children's Books in England* (1932), had taken a socio-historical approach to children's literature; the book appeared in a new edition in 1958 and saw several reprints in the course of the 1960s. The question of the child in a historical context was also explored by the French historian Philippe Ariès, whose *L'Enfant et la Vie Familiale sous l'Ancien Régime* (1960), translated in 1962 under the title *Centuries of Childhood*, presented childhood as a social construct. Ariès' work remains influential – although his methodologies and thesis have been repeatedly challenged by recent scholarship – and his positioning of childhood within a cultural context and emphasis on the importance of the family are particularly significant within the context of increased focus on education, play and child rearing practices during the 1960s.[31] The influence of Donald Winnicott,

---

[29] Elaine Moss, *Part of the Pattern: A Personal Journey Through the World of Children's Books*, p. 31.

[30] Roger Lancelyn Green, *Tellers of Tales: Children's Authors and Their Books of the Last 100 Years* (London: Ward, 1946), p. 5.

[31] Harry Hendrick summarises the impact of Ariès on historical approaches to childhood and explores the shortcomings of Ariès' work in 'Children and Childhood', *ReFresh: Recent Findings of Research in Economic and Social History*, 15 (Autumn 1992), 1–4.

John Bowlby and Benjamin Spock, discussed in the Introduction, helped to launch a new genre of childcare manuals: library catalogue records indicate that the number of books published on the subject of 'child rearing' in 1969 was more than double that of 10 years before. Increased adult interest in children's literature, therefore, was part of a general cultural belief in the importance of childhood and in the power of adults to shape children's experiences for good or ill.

Aspects of children's lives which had previously received little attention from adults began to be highlighted through the work of psychologists and sociologists; the work of Peter and Iona Opie on the folklore and anthropology of children's rhymes and games is a notable example of the ways in which juvenile activities were given new cultural weight. The popular appeal of the Opies' work was great: their book *The Lore and Language of Schoolchildren* (1959) was reprinted four times between 1959 and 1967. That a *Guardian* article of 1960 opens with a casual reference to the appeal of 'being present at the birth of an Opie-ism' testifies to the extent to which their work had gained currency beyond the specialised academic fields of folklore and anthropology.[32] Sandy Hobbs and David Cornwell argue that *The Lore and Language of Schoolchildren* has gained classic status across a range of disciplines; frequent references to the Opies' work in children's literature criticism of the 1960s and 1970s indicates their influence in the field of children's literature.[33] The Opies' anthropology of childhood runs counter to Ariès' argument that the concept of childhood as a distinctive period of life is socially constructed, instead presenting children as involved in generating their *own* unique and specific culture. This viewpoint has important implications for approaches to children's literature: as the 1960s progressed, the idea that children's books should engage directly with real children's experiences of childhood became increasingly important.

The increased professionalisation of fields relating to children's literature resulted not only in more mainstream reviewing of children's books, but also more critical material. Pat Pinsent points to developments in teacher training – notably the introduction of the degree of Bachelor of Education in 1967 – as a phenomenon which allowed for more space for children's literature on university syllabuses.[34] While the subject did not appear on undergraduate English literature syllabuses until the 1970s, its presence on library and education courses encouraged more critical approaches to the subject. Simultaneously, professionals with specialist responsibility for children's libraries began to publish studies arising out of their experience in the field. Surveys such as Geoffrey Trease's *Tales Out of School* and John Rowe Townsend's *Written for Children* were not simply review guides, but identified key trends and examined the purposes and form of children's literature. By the end of the 1960s, children's literature was beginning to constitute an area

---

[32] Nesta Roberts, 'The playground their world' in *The Guardian*, 16 March 1960, p. 7.

[33] Sandy Hobbs and David Cornwell, '"The Lore and Language of Schoolchildren": A Study of Scholars' Reactions', *Folklore*, 102:2 (1992), 175–82.

[34] Pat Pinsent, 'Historical Studies', in *Teaching Children's Fiction*, ed. by Charles Butler (Basingstoke: Palgrave Macmillan, 2006), 6–28, pp. 17–19.

of serious scholarship in its own right, a fact reflected in the introduction to the important essay collection *Only Connect* (1969), a Canadian publication which included essays by both British and North American authors:

> Our primary aim has been to find selections that deal with children's literature as an essential part of the whole realm of literary activity, to be discussed in the same terms and judged by the same standards that would apply to any other branch of writing.[35]

This statement of purpose is notable in its emphasis on the specifically literary aspects of children's books, rather than their educational or psychological significance. This viewpoint was to form one of the major points of conflict in debates about what constituted 'quality' children's literature, as this chapter will show.

Despite the emergence of literary critical approaches like those in *Only Connect*, interdisciplinary approaches to children's literature remained the dominant mode throughout the 1960s and 1970s. 1969 saw the landmark Exeter conference on *Recent Children's Fiction and Its Role in Education*, which brought together teachers, writers, academics and librarians to discuss issues relating to children's literature.[36] As a result of this conference, 1970 saw the establishment of a new journal, *Children's Literature in Education* (*CLE*), creating a space for more extended critical treatments of children's literature. As the name suggests, *CLE* placed the study of children's literature firmly within an educational context, although in practice the journal published articles from a broad range of disciplines. Published jointly in Britain and the United States, it also furthered shared debate between these two countries; a tradition it continues today. Educational interest in children's literature was boosted in 1975 by the Bullock Report, *A Language for Life*, which inquired into the teaching of English and the place of literature in the curriculum.[37] One result of the Bullock Report was the publication of *The Cool Web* (1977), a collection of essays which surveyed the question of children's reading from a variety of perspectives, addressing the experience of the child reader as well as investigating educative approaches. Despite its basis in the field of education, *The Cool Web* included essays from a wide range of perspectives, both professional

---

[35]   Sheila Egoff, G.T. Stubbs and L.F. Ashley, eds, 'Preface', *Only Connect: Readings on Children's Literature* (Toronto, New York: Oxford University Press, 1969), xv–xvii, p. xv.

[36]   Geoff Fox et al., eds, *Writers, Critics, and Children: Articles from Children's Literature in Education* (London: Heinemann Educational Books, 1976), p. ix.

[37]   Margaret Meek et al., eds, *The Cool Web: The Pattern of Children's Reading* (London: Bodley Head, 1977); Alan Bullock, 'A Language for Life' (London: HMSO, 1975), *Education in England*, < http://www.educationengland.org.uk/documents/bullock/> [accessed 02/08/12].

The Cool Web was intended to anticipate the Bullock report, but owing to delays in publication did not appear until two years later.

and literary critical. D.W. Harding's 'The bond with the author', which explores the relationship of author and reader in literature, demonstrated the relevance of the broader field of literary criticism to the field of children's literature.[38] The fact that Harding, a well-respected literary scholar, was employed as a professor of psychology rather than literature is a useful reminder that children's literature scholarship was not unique in crossing disciplinary boundaries.

The range of critical venues for children's literature was further extended by the founding of *Signal Approaches to Children's Books*, launched in 1970 by Nancy Chambers (née Lockwood), who had also edited *Children's Book News*, and her husband Aidan Chambers. *Signal* aimed to function as 'a place where thoughtful writing on any aspect of children's literature, in a variety of registers, would be attended to'.[39] The journal is significant not only for the range and quality of its articles, but also because of its success in moving between 'a variety of registers'. The fact that many of its readers were parents, educators and librarians rather than literary scholars did not preclude the publication of firmly literary critical material such as Aidan Chambers' seminal article on reader-response theory, 'The Reader in the Book', which is discussed at length in Chapter 3. The trend towards academic rather than purely practical approaches to children's literature was also evident in the books published about children's literature during the 1970s, such as Nicholas Tucker's *Suitable for Children?* (1976), a collection of essays on controversies in children's literature, and Mary Cadogan and Patricia Craig's analysis of girls' school stories, *You're a Brick, Angela!* (1976).

The thriving critical environment of the 1960s and 1970s helped to create the sense of a golden age of children's literature. More importantly, the wide-ranging cultural debate surrounding children's literature and childhood helped to produce new definitions of quality in children's literature. While early children's literature reflects many unexamined cultural assumptions, the voices of later critics were instrumental in changing the status quo.

From Primer to Pleasure: Establishing Critical Perspectives on Children's Literature

A large proportion of the critical writing about children's literature published during the early 1960s followed the lead of Harvey Darton in attempting to provide a historical overview of books for children. Roger Lancelyn Green's *Tellers of Tales*, Mary Thwaite's *From Primer to Pleasure* and Marcus Crouch's *Treasure Seekers and Borrowers* all offer a primarily historical approach, while Gillian Avery published a detailed study on Victorian children's literature, *Nineteenth Century Children* (1965). These texts were partially motivated by the desire to record a history which had been neglected by previous scholars, but the process of

---

[38]   D.W. Harding, 'Psychological processes in the reading of fiction' in *The Cool Web*, 58–72. Originally published in the *British Journal of Aesthetics*, 2:2 (1962).

[39]   Nancy Chambers, 'A Note From the Editor', *Signal Approaches to Children's Books*, <http://www.claas-kazzer.de/signal/about.html> [accessed 10/12/07].

tracing the development of children's literature also entailed defining the nature and qualities of children's literature. By documenting a long, continuous history, critics were able to present children's literature as a legitimate and distinctive category.

As Roberta Seelinger Trites has observed, growth and progress are pervasive tropes in children's literature scholarship, and these themes serve to present newer literature as the apogee of a long tradition.[40] This trend is clearly identifiable in the criticism of the 1960s, which typically presents the history of children's literature as a progression towards an increasingly accurate notion of what is valuable to the child reader. This discourse tends to obfuscate the complexities of real childhoods, presenting constructed and culturally specific notions of children's reading as authoritative. Mary Thwaite, for example, points to the fantasy stories of the 'first golden age' – notably Lewis Carroll's *Alice* – as evidence of a new understanding of children:

> The child, at last, was put to the centre, and his [sic] need to wonder and laugh and roam and to live in a world of his own making was recognised [...] the important advance in admitting the need to train the childish imagination and allow it freedom to grow brought far greater benefits than disadvantages.[41]

Thwaite's analysis of the Victorian texts she is discussing betrays her assumptions about childhood and quality in children's literature. Her assertion that the child 'at last' was put to the centre assumes a shared cultural belief in the importance of putting children's needs and desires first – a belief which Hugh Cunningham argues was in fact a relatively new cultural phenomenon.[42] The entire passage enforces particular ideologies about childhood: children have a 'need' for imaginative play and recognition of this is an 'important advance'. Thwaite's language also reveals some unconscious ideologies: while she is critical of the didacticism of early children's books, adults must still allow the imaginative freedom of which she approves, and it must be trained into an appropriate mode.[43] 'Good' children's literature offers the child freedom, she implies – but not too much. While she does not directly address the question of contemporary children's literature, Thwaite's analysis both reflects and reinforces contemporary critical assumptions. Under the guise of documenting the history of children's books she therefore presents an ideal model for children's literature which is similar in form (although different in intent) to the eighteenth- and nineteenth-century religious framework of which she is critical.

---

[40] Roberta Seelinger Trites, 'Historiography and Children's Literature', paper presented at *The Best of Three: The 36th annual Children's Literature Association Conference*, Charlotte, NC, USA, 12 June 2009.

[41] M.F. Thwaite, *From Primer to Pleasure*, p. 81.

[42] Hugh Cunningham, *The Invention of Childhood* (London: BBC Books, 2006), pp. 213–19.

[43] The dominant ideology of the period is, of course, also indicated in the automatic use of the masculine pronoun, even by female scholars. This usage will be reproduced without comment in further quotations.

From Primer to Pleasure is typical of historical overviews of children's literature published during the 1960s in emphasising the value of imaginative freedom in children's literature. Successive critics follow Harvey Darton in painting the history of children's literature as 'the scene of a battle between instruction and amusement, between restraint and freedom, between hesitant morality and spontaneous happiness', with the forces of moralism and didacticism prevailing until the Victorian era, and 'spontaneous happiness' representing the most desirable goal.[44] This discourse frames the history of children's literature as a progression towards ever more imaginative and enjoyable literature. Frank Eyre, writing in 1971, is unusual in depicting the swing between didacticism and pleasure in children's literature as part of a cycle of reaction against previous trends, but concludes,

> With each swing of the pendulum, however, the reaction towards didacticism became less pronounced and the books produced became easier to read and enjoy. It is possible, therefore, to see the whole history of British children's publishing as a development towards freedom – freedom of expression, thought, and, above all, imagination.[45]

Although Eyre recognises that both extremes are essentially reactionary cultural constructions, he ultimately upholds the perception of a progression towards a freer, more imaginative and – implicitly – better children's literature. As critics such as Patricia Demers have argued, the animus against pleasure in early children's books has been overstated, but the prevalence of this narrative in the historical surveys of the 1960s reveals as much about contemporary beliefs about childhood and children's literature as about the values of earlier books for children.[46] A reluctance to appear overly didactic is clearly evident in the critical works of the early 1960s; nevertheless, didacticism was certainly not absent from either the criticism or the literature of the period.

The World of Childhood: Constructing the Child

Children's literature is intimately connected with constructions of childhood itself; indeed, Jacqueline Rose has argued that children's literature exists only as a manifestation of cultural constructions of childhood. Rose's critique of children's fiction as emerging out of 'a conception of both the child and the world

---

[44] F.J. Harvey Darton, *Children's Books in England* (Cambridge: Cambridge University Press, 1982), pp. x, I. Quoted in Peter Hunt, *An Introduction to Children's Literature*, p. 27.

[45] Frank Eyre, *British Children's Books in the Twentieth Century* (London: Longman, 1971), pp. 18–19.

[46] Patricia Demers, *From Instruction to Delight: An Anthology of Children's Literature to 1850*, 2nd edn (Oxford: Oxford University Press, 2004).

as knowable in a direct and unmediated way' has clear antecedents in the discourse about children's literature which emerged during the 'second golden age'.[47] In the rapidly changing social context of the 1960s and 1970s, the intense interest in children's literature was part of a broader cultural endeavour focused on defining and shaping childhood.

Jacqueline Rose argues that the conception of the child which underpins children's fiction 'places the innocence of the child and a primary state of language and/or culture in a close and mutually dependent relation', a conception which is certainly evident in Mary Thwaite's privileging of imaginative liberty in children's literature.[48] This essentially Romantic image of the child is characteristic of the children's literature and criticism from the post-war period up until the mid-1960s. Paul Hazard, in *Books, Children and Men*, presented imagination as a valuable and distinctive characteristic of childhood which set children apart from adults:

> How far removed is the world of childhood? Its inhabitants seem of another species [...] Children are rich with all they do not own, rich with the potential wonders of their universe. Making believe is not only one of their earliest pleasures, it is their vital spark, the token of their liberty. Reason does not curb them, for they have not yet learned its restraints.[49]

Hazard's 'world of childhood' is presented as complete in itself: adults are oppressive intruders upon children's imaginative liberty. The criticism of earlier didactic literature present in Mary Thwaite's work is even more evident in Hazard's criticism of adult reason and his claim that such texts 'effaced from a young heart the sense of freedom and pleasure in play'.[50] The influence of Rousseau and of Romantic constructions of childhood are evident in Hazard's emphasis on the importance of the imagination and the natural instincts of the child, but his thesis is also strongly coloured by his historical context. Hazard was writing on the eve of the Second World War, and his idealised presentation of childhood reflects a sense that adult values had produced an era of war. The 'vital spark' of children's make-believe offered the possibility of a future which could escape the mistakes of the past – a hope equally relevant in the 1950s and 1960s, when the long shadow of the Second World War was darkened by the new threat of the Cold War.

Tom Shippey and Charles Butler have both argued persuasively that the experience of war played an important role in shaping the fantasy literature of writers such as J.R.R. Tolkien, C.S. Lewis, Alan Garner and Susan Cooper, and Hazard's portrayal of childhood and imagination as an escape from adult

---

[47]   Jacqueline Rose, *The Case of Peter Pan, or, The Impossibility of Children's Fiction* (London: Macmillan, 1992), p. 9.

[48]   Jacqueline Rose, *The Case of Peter Pan, or, The Impossibility of Children's Fiction*, p. 9.

[49]   Paul Hazard, *Books, Children and Men*, pp. 1–3.

[50]   Paul Hazard, *Books, Children and Men*, p. 3.

corruption is clearly present in the work of all these writers.[51] Tolkien's childlike hobbits are the least susceptible to the lure of the One Ring, which exerts its most pernicious influence on Men. C.S. Lewis's child heroes repeatedly bring new life and hope to the world of Narnia: in both *The Lion, the Witch and the Wardrobe* (1950) and *The Voyage of the Dawn Treader* (1952), children overthrow corrupt adult regimes in order to assume their rightful roles as benevolent rulers of the kingdom. It is notable that in both books, Lucy – the youngest and most closely connected to Narnia – is castigated for 'making believe' and 'dreaming' when she tries to tell her siblings about Aslan and Narnia, only to be vindicated later in the text.[52] What appears to be make-believe is in fact a clearer view of 'the potential wonders of the universe' which are invisible to Lucy's older siblings, already conditioned by adult ideas of what is possible. The theme of children as repositories of hope and a defence against the forces of evil is also clearly evident in Susan Cooper's Dark is Rising series and Alan Garner's *The Weirdstone of Brisingamen* (1960) and *Elidor* (1965). The turning point of Cooper's *Greenwitch* (1974) depends on the instinctive, unreasoning response of her heroine Jane to the plight of the supernatural Greenwitch:

> 'Oh dear,' she said impulsively, 'I wish you could be happy.'
> She thought, as she said it: how babyish, when you could have wished for anything, even getting the grail back...[53]

'How babyish' – but it is Jane's sympathy, not the reasoned arguments of Will and Merriman, the Old Ones, which ultimately persuades the Greenwitch to come to the aid of the Light. The nature of Jane's role in the quest is, of course, heavily gendered, but it is also emblematic of the kind of instinctive goodness which Paul Hazard presents as a quality of childhood.

The concept of childhood as a period of imaginative liberty during which the child's needs should be put to the fore is consonant with a broader cultural change in the way children were perceived. Peter and Iona Opie, in their survey *Children's Games in Street and Playground*, suggested that children became more rather than less civilised when playing games without the supervision of adults, reinforcing Hazard's emphasis on the negative impact of adult discipline.[54] A responsive, child-centred approach was at the heart of the revolutionary childcare manuals of

---

[51] Tom Shippey, 'Tolkien as a Post-War Writer' in *Proceedings of the J. R. R. Tolkien Centenary Conference*, ed. by Patricia Reynolds and Glen H. GoodKnight (Altadena: Mythopoeic Press, 1995), 84–93; Charles Butler, *Four British Fantasists: Places and Culture in the Children's Fantasies of Penelope Lively, Alan Garner, Diana Wynne Jones, and Susan Cooper* (Oxford: Children's Literature Association and The Scarecrow Press, 2006).

[52] C.S. Lewis, *The Lion, the Witch and the Wardrobe* (London: Fontana Lions, 1986), pp. 27–9, pp. 44–6; C.S. Lewis, *Prince Caspian* (London: Fontana Lions, 1986), pp. 110–13.

[53] Susan Cooper, *Greenwitch* (Harmondsworth: Puffin, 1977), p. 41.

[54] Iona and Peter Opie, *Children's Games in Street and Playground* (Oxford: Clarendon Press, 1969), p. 13.

Doctor Benjamin Spock, who rejected the need for strict discipline and routine. Educational policy in Britain reflected similar ideals; the Plowden Report on 'Children and Their Primary Schools' (1967) stated

> At the heart of the educational process lies the child. No advances in policy, no acquisitions of new equipment have their desired effect unless they are in harmony with the nature of the child, unless they are fundamentally acceptable to him.[55]

The report was heavily influenced by the child development model put forward by Jean Piaget, who portrayed childhood as a series of four stages, each distinctive and important in its own right. It advocated the abolition of corporal punishment – albeit unsuccessfully – and emphasised the value of teacher-led curricula which could be tailored to children's needs. The idea of education which was 'in harmony with the nature of the child' is strongly reminiscent of Hazard's emphasis on the special nature of childhood and the potentially damaging role of education. This trend is very clearly evident in children's literature criticism of the 1960s, which emphasises the need for children's books to address children on their own terms. The North American author and critic Eleanor Cameron outlined the characteristics of a successful children's book in *The Green and Burning Tree* (1962):

> This [a successful book] can only be achieved by the writer's invoking the true aura of childhood through reexperiencing that emotional state he lived in as a child, a state composed of delight in the simplest, most secret, sometimes the oddest things, of sadnesses and fears and terrors one could not or would not explain, of a continuing wonder about much that seems drab and familiar to adults […] He cannot *look back*, he has got to *enter in*. He has got to be a child again.[56]

The influence of Paul Hazard is discernible in Cameron's presentation of the child's world as incomprehensible to adults – filled with things 'one could not or would not explain' – and the consequent need for writers of children's literature to 'become' children in order to enter fully into their readers' experiences. The British critic Margery Fisher rejected the idea that it was possible or desirable for adults to share in the mindset of a child, but echoes Cameron in stating that 'anyone who enters the child's world, whose dreams and wishes in some measure become merged into a child's dreams and wishes, will produce a better book than the writer who writes, as it were, from the top of his head'.[57] Fisher's analysis suggests that children's literature is not an exercise in raising children to adult

---

[55]   Bridget Plowden and The Central Advisory Council for Education (England), *The Plowden Report: Children and their Primary Schools* (London: HMSO, 1967), Volume 1, Chapter 2, <http://www.educationengland.org.uk/documents/plowden/> [accessed 02/08/12].

[56]   Eleanor Cameron, *The Green and Burning Tree: On the Writing and Enjoyment of Children's Books* (Boston, Toronto: Little, Brown, 1969), p. 14.

[57]   Margery Fisher, *Intent upon Reading*, p. 14.

standards – an attitude which Mary Thwaite and Paul Hazard ascribe to earlier eras – but an arena in which the adult must meet the child on his or her own terms. In Thwaite's words, the child is 'put to the centre', and it is this mentality which gives the criticism of the 1960s its distinctive flavour.

The desire to put the child to the centre evident in the children's literature criticism of the 1960s is strongly evident in the books themselves. The theme of entering into the child's imaginative world recurs throughout the 1950s and 1960s. C.S. Lewis's fantasy world of Narnia – literally ruled by children – is more real and important than the everyday world. In Philippa Pearce's Carnegie Medal winner *Tom's Midnight Garden* (1958), the adult Hatty goes 'back in Time to when she was a girl, wanting to play in the garden', meeting the real child Tom in dreams of her girlhood.[58] Children's imaginative play also takes on real life in another Carnegie winner: Pauline Clarke's *The Twelve and the Genii* (1962) centres around a set of wooden soldiers owned by the Brontë siblings and animated by the force of their imagination. When found by another child, Max, a hundred years later, they come to life again. The importance of respecting children's imaginative play is reiterated throughout the book, as when the local parson discusses the importance of the soldiers' different individual personalities:

> Max listened, absorbed. All these soldiers were his friends. This man, towards whom he felt great warmth, understood, and thought of them as real. How he wished he could show him them![59]

The parson is presented as a sympathetic character precisely because of his ability to connect with the soldiers on the same level at which Max experiences them. Similarly, in Lucy Boston's Green Knowe series (1954–1976), discussed in more detail in Chapter 2, the barriers between imaginative play and reality are fluid, and the ability of Grandmother Oldknow to enter into children's experiences is what makes her an appealing character. Texts like these embody the notion of entering into childhood which critics such as Eleanor Cameron identify as essential to the creation of good children's literature: that fact that all three writers were award winners indicates that they were indeed recognised as 'quality' literature.

A focus on entering the child's world is a clear theme in both British children's literature and British culture at large; however, the presentation of childhood in children's books was more nuanced and less isolated from adulthood than the work of figures such as Paul Hazard indicates. On the contrary, entering the child's world in books of this period frequently entails recognition of the child's desire for the autonomy and respect which is enjoyed by adults. In *The Twelve and the Genii*, for example, the animated toy soldiers – to whom the protagonist Max stands *in loco parentis* by virtue of his greater size – are in effect adults with independent desires. A recurring theme throughout the book is Max's respect for the soldiers' dignity, as in the scene when he introduces them to his sister:

---

[58] Philippa Pearce, *Tom's Midnight Garden* (Harmondsworth: Puffin, 1976), p. 215.

[59] Pauline Clarke, *The Twelve and the Genii* (Harmondsworth: Puffin, 1977), p. 135.

'Jane, don't treat him like a toy, or a baby animal, will you?' warned Max. He felt that this would be wrong and insulting. 'He's a small, alive person,' he explained, 'And full of years and wisdom, he says so.'[60]

Whereas Paul Hazard's construction of the imaginative child positions children as 'another species' – and one which is superior to adults – Pauline Clarke implies that children are simply 'small, alive people'. The same theme continues in later texts: in Penelope Lively's Whitbread Award winner *A Stitch in Time* (1976) the imaginative life of the protagonist Maria is treated with as much seriousness as the 'real' events, but part of the emotional impact of the novel rests upon the inability of Maria's parents to recognise that she is not 'just a child', but an intelligent individual. Like *The Twelve and the Genii*, *A Stitch in Time* challenges the idea that children's small size correlates with a lack of intellect or emotional complexity, stating 'It's what you are that matters, not what you look like'.[61] While imagination and fantasy in these texts are presented as distinctive and important qualities of childhood, children are not divorced from adult concerns.

Central to the construction of childhood during the early 1960s is an emphasis on children as imaginative, autonomous and complex beings. The child-centred education policy of the era is clearly contextualised by the portrayal of childhood in children's books, which present their child characters as intellectually capable and deserving of respect. As *A Stitch in Time* demonstrates, this theme continued into the 1970s, and it is this sense that children deserved recognition and respect which helped to fuel many of the movements in education and children's literature throughout the 1960s and 1970s. While childhood is not necessarily presented as being in opposition to adulthood, there is a strong sense that it has a distinctive and important character. Both the critical texts and the children's books of the period present imagination and fantasy as central and necessary aspects of childhood: this construction of the child reader had important implications for the kind of literature which was regarded as 'good' for young readers.

A Fantasy of Freedom: Imagination and Escapism

Critical and cultural constructions of the child as intrinsically imaginative helped to position fantasy as a 'natural' genre for children's literature, an idea which, as Matthew Grenby notes, is a recurring theme in discussions of children's literature.[62] Mary Thwaite's praise of the fantasy literature which emerged during the first golden age highlights the perception that the 'best' children's books were to be found in this genre, a connection which was inevitably strengthened by the fact that many of the most accomplished and highly-praised authors of the 1950s

---

[60]   Pauline Clarke, *The Twelve and the Genii*, p. 79.

[61]   Penelope Lively, *A Stitch in Time* (London: Mammoth, 2000), p. 60.

[62]   Matthew Grenby, *Children's Literature* (Edinburgh: Edinburgh University Press, 2008), p. 144.

and 1960s were writing fantasy. The connection between children and fantasy was more than merely circumstantial, however. In a passage which echoes Paul Hazard's characterisation of children as 'unfettered' by reason, the psychiatrist and author Catherine Storr – writing under the pseudonym Helen Lourie – argues:

> Children pass easily from the incomprehensible adult world to the equally mysterious world of fantasy, partly because they are not steeped in the habit of convention, partly because they are still ignorant of so many of the laws by which our lives are governed that the discovery of new freedoms cannot surprise them.[63]

The assumption that fantasy was in some sense a 'natural' genre for children's literature recurs throughout the criticism of the early 1960s. The Russian poet and critic Kornei Chukovsky argued that fantasy and fairy tales were intrinsic to human nature, and that children who were offered only social realist texts would create their own fantasies: 'It makes no difference whether or not the child is offered fairy tales for, if he is not, he becomes his own Andersen, Grimm, Ershov'.[64] Children's books such as *The Twelve and the Genii*, *A Stitch in Time* and Lucy Boston's Green Knowe series, all of which feature extremely imaginative protagonists, reinforce the idea of fantasy as an essential component of childhood, and therefore of children's literature. In Penelope Lively's book *The Ghost of Thomas Kempe* (1973), the slightly condescending implication of childish credulity in Catherine Storr's analysis is turned on its head by the increasing absurdities of the adults' attempts to find rational explanations for the activities of a ghost. The critical and cultural valuation of imagination worked to position storytelling of all genres as valuable, but the persistent association of childhood with an unfettered imaginative capacity helped to position the fantasy genre as particularly valuable to children.

Critical valuations of fantasy did not focus solely on its appeal to children, but also on its perceived moral and educational value. C.S. Lewis – who along with J.R.R. Tolkien explicitly challenged the idea that fantasy was solely or even primarily the province of childhood – characterised fairy tales as offering the reader access to the numinous: 'the dim sense of something beyond his reach [which] far from dulling or emptying the actual world, gives it a new dimension of depth'.[65] Eleanor Cameron follows Lewis in arguing that the medium of fantasy allows children access to concepts beyond their conscious understanding, including concepts of the divine:

---

[63]   Helen Lourie, 'Where is Fancy Bred?' in *Only Connect*, 106–10, p. 108. The article was originally published in *New Society* (1962), which was aimed at a general adult audience rather than at the world of children's literature; presumably this is the reason for Storr's use of the pseudonym, under which she also published several novels for adults.

[64]   K. Chukovsky, 'There is no such thing as a shark' in *The Cool Web*, 48–50, p. 49. First published in K. Chukovsky, *From Two to Five* (1963).

[65]   C.S. Lewis, 'On Three Ways of Writing For Children' in *Only Connect*, 207–20, p. 215. First published in the *Proceedings* of the Bournemouth Conference (1962).

> The great fantasies often express truths too subtle for the intellect alone; in tales
> of witches and goblins and princesses and animals and dolls there are judgements
> passed on reality, ideas presented which the child may not consciously remember,
> but which he absorbs along with the luminous tissue of the tale itself.[66]

The use of fantasy as a medium for complex concepts and emotions is clearly not
confined either to children's literature or to the literature of any particular period,
but it is particularly evident in the children's books of the 1950s and 1960s. In
particular, 'high' fantasy which involved the creation of a secondary world – either
an entire fantasy universe or as a different plane of existence which lay alongside
the 'real' world – and involved its protagonists in quests which concerned the fate
of that world was a frequent feature of children's books during this period. The
Christian allegory of C.S. Lewis's own Narnia series, praised by the prominent
Canadian librarian Lillian H. Smith for carrying its readers on 'a spiritual journey
towards the heart of reality', set a strong precedent for the resurgence of children's
fantasy as a means of engaging with questions of good and evil, a theme which
Tom Shippey argues was a key factor in producing fantasy for adults during the
post-war period.[67] The fantasy work of British writers such as Alan Garner, Susan
Cooper and William Mayne, and of Americans including Madeline L'Engle and
Ursula Le Guin engages with questions of evil, virtue and belief. Evil appears
both as a hostile and alien force – Susan Cooper's powers of the Dark in *The
Dark is Rising* and IT in Madeline L'Engle's *A Wrinkle in Time* (1962) – and as a
part of human nature. In Ursula Le Guin's *A Wizard of Earthsea* (1968) the evil
which pursues the hero Ged is his own dark shadow, while in William Mayne's *A
Game of Dark* (1971) the fantasy landscape is a manifestation of the protagonist's
psychological landscape. It is notable that the direct Christian allegory of Lewis's
work has few descendants: there is a broadly Judaeo-Christian influence in the
themes of good and evil, but the role of Christianity itself is more ambiguous.
Ursula Le Guin draws heavily upon Taoism for the principles of balance on
which her fantasy world of Earthsea is founded, while Madeline L'Engle employs
explicitly Christian elements but positions Christ as simply one in a long line
of great thinkers which also includes 'Schweitzer and Gandhi and Buddha and
Beethoven and Rembrandt and St. Francis'.[68] Similarly, the supernatural powers of
Susan Cooper's Old Ones are part of a metanarrative which exists outside of time
and includes 'All Gods […] and all the things they have ever stood for'.[69] Narrative
also takes on a spiritual dimension in the work of Alan Garner, in which myth
and storytelling are positioned as essential in shaping identity and understanding.
The use of narrative to provide a philosophical and spiritual framework which

---

[66]   Eleanor Cameron, *The Green and Burning Tree*, p. 47.

[67]   Lillian H. Smith, 'News From Narnia' in *Only Connect*, 170–75, p. 174. First
published in the *CLA Bulletin* (1958); Tom Shippey, 'Tolkien as a Post-War Writer', p. 86.

[68]   Sue Jenkins, 'Growing Up in Earthsea', *Children's Literature in Education*, 16:1
(March 1985), 21–31, p. 21; Madeline L'Engle, *A Wrinkle in Time* (Harmondsworth: Puffin,
1967), p. 82.

[69]   Susan Cooper, *The Dark is Rising*, p. 165.

is outside the boundaries of organised religion is a recurring element of fantasy throughout the 1960s and 1970s; the idea that it could – and should – express 'truths too subtle for the intellect alone' reflects a desire to move away from the overt religious message of earlier eras – which, as historians of children's literature have highlighted, featured heavily in earlier works for children – without sacrificing a moral and spiritual dimension in children's literature.

The popularity of fantasy as a conduit for ethical and moral guidance reflects the same hostility towards overt didacticism that is present in histories of children's literature during this period. This attitude colours the discussion of the Victorian allegorical novel by children's writer and critic Gillian Avery:

> The problem of how much of an allegory a child will understand is not very important. Children can assimilate ideas unconsciously, and as the ideas would in most cases be familiar to them, the symbolic events and characters probably fit automatically into grooves already made in the child's mind. Furthermore, if they are given a beautiful and exciting world to dream over, the child may weave into the fabric of his dream the ideals the story suggests, and thus teach himself in the best possible way.[70]

The idea that 'the beautiful and exciting world' of fantasy could not only impart knowledge in a subtle and unconscious fashion, but could actually lead a child to 'teach himself', resolves the tension between Paul Hazard's portrayal of the child as instinctively good and the desire to offer children education and guidance. Stories – and in particular fantasy stories – allow the child a natural, self-governed education.

Fantasy offered the possibility of discussing broad philosophical and spiritual truths, but the books of the period also display intense concern with the personal and psychological dimensions, as in the case of Mayne's *A Game of Dark*, in which the protagonist's feelings of fear and resentment towards his disabled father are played out through his experiences in a fantasy landscape in which he exists as a squire charged with slaying the malevolent worm which threatens his village. In *Marianne Dreams* (1951) by Catherine Storr – who had training as a psychologist – the protagonist Marianne is able to enter her own drawings in dreams, creating a fantasy world in which her own feelings of frustration and resentment are made manifest. Alan Garner's *The Owl Service* uses supernatural events as a conduit for real emotions. At the climax of the novel, the intense mixture of sexual jealousy, class resentment and hurt in the relationship between the three protagonists is given physical expression through the mythological figure of Blodeuwedd, a woman made from the flowers of the meadow and turned into an owl for her unfaithfulness:

> The skylight smashed under a branch, but the wires bonded in the glass kept out the weight that pressed to enter, and in the darkness the feathers and eyes and the claws hung and moved.[71]

---

[70] Gillian Avery, *Nineteenth Century Children: Heroes and Heroines in English Children's Stories 1980–1900* (London: Hodder & Stoughton, 1965), p. 58.

[71] Alan Garner, *The Owl Service* (Harmondsworth: Penguin, 1969), p. 171.

The novel, which won both the Carnegie Medal and the Guardian Award, was highly acclaimed for its blend of fantasy and realism. A review in the *Times Educational Supplement* praised the novel for the way 'The presentation of a complex psychological theme to children no older than the characters in the story is handled with subtle mastery'.[72] The psychological value of fantasy became increasingly emphasised in critical approaches during the 1970s. The educationalist James Britton, writing in 1971, argued:

> Culture, the common pool of humanity, offers the young child witches and fairy godmothers, symbols which may embody and work upon the hate and love that are part of a close, dependent relationship: he will read of witches and tell stories of his own that arise directly from his needs. In doing so, he performs an assimilative task, working towards a more harmonious relationship between inner needs and external demands.[73]

This analysis shares obvious similarities with ideas about fantasy as a means of developing 'unconscious understanding' such as those posited by Lillian Smith and Gillian Avery, but the role of fantasy here is more personal, helping the child move towards a greater understanding of him or herself rather than towards more abstract truths. In his landmark discussion of fairy tales, *The Uses of Enchantment* (1976), Bruno Bettelheim addresses fantasy from a psycho-analytical viewpoint, presenting it as fundamental to psychological development:

> The unconscious is the source of raw materials and the basis upon which the ego erects the edifice of our personality. In this simile our fantasies are the natural resources which provide and shape this raw material, making it useful for the ego's personality-building tasks. If we are deprived of this natural resource, our life remains limited; without fantasies to give us hope, we do not have the strength to meet the adversities of life. Childhood is the time when these fantasies need to be nurtured.[74]

Bettelheim recasts the Romantic image of childhood as characterised by imagination and fantasy as part of the developmental process, giving it a more overtly utilitarian role and moving back towards a didactic view of children's literature.

The utilitarian emphasis of psychological interpretations of the role of fantasy partly reflects an increasing tension in attitudes towards fantasy as the 1970s progressed. The cultural interest in both fantasy and children's literature which emerged during the 1960s produced a reaction among those who regarded

---

[72] Anonymous review, 'Dichotomy of Adolescence', *The Times Educational Supplement*, 25 August 1967, photocopy, Penguin Archive, Bristol University, DM/1107/PK66.

[73] James Britton, 'The role of fantasy' in *The Cool Web*, 40–47, p. 47. Originally published in *English in Education*, 5:3 (1971).

[74] Bruno Bettelheim, *The Uses of Enchantment: The Meaning and Importance of Fairy Tales* (Harmondsworth: Penguin, 1991), p. 121.

the emphasis on imagination and fantasy as essentially escapist in nature. The philosopher Mary Warnock criticised the popularity of children's books among adults in terms which presented the imaginative fantasies of children's books as essentially simplistic and regressive, arguing that the appetite for 'curling up, metaphorically thumb-sucking, lost in *The Secret Garden* or *Sara Crewe*' was 'imaginatively lazy'.[75] Warnock's argument reflects an anxiety about the growing cultural visibility of children's literature and the trend for adults to read books published for children, and a tendency to elide the fantasy genre with children's literature. Both trends have re-emerged in recent years in responses to Harry Potter: author and critic A.S. Byatt criticised the Harry Potter books as 'jokey latent fantasies', arguing that their popularity among adults reflects a desire for comfort reading and a lack of discrimination.[76] The close association between fantasy and childhood tended to position fantasy as inherently child*ish*. Whereas critics like Mary Thwaite and Paul Hazard, and books like *The Twelve and the Genii* had presented an imaginative return to childhood in a positive light, Warnock's analysis suggests that childhood – and fantasy – should be 'grown out of'. Psychological analyses of fantasy enabled children's literature critics to respond to such charges of escapism. Wendy Jago, in a rebuttal of Mary Warnock's criticisms of children's literature, cites the psychologist Jerome Bruner in support of her assertion that far from being escapist, fantasies such as Ursula Le Guin's *A Wizard of Earthsea* helped both children and adults to access an 'honest reality' and provided a means of exploring the complexities of a rapidly changing world.[77] Dick Cate also takes a psychological approach in his analysis of the potentially regressive nature of fantasy in Frances Hodgson Burnett's *A Little Princess* and George Eliot's *The Mill on the Floss*:

> Sara always seems to have her fantasy under control. Maggie Tulliver, too, has a doll. But Maggie, from the start, seems to run *to* her dolls and *away from* life, whereas for Sara the doll leads *out* to Ermengarde and Becky.[78]

Psychological analyses of the role of fantasy help to position it as a tool which 'leads out' – in Bettleheim's terms, the 'building block' for a successful adulthood. This tension between the appeal of fantasy and imagination is clearly evident in a number of the children's books of the period. In *Tom's Midnight Garden*, Hatty's recreation of the garden of her childhood serves to demonstrate the value of growing up: although the reader shares Tom's grief at the loss of the garden,

---

[75]   Mary Warnock, 'Escape into Childhood', *New Society*, 13 May 1971, p. 823.

[76]   A.S. Byatt, 'Harry Potter and the Childish Adult', *The New York Times*, 7 July 2003, <http://www.nytimes.com/2003/07/07/opinion/harry-potter-and-the-childish-adult.html?scp=10&sq=A.S.Byatt&st=nyt&pagewanted=1> [accessed 03/01/10].

[77]   Wendy Jago, '"A Wizard of Earthsea" and the Charge of Escapism', *Children's Literature in Education*, 3:2 (1972), 21–9, p. 29.

[78]   Dick Cate, 'Forms of storying: the inner and outer worlds: uses of narrative' in *The Cool Web*, 24–31, p. 25. Originally published in *English in Education*, 5:3 (1971).

ultimately both the reader and Tom learn to see Hatty's progression out of the fantasy garden and into adulthood as both inevitable and desirable. Similarly, in *A Stitch in Time* Maria begins by thinking 'I want to be me as I am now for ever and ever', existing happily in a world peopled by imaginary friendships, but by the end of the book she can think with satisfaction of growing up:

> And into her head came the idea of mysterious and interesting future Marias, larger and older, doing things one could barely picture. They seemed like friends she had not yet met.[79]

The idea that fantasy must ultimately be left behind is even more strongly apparent in Philippa Pearce's later novel *A Dog So Small* (1962), in which a child's unhappiness, manifested in his desperate longing for a dog, leads him to become so caught up in the fantasy of his imagined pet that he is seriously injured, only narrowly avoiding being killed in a road accident. While these texts suggest that fantasy helps to give childhood its distinctive quality, they also present it as a tool for helping children develop and move into adulthood. When fantasy is not held in check, it becomes destructive. Peter Dickinson's Changes trilogy depicts a contemporary Britain in which fantasy has literally taken over: the dreams of a drugged Merlin have cast a spell over the country which induces all but a few to react violently against the mechanical apparatus of the modern age, producing a pseudo-medieval state. The trilogy ranges over a wide range of themes, but the first book in particular, *The Weathermonger* (1968), suggests the dangers of a society which rejects reason and becomes ruled by superstition and fantasy.

At the end of the 1960s and in the 1970s, new tensions emerged around fantasy. While earlier critics had praised the genre for its capacity to offer 'truths too subtle for the intellect alone', the question of precisely what such 'truths' might be came increasingly into focus. In an article of 1971, the academic and critic David Holbrook questioned the Christian values contained within the Narnia series, arguing that 'under cover of his apparent religious intentions and his mask of benignity C.S. Lewis conveys to his readers a powerful unconscious message that the world is full of malignancy'.[80] Children's literature was subjected to similar ideological scrutiny by critics such as Bob Dixon, who criticised the predominately white, middle-class, male-dominated world of children's literature, criticisms which can easily be related to the work of fantasists such as C.S. Lewis, Susan Cooper and Pauline Clark. As the 1970s progressed, the numinous values of fantasy began to be rejected in favour of an increasing engagement with the 'real' child. While fantasy remained an important force in children's literature, the new fantasy writers who emerged in the 1970s – such as Diana Wynne Jones,

---

[79]   Penelope Lively, *A Stitch in Time*, p. 48; p. 136.

[80]   David Holbrook, 'The Problem of C.S. Lewis' in *Writers, Critics and Children: Articles from Children's Literature in Education*, ed. by Geoff Fox et al. (London: Heinemann Educational Books, 1976), 116–24, p. 124. Article first published in *Children's Literature in Education*, 1971.

Helen Cresswell and Margaret Mahy – moved away from the 'high' fantasy which had characterised the 1950s and 1960s, integrating fantasy more closely with everyday concerns. The abstract characterisation of children's literature as a means of 'entering the child's world' was to give way to a strong focus on the social role of literature.

What Do Stories Tell Us? Didacticism and Ideology in the Early 1960s

The dominance of fantasy in children's literature during the 1950s and 1960s entailed an emphasis on the aesthetic and pleasurable aspects of literature rather than its social or ideological features. The concept of imagination as a means of allowing children to learn and develop without the inhibitions of adult instruction helped to position fantasy as inherently pleasurable and non-didactic. Nevertheless, as the discourse of the value of fantasy makes clear, the aversion to didacticism did not mean that children's stories were not expected to teach children something. Margery Fisher, writing in 1961, observes, 'It is the fashion nowadays to decry the story along with a moral, but no story can be written without one, though it may not take the sermon form familiar to the child of the last century.'[81] Gillian Avery strikes a similar note in her evaluation of the 'moral' Victorian tales:

> Nor should one complain about the moral. Juvenile writers have rarely discarded that and it lurks in the 'pulp' and in the 'prestige' story for the young alike even today.[82]

C.S. Lewis had certainly not shied from the moral in his Narnia books, and later fantasies which turned upon the conflict between good and evil were similarly laden with moral significance. In fact, the fantasy genre arguably offered more rather than less scope for overt moral statements. Susan Cooper's Dark is Rising series ends with a speech which is reminiscent of the sort of moral homilies which concluded Victorian children's stories. Merriman Lyon tells the child protagonists – and the book's readers –

> 'The responsibility and the hope and the promise are in your hands – your hands and the hands of the children of all men on this earth [...] you may not lie idly expecting the second coming of anybody now, because the world is yours and it is up to you. Now especially since man has the strength to destroy this world, it is the responsibility of man to keep it alive, in all its beauty and marvellous joy.'[83]

This lesson of responsibility and hope is at the heart of the series; although its appeal to modern sensibilities lessens the impression of didacticism, no reader can be left in doubt that Cooper intends her readers to learn something from their reading.

---

[81] Margery Fisher, *Intent upon Reading*, p. 17.

[82] Gillian Avery, *Nineteenth Century Children*, p. 28.

[83] Susan Cooper, *Silver on the Tree* (Harmondsworth: Puffin, 1979), p. 282.

Didacticism was also present in the historical novels which predominated during the 1950s and early 1960s. In Sheena Porter's Carnegie Medal winner *Nordy Bank* (1964), the tension generated by the mysterious forces affecting the protagonist Bron on a camping trip affords the author an excuse to deliver some detailed instruction on historical fact:

> Bron said, loudly and unexpectedly, 'No. You are both quite wrong. It is Iron Age. [...] The Romans built their forts in advance of a line, each one further out into the wild, like beads on a string. They were not haphazard builders, and roads joined all their buildings. Each fortress was connected with a base, and was set in a valley or on high open ground to be accessible to it. That,' she looked down to Nordy Bank, 'was placed so as to be as difficult of access as possible.'[84]

Similarly, *The Load of Unicorn* (1959) by Cynthia Harnett – who was awarded the Carnegie Medal in 1951 for *The Wool-pack* (1951) – not only includes detailed descriptions of the process of scribing and printing in fifteenth-century England, but also provides informative sketches detailing tools such as the pot used to dust wet ink with sand.[85] That historical novels ought to provide children with such details of the period they described was largely taken for granted: in 1961 the writer and historian Marion Lochhead notes a trend away from the overtly didactic and towards human interest, but her assertion that 'The question of what heroes and heroines and the common people of history were like, especially when young, of what they wore and what they ate, how they talked, what games they played – all that must always interest modern children of any intelligence and curiosity' indicates an assumption that historical novels ought not only to move and entertain their readers, but also to provide them with a detailed and accurate picture of the period.[86]

Historical novels were in part a means of conveying information about the customs and beliefs of the past, but by 1963, the author and critic Naomi Lewis was already questioning whether children's books might also perpetuate outdated beliefs:

> A great many attitudes have been sanctified for years or centuries by customs and tradition, and fiction, in one form or another, has had no small part in carrying on the word. It might be (or have been) that bullfighting is in some way 'noble', or that slaves are contented, or that women or the poor were physiologically incapable of being educated, or that the better-dressed and prettier side in any historic rebellion was automatically right. I see no point in deliberately perpetuating such ideas through books.[87]

---

[84]   Sheena Porter, *Nordy Bank* (London: Oxford University Press, 1971), pp. 36–7.

[85]   Cynthia Harnett, *The Load of Unicorn* (London: Methuen, 1959), illustration p. 164.

[86]   Marion Lochhead, 'Clio Junior: Historical Novels for Children' in *Only Connect*, 233–43, p. 243. Originally published in *Quarterly Review* (January 1962).

[87]   Naomi Lewis, *The Best Children Books of 1963* (London: Hamish Hamilton, 1964), p. 8.

By the early 1960s, a number of children's writers had engaged in precisely the kind of ideological challenging of ideas which Lewis suggests is necessary. Geoffrey Trease in particular stands out for his attempts to re-examine historical assumptions: his first book, *Bows Against the Barons* (1934), published by the left-wing imprint Lawrence and Wishart, was an explicit attempt 'to expose even to children the falsity of the romantic Merrie England image'.[88] Rosemary Sutcliff's novels also offered new perspectives on history, exploring the experiences of the vanquished as well as the victors, and depicting not only conventional heroes but also the poor and disenfranchised. *Warrior Scarlet* (1958) explores the experience of a disabled boy in a warrior society, while *Knight's Fee* (1960) and *Witch's Brat* (1970) both focus on characters who are perceived as social outsiders. The degree to which Sutcliff challenges the ideological status quo should not be overstated, however: Peter Hunt has argued that the nostalgic dimension of her historical landscapes 'extends to a regret at the loss of simple (right-wing) virtues such as valour and obedience and discipline, and the nostalgic acceptance of 'traditional' (right-wing) values', and the narrative arc of books like *Knight's Fee* essentially follows a traditional rags-to-riches pattern.[89] Nevertheless, the new perspectives offered by writers such as Rosemary Sutcliff and Geoffrey Trease presage some radical approaches to ideology in children's books during the 1970s.

Implicit Ideologies: The Status Quo in Children's Literature

The essential traditionalism in books by writers like Rosemary Sutcliff helped to create the perception of a lack of didacticism in the children's literature of the 1950s and early 1960s. The discourse around children's literature depended on a broad consensus about who the child reader was and what he or she needed, and tended to support the status quo, particularly in terms of class, gender and ethnicity. Despite the concern to avoid didacticism in children's books, therefore, both the criticism and the children's literature of the period reveal a host of unexamined ideologies which were presumed to be suitable lessons for child readers. Concerns about the issues surrounding the depiction of race and Empire, for example, are striking in their absence. Both Marcus Crouch and Mary Thwaite praise *Little Black Sambo* (1899) – a book which was heavily criticised during the 1970s for its perceived racism – without any apparent sense of a need for the kind of caveats with which John Rowe Townsend defends the book during the 1970s.[90]

---

[88]   Geoffrey Trease, quoted in Belinda Copson, 'Geoffrey Trease (1909–1998)', *British Children's Historical Novels*, <http://www.collectingbooksandmagazines.com/history.html> (1999) [accessed 28/08/2009].

[89]   Peter Hunt, *Children's Literature* (Oxford: Blackwell, 2001), p. 134.

[90]   Marcus Crouch, *Treasure Seekers and Borrowers*, pp. 27–8; M.F. Thwaite, *From Primer to Pleasure*, p. 206; J.R. Townsend, *Written for Children*, p. 155. Interestingly, Townsend does not mention *Little Black Sambo* in the 1965 edition of *Written for Children*, suggesting that his praise of the book in 1975 was motivated by a desire to reclaim it from its ideological ignominy.

Similarly, Thwaite comments without apparent irony on the ideal of Empire in Ballantyne's adventure stories:

> This world of Ballantyne is the Empire in the making – the white man opening up the wilderness and bringing trade, medicines, rough justice, and, above all, Christianity, to the savage.[91]

This ideal of Empire was not absent from the children's books of the period. There are uncomfortable imperialist overtones to Roald Dahl's popular *Charlie and the Chocolate Factory* (1964; first British edition 1967), in which Willy Wonka's chocolate factory relies on an apparently unpaid workforce "'Imported direct from Africa!'".[92] In the 1970s, attempts were made to make the book less racially offensive: the Oompa-Loompas were changed from black to white, and their country of origin from Africa to the fictional Oompa-Loompa Land. Nevertheless, from a post-colonialist perspective the passages which remain are problematic:

> '"Look here," I said,' [said Willy Wonka,] '"if you and all your people will come back to my country and live in my factory, you can have *all* the cacao beans you want!"' [...] 'So I shipped them all over here, every man, woman, and child in the Oompa-Loompa tribe. It was easy. I smuggled them over in large packing cases with holes in them, and they all got here safely. They are wonderful workers. They all speak English now. They love dancing and music. They are always making up songs.'[93]

Wonka's capitalist benevolence, which involves removing the Oompa-Loompas from their homeland and proving them with a 'better life' as his workers, is closely related to the image of the 'white man opening up the wilderness' which Thwaite identifies in Ballantyne. Although it is possible to detect a degree of irony in Dahl's exaggerated use of racial stereotypes, the depiction of the Oompa-Loompas as happy in their subjugation is still troubling, even after the alteration of their race.

The depiction of the Oompa-Loompas in *Charlie and the Chocolate Factory* is notable for its conspicuously problematic elements; in a large proportion of other books from the 1950s and early 1960s the problem of race is conspicuous by its absence. Of the books which were awarded the Carnegie Medal in the years 1960–1969, only Lucy Boston's *A Stranger at Green Knowe* (1961) features a non-white protagonist in a modern setting; Rosemary Harris's Biblical retelling *The Moon in the Cloud* (1968) has an Egyptian setting, but the ethnicities of her characters are never explicitly referred to. As the 1960s progressed, this lack of diversity in children's literature was to become a major ideological focus.

---

[91]　M.F. Thwaite, *From Primer to Pleasure*, p. 206; p. 168.

[92]　Roald Dahl, *Charlie and the Chocolate Factory*, Allen and Unwin edition (1967), p. 60. Quoted in Jessica Yates, 'Censorship in Children's Paperbacks', *Children's Literature in Education*, 11:4 (1980), 180–91, p. 185. Yates's article includes a detailed comparison of the original text and the edited version.

[93]　Roald Dahl, *Charlie and the Chocolate Factory* (Harmondsworth: Puffin, 1995), pp. 94–5.

The unthinking adherence to the status quo during the 1960s is equally evident in the portrayal of gender and class in the Carnegie winners of the decade, which feature predominately middle-class characters in traditional gender roles. The first meeting of the two families in Sheena Porter's *Nordy Bank* positions the characters in a firmly middle-class milieu:

> Mrs. Furness made a sympathetic noise and led the way into the sitting-room. [The dog] Lucy, who was lying curled in a very large armchair, put her ears back and wagged her tail very quickly in a guilty way. [...]
>
> Mrs. Furness noticed the faint surprise in Bron's mother's face. 'Lucy isn't usually allowed on the chairs,' she said, 'but this is a special concession that Margery's persuaded me into, because she's having her first litter in about a week.'[94]

The social embarrassment arising out of this situation – underlined by Bron's mother's unspoken but evident surprise – bespeaks a particular social setting; the fact that the reader is expected to appreciate the interchange here presumes a reader of a similar social background. Similarly, in Pauline Clark's *The Twelve and the Genii*, there is an undeniably middle-class element to the explanation that 'When Max, who was eight, made speeches with long words, his mother could not deny him', with its implication of a highly literate and intellectually focused family.[95] The critic Margery Fisher's assertion that 'The sensible author lets his young heroes and heroines take the problems of class, such as they are, in their stride', is indicative of an attitude that class was an unsuitable topic for children's literature: a large proportion of writers allowed their readers to 'take the problems of class in their stride' by effacing them altogether.[96]

The absence of working-class characters in children's literature of the 1950s and early 1960s is paralleled by the absence of active female protagonists and the gendered assumptions in both children's literature and criticism. Max in *The Twelve and the Genii* plays the role of 'chief Genius', while his sister 'being a girl, was really perhaps more interested in feeding the Twelves than seeing them on parade', while in Susan Cooper's *Over Sea, Under Stone* (1965) the differing contents of girls' and boys' pockets contributes to a significant plot point.[97] More significantly, the most active and daring roles were typically afforded to boys; author Philippa Pearce recollected, 'In the first books I wrote, the central character was a boy or boys, because I somehow thought that was right'.[98] The influence of such gendered assumptions is particularly evident in the work of American author Ursula Le Guin, whose Earthsea series was a conscious attempt to write against the tradition of white dominance in science fiction and fantasy: despite the ideological

---

[94] Sheena Porter, *Nordy Bank*, p. 8.

[95] Pauline Clark, *The Twelve and the Genii*, p. 13.

[96] Margery Fisher, *Intent upon Reading*, p. 287.

[97] Pauline Clark, *The Twelve and the Genii*, p. 95; Susan Cooper, *Over Sea, Under Stone* (Harmondsworth: Puffin, 1968), pp. 138–140.

[98] Philippa Pearce, 'Interview with Kimberley Reynolds and Nicholas Tucker, 1995', in *Oral Archives*, 289–305.

consciousness with which Le Guin approached the series, the first three Earthsea books conform to the masculine dominance of traditional high fantasy. Writing in 1992, Le Guin reflected on the ways in which gendered thought had influenced her writing, commenting that when she wrote the first three books in the series, she was 'writing partly by the rules as an artificial man'.[99] *Tehanu* (1990), the fourth book in the series, radically subverts the constructions of gender and power on which the original trilogy is based.

Gendered assumptions are evident not only in the characterisation of boys and girls in children's books of the early 1960s, but also in the perceived differences between the reading needs of the different sexes. Gillian Avery asserts that in the nineteenth century

> The writers of juvenile literature recognized at an early stage that in the boy they had an entirely different animal. Girls were malleable, suggestible, sensitive to correction; it was possible to reform them and improve them through their reading. But boys would not stomach much of this sort, and from early days were allowed to go their own way.[100]

This assessment of nineteenth-century attitudes does not challenge the characterisation of boys as wilful and less malleable than their sisters: the assertion that boys were 'recognised' as different implies that the difference was biological rather than socially constructed, and Avery draws no strong distinction between boys and girls of the Victorian era and those of her own. Margery Fisher too presents boys and girls as intrinsically different in both how and what they read:

> For girls, character-drawing is always an essential part of fiction. Schoolboys demand more fact and less feeling.[101]

The concept of 'books for boys' and 'books for girls' retains a strong currency today but in the 1970s, such gendered assumptions were to be radically challenged. During the late 1960s and the 1970s, the implicit ideologies of children's books were increasingly examined, and a new era of didacticism emerged.

The New Didacticism: Images of Society in Children's Books

Despite uneasiness about children's literature written with overt moral and didactic intent, the 1975 Bullock report on literature and education emphasises the 'civilising' role of literature and asserts:

> In Britain the tradition of literature teaching is one which aims at personal and moral growth, and in the last two decades this emphasis has grown. It is

---

[99]   Ursula K. Le Guin, *Earthsea Revisioned* (Cambridge: Green Bay Publications, 1993), p. 7.

[100]   Gillian Avery, *Nineteenth Century Children*, p. 138.

[101]   Margery Fisher, *Intent upon Reading*, p. 17.

a soundly based tradition, and properly interpreted is a powerful force in English teaching.[102]

The concept of literature as a tool for 'personal and moral growth' was consonant with the attitudes of the 1950s and early 1960s, but in the late 1960s and 1970s there was an increased emphasis on the socialising aspects of literature and its function within contemporary society. The social consensus evident in the children's literature and criticism of the early 1960s increasingly came under challenge as the decade progressed and a changing social environment in Britain altered the status quo. New political and ideological movements were emerging: the publication of Betty Friedan's *The Feminine Mystique* in 1963 marked a key moment in the feminist movement; the rise in immigration in Britain and the civil rights movement in America helped to increase awareness about issues of race; and the changing social and educational structure of Britain was radically altering perceptions of class. Children's literature did not remain untouched by this broader political context: on the contrary, the perception of children as innocent, malleable and free of adult prejudices which is evident in the critical and literary work of the 1950s and early 1960s made childhood a natural focus for those hoping to effect political change. High levels of social funding also helped to focus attention on a broader demographic of children: teachers and librarians tasked with providing books for children in urban centres were directly faced with the question of how well working-class, ethnically diverse children were served by the existing canon of children's literature. As a consequence, whereas the early 1960s had seen an emphasis on fantasy and imagination, by the mid-1960s there was an increasing focus on books as a means of social activism and a corresponding move towards more overtly didactic and ideologically focused texts.

The changing social and political environment of Britain helped to expose some of the implicit ideologies in children's literature. The left-wing writer and poet Bob Dixon attacked the literary canon for inculcating racist, sexist and classist ideologies in children, arguing, 'Much of the material in children's books is anti-social, if not anti-human and is more likely to stunt and warp young people than help them grow'.[103] Dixon was one of a number of critics in the 1970s to apply contemporary ideologies to the literary canon. He identified strongly sexist motifs in classic books for girls such as *Little Women* (1868) and *What Katy Did* (1872), arguing that such themes could not be excused by the context in which they were written. On the contrary, he argued, 'If books are read now – and these are certainly very widely read indeed – then surely we have to apply contemporary standards in evaluating them'.[104] This thesis was put into practice by Mary Cadogan

---

[102] Alan Bullock, 'A Language for Life'.

[103] Bob Dixon, *Catching Them Young 1: Sex, Race and Class in Children's Fiction* (London: Pluto Press, 1977), p. xiv.

[104] Bob Dixon, *Catching Them Young 1: Sex, Race and Class in Children's Fiction*, p. 10.

Dixon's criticisms were not confined to children's literature: the anti-Semitism of Dickens's Fagin and the racist portrayal of Shakespeare's *Othello* also came under attack.

and Patricia Craig, who applied contemporary feminist ideologies in their study of girls' adventure stories *You're a Brick, Angela!* Cadogan and Craig's work is also notable for the sensitivity to other issues which would have received little attention a decade earlier, for example in their comments on class and imperialism:

> The imperialism which impregnates *Terry the Girl Guide* was an exhortation to its young readers to work together to maintain the British Empire and to protect the weak. However, the author – and the book's heroine – had little sympathy to spare for the lower orders near at hand, who, it seemed, required repression rather than help or protection.[105]

Whereas Thwaite, writing a little over a decade earlier, had been able to refer unselfconsciously to Ballantyne's Empire-building heroes, Cadogan and Craig's treatment takes for granted that both imperialism and a lack of sympathy for the working classes are reprehensible aspects of the text under discussion. A consciousness of the ideological issues inherent in certain texts, particularly those dealing with race and gender issues, was increasingly integrated into children's literature criticism.

The drive to recognise outdated ideologies in children's books emerged directly out of the work of those engaged with real child readers. Janet Hill, a librarian in the ethnically diverse London borough of Lambeth, fiercely criticised the lack of diversity in children's literature for its effects on readers of colour:

> Many books are blatantly biased and prejudiced. How is an African child growing up in this country likely to react to some of the patronising, insensitive and outmoded tales of the noble white man and the native that are still in print? Despite the rich variety of adult novels by African, Indian and West Indian writers, there are hardly any for children.[106]

Such criticisms had a direct effect on children's literature: a number of books were revised or cut in response to ideological criticisms. In 1971 the American critic Lois Kalb Bouchard launched a fierce attack on the depiction of race in *Charlie and the Chocolate Factory*, arguing that 'the West has been treated to "dark Africa" too many times and it is racism to perpetuate the myth and image of darkness'; these criticisms, and those of others, prompted the revision of the text when it appeared in a new edition.[107] Books such as *Little Black Sambo*, which had been widely recommended in the early critical texts, fell out of favour, while classic texts like the Grimms' story 'The Jew in the Bush' were silently edited in order

---

[105] Mary Cadogan and Patricia Craig, *You're a Brick, Angela!: A New Look at Girls' Fiction From 1839 to 1975* (London: Gollancz, 1976), pp. 147–9.

[106] Janet Hill, quoted in Rosemary Stones, 'Multi-cultural Publishing: What it Took to Get Us Where We Are' in *Diversity in Publishing*, <http://www.diversityinpublishing.com/Recommended-Reads/MEDIA-ARTICLES/Multi-cultural-Publishing-What-it-took-to-get-to-where-we-are> [accessed 11/02/08].

[107] Jessica Yates, 'Censorship in children's paperbacks', p. 184.

to better reflect contemporary values.[108] Simultaneously, some publishers began to make efforts to publish more diverse literature: Aidan Chambers, discussed in Chapter 3, was one of those editors who made a conscious effort to include more writers of colour on his list.

Efforts to change the underlying ideologies of children's literature formed a key part of social activism. The Children's Rights Workshop, founded in 1973 by Rosemary Stones and Andrew Mann, published a series of pamphlets offering guidelines on issues such as racism and sexism in children's literature. The introduction to the pamphlet on *Sexism in Children's Books* (1976) states:

> One of the purposes of these 'Papers…' is to inform a wider public of the value of the concept of sexism as a means to understanding and as a critical tool, particularly in relation to children's literature. As this pamphlet hopefully shows, sexism in literature is expressed in the use of vocabulary and in the presentation of people, roles and situations. […] Language is central to the speech, thinking and culture of any society. To tackle the assumptions behind language, by using alternative words and thus exploring alternative concepts, is the challenge of the McGraw-Hill Guidelines.[109]

Guidelines like these attempted to tackle implicit ideologies not only on the level of plot and characterisation, but also at a linguistic level. Children's literature itself had an uneasy relationship with such guidelines – Elaine Moss, writing in 1980, commented that they could only be relevant to 'those who are interested in the sociological content of literature but unmindful of its peculiar essence, part of which is the beauty of a language they seek to put in splints'.[110] Nevertheless, the ideological influence of bodies such as the Children's Rights Workshop is discernible in the appearance of books such as Gene Kemp's inventive Carnegie winner *The Turbulent Term of Tyke Tiler* (1977), which forces the reader to confront unexamined ideologies about gender by withholding mention of Tyke's gender until the final pages of the book. The book also won the Other Award, established in 1975 by the Children's Rights Workshop in order to raise the profile of 'those writers and illustrators who are making available to children a wider and more accurate representation of human experience and situation'.[111]

The concern that there should be a children's literature which reflected socially progressive ideologies is evident in the books published during the late 1960s and 1970s. The desire to challenge prevailing ideologies about issues such as race,

---

[108] Perry Nodelman, 'The Case of the Disappearing Jew', *Children's Literature in Education*, 10:1 (1979), 44–8.

[109] Children's Rights Workshop, *Sexism in Children's Books: Facts, Figures & Guidelines* (London: Writers and Readers Pub. Cooperative, 1976), p. 2.

[110] Elaine Moss, 'The Seventies in Children's Books', in *Part of the Pattern*, 136–60, p. 141. Originally published in *Signal* (1980).

[111] Pat Triggs, 'The Other Award 1981', *Books For Keeps*, 11 (November 1981), <http://www.booksforkeeps.co.uk/issues/11/29676> [accessed 01/09/09].

class and gender contributed to a move towards more overtly didactic books. Robert Leeson's *The Third-Class Genie* (1975), for example, offers an explicit lesson on revisionist history in an episode in which the genie – conjured out of an appropriately modern beer can – provides his young master with a version of the Crusades as told from a Middle Eastern perspective. The scorn with which the protagonist's history teacher meets this 'completely new version of history' is offset by the reaction of the headmaster:

> "I read it with some fascination. I served for years in the Middle East and I came to realise that the Arabs have quite a different view of history from ours."

> "That's right, sir. They thought the Crusaders were a pack of barbarians."

> Cartwright nodded. "The trouble was, their civilisation was on the way down while ours was on the way up. We owe them a lot."[112]

The idea that history is dependent on the perspective from which it is viewed had already been explored by Rosemary Sutcliff, but this scene is much more overtly didactic. Similarly, in Bernard Ashley's *The Trouble with Donovan Croft* (1974), winner of the Other Award in 1976, the sympathetically portrayed father explicitly condemns racists as 'small-minded bigots', while the racist teacher is introduced as a figure of fear, 'short, fat and old (at least forty-five) with a loud shouting voice which always took the mickey out of you'.[113] The reader is left in no doubt about the appropriate social lesson to be drawn from the book. This overt didacticism was an inevitable consequence of the desire to challenge the ideological status quo in children's literature. Whereas moral lessons supporting the status quo appeared relatively unobtrusive, the didactic element of even such subtly ideological texts as *The Turbulent Term of Tyke Tiler* was more readily apparent. While the shift towards more overt didacticism was by no means universal, and many writers continued in the traditions established during the 1950s, the desire for children's literature to provide socially progressive ideologies helped to reduce the emphasis on pleasure over utility which had characterised the discourse on children's literature at the start of the 1960s. This shift towards didacticism was part of a broader change in perceptions of childhood: the idealised post-war construction of the child as innocent and imaginative was giving way to attempts to access the 'real' child.

Reconstructing Childhood: Social Realism

A key effect of the social policy of the 1950s and the early 1960s was an increasing state focus on childhood. The concept of the child as a focus for hope in a post-war world evident in much of the criticism of this period encouraged investment

---

[112]   Robert Leeson, *The Third-Class Genie* (London: Collins, 2000), p. 54; p. 100.

[113]   Bernard Ashley, *The Trouble with Donovan Croft* (Harmondsworth: Puffin, 1977), p. 94; p. 10.

in education and libraries, creating a body of professionals who were directly concerned with offering opportunities to children. By the beginning of the 1960s, the experiences of such professionals were already leading them to question the impact of the gap between the idealised middle-class childhood presented in many children's books and the lives of real children. The effects of earlier educational reforms were also beginning to make themselves felt: the increased social mobility fostered by the opportunities established in the 1944 Education Act meant that many of those entering the fields of education, librarianship and publishing in the 1960s had themselves come from working-class backgrounds. This so-called 'educated out' generation had personal experience of encountering a literature which did not reflect their own lives, and were passionate about extending opportunities to a new generation of working-class children. Children's authors led the way in addressing the issue: while an essentially middle-class conception of childhood is evident in the critical monographs of the early 1960s, authors' attempts to portray more 'ordinary' childhoods are evident from the late 1950s. The author and critic Wallace Hildick was one of many people whose experiences as teachers in working-class areas led them to seek a more diverse children's literature:

> I [...] had had many awkward moments in the classroom trying to present children's books with middle-class settings and values that were often foreign to my pupils. I too felt that in the interests of identification and the pleasure of recognition, it would be a good thing if these children could at least occasionally read about their own kind.[114]

In response to this problem, Hildick produced *Jim Starling* (1958), set in an ordinary day school rather than the more traditional boarding school. During the same period, John Rowe Townsend was encountering similar issues in his work as a journalist and children's book reviewer for the *Guardian*, where he became conscious of the profound gap between the 'harmless and hygienic and middle class' nature of the books he was reviewing and the poverty he witnessed accompanying the N.S.P.C.C around city slums.[115] Townsend's first novel, *Gumble's Yard* (1961), was widely acclaimed for its realistic take on working-class life. The setting of the book, which centres around the efforts of a group of children to cope alone after they are abandoned by their caregivers, is far removed from the cosy middle-class world of books like *Nordy Bank* and *The Twelve and the Genii*:

> Our house, like all the others in Orchid Grove, had a living room and a scullery and two bedrooms. Our back bedroom was in a bad state because the roof needed repairing. We four children all slept downstairs in the living room. We had a big iron bedstead, and Harold and I slept with our heads at one end and Sandra and Jean at the other. There was room for all of us, and we had some blankets and old coats to keep us warm, and it was a very good arrangement.[116]

---

[114] Wallace Hildick, *Children and Fiction* (London: Evans, 1970), p. 32.

[115] Kimberley Reynolds and Nicholas Tucker, 'Interview with John Rowe Townsend and Jill Paton Walsh, 2 May 1995', in *Oral Archives*, 262–88, p. 275.

[116] John Rowe Townsend, *Gumble's Yard* (Harmondsworth: Puffin, 1967), p. 16.

The depiction of a poor working-class household like this was strikingly different from the environments portrayed in the majority of children's books in this period: the same year that *Gumble's Yard* was published, the Carnegie Medal was awarded to *A Stranger at Greene Knowe*, which takes place in a country house complete with a moat and its own chapel. By the late 1960s, however, the sense of a gap between children's literature and the lives of real children which had motivated E.W. Hildick and J.R. Townsend to produce their books in working-class settings was becoming a dominant part of the discourse on children's literature. Librarians such as Janet Hill and Elaine Moss, and social activists like Leila Berg and Robert Leeson, were increasingly arguing that the gap mattered.

The post-war construction of childhood as intrinsically imaginative and allied to fantasy had helped to create the sense that the lack of social realism in children's texts was unimportant: the dominance of fantasy and historical fiction reflected an idea that childhood reading was about stepping into another world. This sense was particularly acute in the case of working-class children: Wallace Hildick asserts that the lack of working-class settings in children's books was partly due to a belief that 'children in poor or drab surroundings disliked reading about such circumstances and craved nothing less than total escape'.[117] This belief was replaced towards the end of the 1960s by a widespread view that it was important for children to be able to identify with what they were reading. Robert Leeson, one of those who advocated greater social realism in children's literature, reflected that recognising his own experiences in a book 'gave an added and a very special pleasure' to his childhood reading, commenting 'if you do not appear in the literary world of your society, you don't exist'.[118] Elaine Moss, reflecting on her experiences of selling books from a market stall in the East End of London, made a similar argument. For children approaching reading for the first time, she commented, 'identifying lights the vital spark'.[119] Aidan Chambers took a similar position; as Chapter 3 will show, his sense that children and young people needed books which talked about their experiences was fundamental to his approach to editing the Topliner list.

The journalist and social activist Leila Berg was one of the most active proponents of more social realism in children's books, arguing that improving the representation of working-class children in children's literature was key to overcoming a social situation which profoundly disadvantaged such children. Whereas literate middle-class families offered children a book-friendly environment which made the development of literacy natural and pleasurable, Berg argued, lack of time, money and education in working-class families created a situation which was profoundly inimical to reading. Her position was borne out by the Plowden Report of 1967, which noted that '29 per cent of all homes have five books or less, and emphasised the importance of the home environment in determining

---

[117] Wallace Hildick, *Children and Fiction*, p. 32.

[118] Robert Leeson, quoted in Nicholas Tucker, 'Setting the Scene' in *Children's Book Publishing in Britain Since 1941*, 1–19, p. 10.

[119] Elaine Moss, 'A Mirror in The Market Place', in *A Part of the Pattern*, 119–23, p. 122. First published in *Signal* (1972).

educational outcomes.[120] Leila Berg actively campaigned for educational and social initiatives which would help to provide socially disadvantaged children with the support that 'the book child' received at home, but argued that if public institutions could not provide such support:

> [...] at least the first books they are given might help to bridge that gap – might underline their identity, cherish it, and build from there, which after all is one of the things that has been happening with 'the book-child' for five years. But what is it they are given? They are given readers about a family that lives in a detached house [...] If anything could completely confirm for this child what he has already dimly suspected through his growing five years – that he and his family and friends and his street are worthless and expendable – it is the orthodox school reader. As far as they are concerned, he does not exist.[121]

Leila Berg's ideas about the value of social realism had a direct impact on children's literature through the Nippers series of school readers, which she developed under the aegis of Macmillan Education in an attempt to provide children with books which reflected the reality of working-class life. Nippers were a response to reading schemes such as Ladybird's Key Words Reading Scheme, launched in 1965, which centred around the activities of white, middle-class Peter and Jane and their family. The books attempted to reflect both the lifestyles and the language of urban working-class families, as in *Grandad's Clock* (1975):

> [My grandad] used to work at the sugar factory. Worked there fifty years.
>
> He liked it there. Specially the band. He used to play trumpet in the band.
>
> He came home and he said, "They've given me a clock. Factory's given me a clock. For working there fifty years."
>
> "Ay, that's lovely," said our Mam, putting on the chips.
>
> "Don't soft-soap me, queen," said Grandad.[122]

The illustrations show the family crammed into their tiny kitchen, and rather than the conservative cardigan and dress worn by the neatly-groomed Mother of Peter and Jane, Mam is dressed in flares and a pinny, with her hair wrapped up in a turban. The books not only depict working-class lifestyles, but also reflect a more working-class (and distinctly left-wing) outlook on life: it is evident that Grandad feels that a clock is a poor reward for 50 years of working life. The series

---

[120] Bridget Plowden and The Central Advisory Council for Education (England), *The Plowden Report*, Volume 3, Chapter 3, <http://www.educationengland.org.uk/documents/plowden/plowden1-03.html> [accessed 03/07/12].

[121] Leila Berg, *Reading and Loving* (London: Routledge, 1977), p. 75.

[122] Leila Berg, *Grandad's Clock* (London: Macmillan, 1976), <http://www.aspects.net/~leilaberg/Grandad.htm> [accessed 02/09/09].

caused significant controversy, not only on literary grounds, but also because of the image of childhood it presented. *Fish and Chips for Supper* (1968), one of the first in the Nippers series, provoked accusations of immorality for its depiction of a family with a leaking roof and washing lines stretched across the stairs, which critics perceived as either false or unacceptably lacking in optimism for young readers. Many opponents of the series rejected the realism of the books entirely: one headteacher wrote, 'I must express my complete dislike of the world portrayed in your latest readers. Most working-class families have now reached what was previously a middle-class environment and standard of living.'[123] Nevertheless, the kind of social realism depicted in the Nippers series became increasingly acceptable in children's literature. Whereas middle-class childhoods were a dominant feature of the books awarded the Carnegie Medal during the 1960s, during the 1970s the award recognised books such as Robert Westall's *The Machine Gunners* (1975), Jan Mark's *Thunder and Lightnings* (1976) and Gene Kemp's *The Turbulent Term of Tyke Tiler*, all of which offered frank portrayals of working-class children. This scene from *Tyke Tiler* is characteristic of the changes which had occurred in depictions of childhood:

> 'Look out,' [Danny] yelled as I kicked the door open. 'Patty's among that lot.'
>
> That lot was a collection of beer bottles, milk bottles, cider bottles, pop bottles in a corner by the sink. Fatty's nose twitched round one labelled 'Newcastle Brown' [...] the bottles flew like skittles, crashing, banging, rolling, splintering into pointed daggers. Danny's mum flew in, like an angry rhino, belted Danny twice round the head and told us to get out, so we moved at speed.[124]

This is a strong contrast to the delicate disapprobation of dogs on the furniture in *Nordy Bank*! The untidiness of the house, the mention of beer and cider bottles, and the casual reference to Danny's mother 'belting' him, are all features which would have been highly controversial only a few years before.

The trend for more social realism in children's books affected characterisation as well as setting. Writing in 1965, Gillian Avery complained:

> [Writers for children] omit (instinctively, not consciously, one feels) all unpleasant traits in a child's personality; all crudity and coarseness. Their children hardly seem to have a physical nature, beyond a good appetite. Family relationships are smooth, mother is always right, father never irks his sons.[125]

The characterisation of the children in John Rowe Townsend's *Gumble's Yard* illustrates the validity of some of Avery's criticisms. Although the family relationships in the book are far from smooth, the children themselves are

---

[123] Leila Berg, *Reading and Loving*, p. 97.

[124] Gene Kemp, *The Turbulent Term of Tyke Tiler* (London: Faber and Faber, 2002), p. 46.

[125] Gillian Avery, *Nineteenth Century Children*, p. 227.

scrupulously honest and polite to authority figures despite their poverty, and only the barest traces of a regional accent are discernible in their speech. By contrast, in *Tyke Tiler*, Tyke's friend Danny is a kleptomaniac with a heavy speech impediment (evident in his rendition of 'Fatty' as 'Patty' in the passage above), Tyke is affectionately described as a 'disobedient, under-educated, loud-mouthed ruffian', and the children's dialect is much more apparent.[126] The appearance of such books on the Carnegie list is indicative not only of a shift to a construction of quality which incorporated the ideological impact of the work, but also of a change in the parameters of more traditional measures of quality. Whereas children's literature up until the 1960s had tended to privilege a particular form of writing, the move towards more realistic portrayals of childhood allowed for a definition of literary quality which valued the authenticity of the language used.

What's His Problem? Social Realism and the 'Problem Novel'

The dominant theme of criticism in the early 1960s was the concept of 'stepping into the child's world'. The move towards more social realism in children's books, however, accompanied a radical change in perceptions of how children experienced the world. The author Nina Bawden characterised her books as growing out of a desire to write 'not as a grown-up looking back, but as a former child', but her return to childhood is neither idyllic nor escapist in the manner of Hazard.[127] On the contrary, she tackled difficult real life experiences, including evacuation in *Carrie's War* (1973) and bereavement and child abuse in *Squib* (1971). Such issues became increasingly represented in children's books as authors sought to reflect the reality of children's lives. An Rutgers van der Loeff argued against the perception that the child's world was radically removed from that of adults, commenting:

> Children want to be part of the world and to know about life and people everywhere. They are part of this new world we are making. In the western world we tend to set children apart, to cut them off instead of integrating them in family and local affairs. They are, therefore, not prepared for the shocks life brings – when it brings them.[128]

The idea that children's literature should help prepare children 'for the shocks life brings' led to an increasing number of books focusing on particular social issues and life experiences. American writers led this trend: Judy Blume tackled a range of contemporary issues, including puberty in *Are You There, God? It's Me, Margaret* (1970) and *Then Again, Maybe I Won't* (1971), bullying and body image in *Blubber* (1974), and – most controversially – teenage sexuality in *Forever* (1975). Her books were published in the United Kingdom by Pan

---

[126] Gene Kemp, *The Turbulent Term of Tyke Tiler*, p. 21.

[127] Nina Bawden, 'The Imprisoned Child' in *The Thorny Paradise: Writers on Writing for Children*, ed. by Edward Blishen (Harmondsworth: Kestrel, 1975), 62–4, p. 62.

[128] An Rutgers van der Loeff, quoted in 'Through Literature to Life?', p. 103.

Piccolo in the late 1970s. Paul Zindel's novels for teenagers, published in the United Kingdom on Bodley Head's Books For New Adults imprint and in Aidan Chambers' Topliner imprint, took a harder-hitting approach to social issues: *The Pigman* (1968) is a bleak exploration of the relationships between the generations and social responsibility, while *My Darling, My Hamburger* (1969) addresses sexual relationships and abortion. In the United Kingdom, Bernard Ashley addressed a range of social issues, including foster care and racism in *The Trouble With Donovan Croft*, the problems of changing school in *All My Men* (1977) and organised crime in *A Kind of Wild Justice* (1978), while Joan Lingard explored the Irish Troubles in *The Twelfth Day of July* (1970) and its sequels. Whereas the fantasy novels of the 1950s and early 1960s had dealt with real life experiences obliquely, during the 1970s realism increasingly became a feature of fantasy novels. The genie of Robert Leeson's *The Third-Class Genie* is very much part of the working-class community in which he is found, and his presence helps to expose the racial and class prejudices of the community, while in Diana Wynne Jones's *The Ogre Downstairs* (1974) the tensions of a new step-family are played out over a magical chemistry set. Michael de Larrabeiti adopted fantasy in order to explore class conflict in *The Borribles* (1976), a parody of Elizabeth Beresford's *The Wombles* in which the childlike working-class Borribles are pitted against the upper-class Rumbles. Such realistic and overtly ideological fantasies reflect the shift in thinking about children's literature represented in the growth in social realism for children.

The shift towards more socially conscious, realistic writing for children in the late 1960s and 1970s was widespread, but the trend was not universally accepted as a good thing. Frank Eyre criticised the vogue for trends and guidelines, commenting that while demands for books on specific topics might be useful to those writers already drawn towards such a style of writing, 'There are other kinds of writers for children, who do not need to be directed into such service'.[129] The emphasis on the therapeutic and socialising qualities of literature was also questioned by critic and lecturer in psychology Nicholas Tucker, who cautioned:

> I [...] believe that too much insistence on children's literature as a kind of spiritual tonic for the young may lead to a downgrading of its status as literature, in some cases for all ages. One should not have to defend literature on the grounds that it is necessarily good for you; a book is something that exists primarily to provide the reader with a literary experience, something he cannot get elsewhere from other means.[130]

Tucker's concerns reflect the degree to which the boundaries between the literary and the educational were blurring, a perhaps inevitable consequence of the

---

[129] Frank Eyre, *British Children's Books in the Twentieth Century* (London: Longman, 1971), p. 79.

[130] Nicholas Tucker, ed., 'Introduction', *Suitable for Children? Controversies in Children's Literature* (Sussex: University of Sussex, 1978), 15–28, p. 17.

primary focus on children's literature as a means of addressing social inequalities. Joan Aiken, winner of the Guardian Fiction Award for *The Whispering Mountain* (1969), also questioned the effect of didacticism on literary quality, characterising wholesome-but-dull novels as 'Filboid Studge':

> There's a whole range of it – from The Awfully Sudden Death of Martha G-, through A Hundred and One Things to Do on a Wet Saturday and not Plague Daddy – and Sue Jones has a Super Time as a Student Nurse – to the novels (some of them quite good) intended to show teen-agers [sic] how to adjust to the colour problem and keep calm through parents' divorce and the death of poor Fido. […] I suppose they serve some purpose. But just the same I count them as Filboid Studge. And how insulting they are! Adults are not expected to buy books called Mrs Sue Jones – Alcoholic's Wife, or A Hundred and One Ways to Lose Your Job and Keep Calm.[131]

Aiken's inventive brand of alternative history, which seamlessly blends fantasy and reality, resists the trend for focusing on contemporary issues and any hint of Filboid Studge. The continuing popularity of Aiken's work, and the recognition afforded to books such as Peter Dickinson's alternative history novel *The Blue Hawk* (1975), which deals with the fall of a priest-ruled empire, and Diana Wynne Jones's alternative world fantasy *Charmed Life* (1977) – both recipients of the Guardian Award – demonstrates that contemporary realism did not wholly dominate children's literature during the 1970s. Nevertheless, the 'problem novel' was sufficiently pervasive to provoke Nina Bawden's ironic observation, 'We all know the story about the mother who went to the library to get a suitable novel for her fifteen year-old and was asked by the librarian, "What's his problem?"'[132] The resistance to didacticism evident in the early 1960s had been replaced by a widespread emphasis on children's literature as an educative and social tool.

Something for the Big Ones: The Changing Age of the Child Reader

A key aspect of the shift towards more social realism in children's literature during the 1960s and 1970s was a growing emphasis on the needs of the adolescent reader. In the post-war period, the duration of childhood was extended both legislatively and socially. The educational reforms of the post-war years had acted to retain more children in school into their teenage years, first through the widening of access to secondary education instituted in the 1944 Education Act, then through the extension of compulsory education to age 16, enacted in 1972.[133] Simultaneously,

---

[131] Joan Aiken, 'A Free Gift' in *The Thorny Paradise*, 36–52, p. 48. It is interesting to note that the contemporary publishing industry *does* offer adults titles very much in this vein.

[132] Nina Bawden, 'A Dead Pig and My Father' in *Writers, Critics and Children*, 3–14, p. 5. Originally published in *Children's Literature in Education*, 14 (May 1974).

[133] David Childs, *Britain Since 1945: A Political History*, p. 189.

a buoyant economy in the 1950s and early 1960s – combined with an increasing tendency for young people to retain their earnings rather than giving them up to their parents – helped to produce a new generation of affluent adolescents, a phenomenon which John Springhall identifies as fundamental to the identification of teenagers as a distinctive social group.[134] Both culturally and educationally, the 1960s and 1970s saw a focus on adolescence; this focus is reflected in the children's literature of the period, which increasingly aimed to serve readers in their teenage years.

At the beginning of the 1960s, the concept of a specialist literature for the adolescent was only just beginning to emerge in Britain: the librarian and critic Sheila Ray identifies the 'career novel' as the only genre aimed directly at teenagers during the 1950s.[135] Writing in 1961, Margery Fisher argued the case for a specialist children's literature, but presented adolescents as served by existing adult literature. Her comments on children's stories about the theatre suggest that the boundaries between children's and adult literature are fluid:

> Too much of the danger and difficulty of real life must be left out if the subject is a girl or a boy in the late teens (unless, as Pamela Brown does, you keep your character at the permanent emotional age of fourteen or so) and children of ten or twelve who want to read about the stage will naturally enjoy theatrical technique more than theatrical perils. A girl of thirteen or so will do better to read some of the best adult novels of the theatre.[136]

Fisher presents the difference between children's and adult literature as primarily rooted in the scope of the content, with genre fiction forming a natural bridge to adult novels. A similar perception is evident in the selection of titles which made up the first specialist publishing imprint for teenagers: as Chapter 2 will show, Penguin's Peacock list included a preponderance of adult titles on its launch in 1961. The assertion that teenage readers 'will do better to read some of the best adult novels' betrays an underlying assumption of a literate and committed reader, but by the mid-1960s both the experiences of those working in education and the work of social activists such as Leila Berg were demonstrating that the vast majority of adolescent readers did not fall into this category. Whereas earlier generations of adolescents had left school after acquiring basic literacy, the increasing retention of adolescents in secondary education confronted educationalists with the fact that many adolescents could read on a functional level, but lacked the skills or the desire to read for pleasure. The Newsom report of 1963 focused attention on the 'unrealised talent' of the high percentage of children in secondary modern schools, arguing that the changing social context demanded

---

[134]   John Springhall, *Coming of Age: Adolescence in Britain, 1860–1960* (Dublin: Gill and Macmillan), p. 216.

[135]   Sheila Ray, 'The Development of the Teenage Novel' in *Reluctant to Read?*, ed. by John Foster (London: Ward Lock Educational, 1977), 46–67, p. 47.

[136]   Margery Fisher, *Intent upon Reading*, p. 187.

that 'more and more people need to [read and write] with greater competence'.[137] One of the key outcomes of the report was the extension of the school leaving age in 1971. In the world of children's literature, concerns about the so-called 'reluctant' adolescent reader prompted a growing sense of a need for a specialist teenage literature. Elaine Moss, writing in 1968, identified a need to provide for those readers who could not move easily into the realm of adult fiction:

> Academic fourteens nourish themselves on Dickens and the Brontës, Golding and Orwell, with Ian Fleming as a snack between meals. Libraries and bookshops attract them the way coffee bars and record shops attract their less intellectual contemporaries. Yet reading in adolescence is just as important for the non-academic young who constitute a large percentage of the secondary-school population, the section the school-leaving controversy is all about.[138]

The same argument was made by Aidan Chambers, whose book *The Reluctant Reader* (1969) was a direct response to the issues addressed by the Newsom Report. Chambers argued for the development of a literature which attended to the needs of the 'non-academic young'; Chapter 3 addresses his attempts to do so through the paperback imprint Topliner. The focus on the less-able adolescent reader during the 1960s is also evident in the establishment of Heinemann's Pyramid series, the second specialist teenage imprint. Pyramids were original novels of 27,000 words or less, designed especially to appeal to the reluctant reader. The new focus on readers who could not or would not access much of the children's literature canon was to contribute to a changing view of children's literature.

The move towards more literature specifically for teenagers was intimately connected with the move towards more social realism in children's literature; in particular, the desire to reflect the lives of the working-class children who compose the majority of the secondary-modern population which the Newsom Report identified as 'underachieving'. Discussing the structure of education at the secondary modern level, the Newsom Report asserted:

> Most boys and girls, and especially those with whom we are concerned, want their education to be practical and realistic. They feel a good deal better if they can see that it is vocational. They like to have some say in choosing what they shall learn. We believe that these four words – practical, realistic, vocational, choice – provide keys which can be used to let even the least able boys and girls enter into an educational experience which is genuinely secondary.[139]

The same view is evident in the construction of teenage literature during the 1960s and 1970s. Realistic fiction dominated Aidan Chambers' Topliner list, and

---

[137] John Newsom, 'Half Our Future' (London: HMSO, 1963), *Education in England*, <http://www.educationengland.org.uk/documents/newsom/> [accessed 09/09/09].

[138] Elaine Moss, 'Reluctant at Fifteen' in *Part of the Pattern*, 31–3, p. 31. First published in *The Times* (1968).

[139] John Newsom, 'Half Our Future', <http://www.educationengland.org.uk/documents/newsom/>.

featured prominently on Bodley Head Books for New Adults, which published titles by authors such as Paul Zindel, focusing on the lives of contemporary adolescents. Zindel was one of a number of influential young-adult authors from America, which had begun to develop a literature for young adults during the 1950s. The influence of J.D. Salinger's seminal novel *The Catcher in the Rye* (1951) – written as adult literature, but rapidly adopted by young adults – had helped to establish realism as a central genre in young adult fiction, and the impact of Salinger's first-person narration and focus on the personal concerns of contemporary adolescents is clearly discernible in the work of Paul Zindel, Robert Cormier and even Judy Blume, all young adult authors who enjoyed a wide readership in Britain.

The needs of the reluctant and less-able reader were central to the early debate around teenage literature in Britain, but the development of the genre also owed much to the perception that young adults needed guidance in a rapidly changing world. The Newsom report asserted,

> As the life of our society becomes more complex, new demands are continually made on all of us; and this is as true in relation to our personal lives as it is in relation to the changing economic life of the country as a whole. The amount which men and women need to understand, and the range of experiences with which they are required to deal in all the daily business of living, are continually extending.[140]

The perception that the experience of adolescence was radically – and disturbingly – different from that of previous generations is clearly evident in the media of the period. A review of the *Guardian* during this period reveals articles addressing the question of teenage irresponsibility, the 'generation gap' between teenagers and their parents and the problem of teenage unemployment.[141] The strength of anxiety about youth culture is also evident in *The Vulnerable Generation* (1971), a book by headmistress Elizabeth Manners, which portrays young adults as restless and directionless: the book was written in response to the high levels of media attention devoted to Manners' lecture on the same subject. In the context of this complex society, novels for adolescents were presented as a means of offering young people guidance and meaning. Rosemary Sandberg, editor of Fontana Lions, made the case for teenage books as an educative and socialising resource:

> Coming to terms with school problems and with the community in general can be an even more complex and confusing business. Before them, older children glimpse the tumult of the adult world into which they are being propelled [...]

---

[140] John Newsom, 'Half Our Future', <http://www.educationengland.org.uk/documents/newsom/>.

[141] A.J. Rowman, 'Irresponsible teenagers', *Manchester Guardian*, 9 April 1958, p. 6; Ann Chesney, 'The young idea', *Guardian*, 9 December 1964, p. 8; Malcolm Stuart, 'Plight of the school leavers', *Guardian*, 28 September 1971, p. 8.

> Here, again, the role of books is all important. The protagonist they trust in a book can underline the value of the young person as an individual, can offer a reason for behaving in one way as opposed to another, can restore a little hope.[142]

The theme of coming to terms with personal problems and seeking to establish a place within 'the community in general' is a recurring one throughout the teenage literature of the 1960s and 1970s. Hester Burton in *A Time of Trial* (1963) and Kathleen Peyton in *The Edge of the Cloud* (1969), both winners of the Carnegie Medal, relate adolescent experience to broader societal concerns by setting their stories in the context of significant historical events. In *The Edge of the Cloud* (1969), the individual and personal fears faced by Christina in relation to her fiancé Will's career as an aeroplane pilot are used as a reference for wartime experience:

> She knew now that life was suddenly dangerous for very many more people than just Will. She would no longer be alone with her fears. In fact, she had the advantage of being proved and tried: she had come through, all calm and collected, to please Will, and now she knew she had the practice, or the strength, or the courage – whatever it was – to face anything that might happen.[143]

This passage, which takes place immediately after Christina's wedding, positions the personal concerns of adolescence as directly relevant to the experience of adult life. Similarly, in *A Time of Trial*, Margaret Pargeter's move into adolescence and adulthood is explored not only through the personal experience of her blossoming love affair, but also through Margaret's exposure to political unrest and social inequity.

The sense that adolescents required guidance in an increasingly perilous world is reflected in the dominance of the 'issues' novel in teenage literature. One of the first authors to write especially for adolescents was Josephine Kamm, who explored topics such as unmarried motherhood and inter-racial relationships. Her book *Young Mother* (1965) reflects a heavily didactic impulse. The scene in which the titular young mother, Pat, discusses her sexual experience with a social worker is characteristic in emphasising Pat's own responsibility for her pregnancy:

> [Pat] realized then what she had been deliberately trying to forget – that she was herself in some way responsible for what had occurred. 'It wasn't quite like what I said,' she whispered at last. 'I didn't know it was going to be that sort of party, you must believe me. But other girls had done it – Cynthia had lots of times – and I didn't want to be left out. I might have got away from him at the beginning, but I just felt I couldn't; and I didn't really hate it, not after the start.'[144]

---

[142] Rosemary Sandberg, 'The Relevance of Books for Older Children' in *Teenage Reading*, ed. by Peter Kennerley (London: Ward Lock Educational, 1979), 29–34, pp. 31–2.

[143] K.M. Peyton, *The Edge of the Cloud* (Harmondsworth: Puffin, 1979), pp. 191–2.

[144] Josephine Kamm, *Young Mother* (London: Heinemann Educational Books, 1968), p. 45.

The passage offers its readers strong warnings against attending parties without adult supervision, succumbing to peer pressure, or indeed seeking sexual pleasure. The portrayal of Pat as 'in some way responsible' is deeply problematic from a modern perspective: as her comment 'I might have got away from him' implies, her sexual experience with a much older man is barely consensual, and the book places no responsibility on the shoulders of the father of her baby. Nevertheless, Elaine Moss praised the book for its moral and educational dimensions, commenting, 'This is not a study in depth, but it is a skilful and honest sketch of a bad situation – required reading for headstrong girls, and for parents who think it "square" to stay in the house when their teenage children give parties.'[145] The perception that specialist teenage literature was primarily valuable as a socialising tool is similarly evident in Peter Hollindale's 1974 guide *Choosing Books for Children*, in which Hollindale asserted that 'the need for a specialist literature has faded', reaffirming Margery Fisher's assessment that older children could be largely served by adult literature, but commented that it did have a function in addressing specific adolescent concerns:

> In particular there are perhaps three major adolescent concerns where good novels can help: the beginning of important sexual relations, of work, and of sensitive (though often hidden) class consciousness.[146]

These themes are reflected in much of the teenage literature of the period. Josephine Kamm's oblique and heavily didactic approach to teenage sexuality partly reflects the controversy attached to this subject in 1965; a more frank approach to sexual relations emerged during the 1970s with books such as Gunnel Beckman's *Mia* (1974) and Judy Blume's landmark novel *Forever* (1975), although – as Roberta Seelinger Trites has demonstrated – didacticism was still a key feature and often a primary aim of such texts.[147] In K.M. Peyton's Flambards trilogy the changing class structure of Britain in the first part of the twentieth century is central to Christina's personal and romantic journey: in *Flambards* (1967), the first novel of the series, Christina has no way of 'bridging the gulf' between herself and working-class Dick; at the end of the trilogy she is able to marry Dick and assume control over the manor house where he was once a servant, although the characterisation of both Dick and Christina reveals a number of lingering assumptions about class characteristics.[148] As Chapter 3 will show, the themes of sex, class and work were also strongly present in the books selected for the Topliner list. The hostility towards didacticism evident in discussions of fantasy during the early 1960s is strikingly lacking here: in the realm of teenage reading, the provision of guidance was positioned as a primary function of literature.

---

[145] Elaine Moss, 'Review of *Young Mother*' in *Part of the Pattern*, 23, p. 23. First published in *The Spectator* (1964).

[146] Peter Hollindale, *Choosing Books for Children* (London: Elek, 1974), p. 135.

[147] Roberta Seelinger Trites, *Disturbing the Universe: Power and Repression in Adolescent Literature* (Iowa City: University of Iowa Press, 2002), pp. 86–96.

[148] K.M. Peyton, *Flambards* (Harmondsworth: Puffin, 1976), p. 99.

The perception that young people needed literature to guide them in a changing and unfamiliar world is evident in the work of other writers and critics of the period. Robert Westall, discussing teenage literature as a genre, argued:

> This is the teenage vacuum. Increasingly abandoned by adult authority; their own hierarchies unwittingly destroyed; increasingly cut off from meaningful dialogue with helpful adults; increasingly exposed to the fragmented disasters of the media, the young wander increasingly lost. [...] Perhaps we have to create new myths. If so, I can think of no one better qualified than those I shall call the teenage novelists. I have read a lot of teenage novels recently, and I have read few without integrity and a desire to offer something good.[149]

The attempt to 'create new myths' and make sense of social hierarchies is clearly discernible in the literature for adolescents of the period. Westall identified his own novel *The Machine Gunners* as an attempt to address the need for a meaningful social context, commenting, 'That is why *The Machine Gunners* is about a gang; it hopes to serve a hunger for social-structure in the young which, at the moment, we are very far from meeting'.[150] The need for myth and narrative is directly explored by Alan Garner in his two novels for adolescents, *The Owl Service* and *Red Shift* (1973); Charles Butler characterises Garner as attempting to develop ways of writing fiction which would 'function effectively as a transmitter of mythic energy'.[151] In *The Owl Service*, the relationship between the three protagonists is both shaped and explained by the underlying myth of Blodeuwedd, and it is only by 'reading' the myth in a creative and positive light that they are able to avoid disaster in the real world. At the climax of the novel, Roger is able to avert the looming destruction arising from the conflict between the three by 'rereading' the myth, focusing on Blodeuwedd's beneficial aspect as flowers, rather than the destructiveness of her owl form:

> 'You've got it back to front, you silly gubbins. She's not owls, she's flowers. Flowers. Flowers, Ali.' He stroked her forehead.[152]

Robert Leeson has criticised the novel for placing its resolution in the hands of middle-class Roger rather than working-class Gwyn, but Gwyn's inability to effect this rereading reflects his sense of disassociation from his own heritage of language and story: his determination to escape his Welsh, working-class roots has led him to buy elocution records which 'teach you to speak properly', and he uncomfortably dismisses the stories of the Mabinogion as '"Fine if you like that sort of thing – wizards and blood all over the place"'.[153] If Roger's ability to reread

---

149 Robert Westall, 'The Vacuum and the Myth' in *Teenage Reading*, 35–42, pp. 38–40.
150 Robert Westall, 'The Vacuum and the Myth', p. 42.
151 Charles Butler, *Four British Fantasists*, p. 203.
152 Alan Garner, *The Owl Service*, p. 173.
153 Alan Garner, *The Owl Service*, p. 114; p. 50.

the myth arises partly out of his position of privilege, Garner is not uncritical of that privilege. The importance of myth and story in creating meaning and direction for adolescent lives is even more powerfully expressed in *Red Shift*, in which the protagonist, Tom, rejects the symbolic aspects of the votive axe that has served as a talisman for his relationship with Jan and which they have affectionately termed their Bunty:

> 'It was an axe. Beaker Period. It was a votive axe. The best ever found.'

> '"Was?"' said Jan. 'Bunty "was"?'

> 'It wasn't a Bunty. It was an artifact. Not a toy.'[154]

Tom's rejection of the symbolism of the axe is linked with his inability to accept or negotiate the relationship Jan offers him; at the end of the novel he is isolated, alone, and – the cryptic endpapers imply – suicidal. It is questionable whether *Red Shift* offers its adolescent readers new myths by which to live, but the novel powerfully expresses Garner's belief in the need for myth and narrative. The recurring idea that young adults were particularly in need of stories which gave meaning to modern life, evident in the work of both Robert Westall and Alan Garner, reflects the degree to which adolescents during the 1960s and 1970s were perceived as *outside* the structures which had guided previous generations. Roberta Seelinger Trites' assertion that adolescent literature is ultimately about power is fundamentally relevant to this attempt to inscribe meaning on adolescence: literature which provided teenagers with guidance on how to live also offered adults the opportunity to attain some control over adolescents who – as the media reports show – were perceived as out of control.

Alan Garner's demanding and complex narrative in *Red Shift* is indicative of a move towards teenage literature which did not assume a reluctant or unaccomplished reader. In the 1970s, the growing acceptance of a specialist teenage literature accompanied the emergence of more stylistically demanding work written especially for young adults. Jill Paton Walsh, Jane Gardam and Lynne Reid Banks all produced novels which straddled the boundary between teenage and adult literature, demanding literate and engaged readers; Jill Paton Walsh observed that despite perceptions that *Unleaving* (1976) could have been published as an adult novel, if she had intended it for adult readers she would have 'approached it quite differently'.[155] Increasing stylistic complexity emerged in works such as Robert Cormier's *I Am the Cheese* (1977), in which the story of the protagonist Adam is revealed through an elliptical narrative style and fragmented chronology. The postmodernist narrative techniques adopted by Cormier were also used by Aidan Chambers in *Breaktime* (1978), in which the story is told through a combination of third-person narration, notes, excerpts from other texts, first-

---

[154]   Alan Garner, *Red Shift* (London: Lions, 1975), p. 158.

[155]   Jill Paton Walsh, 'Seeing Green' in *The Thorny Paradise*, 58–61, p. 61.

person stream-of-consciousness and graphic narrative. The emergence of texts like these indicates that the quality of teenage literature was not judged purely on its perceived moral or educational value, but also increasingly developed a status as a literature which could be assessed according to other criteria.

Teenage literature remained a strongly debated topic in children's literature throughout the 1960s and 1970s, with many commentators continuing to argue that a specialist literature for adolescents had no real legitimacy. Nevertheless, both the discourse surrounding the 'reluctant reader' and the emergence of stylistically complex works for young adults indicates an increasing acceptance of teenage literature as a distinctive category. The awarding of the Carnegie Medal to *The Edge of the Cloud*, and of the Whitbread Children's Award to Jill Paton Walsh's *The Emperor's Winding Sheet* (1974) demonstrates that despite the controversy over teenage literature, books aimed at readers between the ages of 13 and 18 were recognised as part of 'quality' children's literature. The tendency to justify teenage literature on the grounds of its socialising and educative function also helped to support the increasing focus on the didactic aspects of children's literature which was apparent in the move towards greater social realism.

Suitable for Children? Realism and Depressive Literature

The move towards more social realism in children's literature, and the perception that it should serve a wider age range than had previously been assumed, resulted in a shift towards bleaker, more hard-hitting narratives. Writing in 1961, Margery Fisher had commented on the need to exclude 'much of the danger and difficulty of real life' from children's stories; a perception already being challenged by John Rowe Townsend's depiction of child abandonment in *Gumble's Yard*. By the 1970s, the essentially hopeful and hygienic representation of real life problems in *Gumble's Yard* was no longer the default mode in children's literature. Alan Garner's *Red Shift* reflects a much bleaker and more graphic representation of reality; the historical sections of the book feature rape and genocide, while Tom's isolation and hopelessness at the end of the novel are a striking contrast from the message of hope emphasised by earlier novels for children. Some of the same bleakness is present in *Josh* (1971) by Australian author Ivan Southall, which explores the hostility and violence between 14-year-old town-dweller Josh and the children in the country town where he has come to stay:

> 'You're the champion, you are, kid. I reckon they ought to strike you a medal. You know what I'm telling you? You get sick, you get sicker than a dog and put yourself to bed, because if you turn up at cricket and pinch a game from another fellow you'll be the sorriest kid ever.'

> Josh, bewildered, bewildered, moaning inside, fighting to stop it from showing.[156]

---

[156] Ivan Southall, *Josh* (London: Angus and Robertson, 1971), p. 122.

The stream-of-consciousness narrative style of *Josh* makes the experience of his pain and bewilderment more direct for the reader, and while the reasons for the conflict are ultimately explained, there is no easy resolution; John Rowe Townsend observes that 'The taste remaining in the mouth is of bitterness and alienation'.[157] Despite the stylistic and emotional challenges posed by *Josh*, it was met with critical approbation and was awarded the Carnegie Medal in 1971. Dark and threatening emotions are similarly vividly represented in *Carrie's War*, Nina Bawden's highly-acclaimed novel on evacuee experience during the Second World War:

> Carrie felt as if she were suffocating. Mr Evans's face seemed to hang over her, pale and sweaty, like cheese. [...] This was like a bad dream coming true. Feeling so frightened without quite knowing why, and Mr. Evans's pale eyes boring into her, and no escape anywhere ...[158]

The novel is not unremittingly bleak – its portrayal of happiness is equally vivid – but it does present fear and powerlessness as integral aspects of childhood. In a speech delivered at a National Book League conference on the subject of realism in children's fiction, Nina Bawden argued, 'Books that don't take account of children's fears will never mean much to them, and books can help by bringing fears out into the open. It's reassuring for a child to know others have felt the same way'.[159]

The move to portray a broader range of life experiences and concepts introduced bleaker and more ambiguous themes to books for children and young people. Paul Zindel and Gunnel Beckman addressed the topic of abortion in *My Darling, My Hamburger* (1969) and *Mia* respectively; death and grief were explored by Katherine Paterson in *A Bridge to Terabithia* (1977) and Lois Lowry in *A Summer to Die* (1977); and Ann Schlee portrayed a bleak totalitarian regime in her science fiction novel *The Vandal* (1979), winner of the Guardian Award. The extent to which real life should be represented in books for children, however, remained a source of conflict. Nicholas Tucker, writing in 1976, asserted 'books should be about desirable experience rather than realistic experience. It is asking too much of a child to expect him to see life in the raw as it actually is.'[160] American authors Paul Zindel and Robert Cormier were frequently criticised for their bleak portrayals of adolescent life, which the teacher and critic Myles McDowell identified as unsuitable for child readers:

> There is such a cynical, depressive quality to Zindel's books, which seems to me to be destructive of values before values have properly had time to form. It

---

[157] John Rowe Townsend, *Written For Children*, p. 285.

[158] Nina Bawden, *Carrie's War* (Harmondsworth: Puffin, 1974), pp. 77–8.

[159] Nina Bawden, quoted in 'Through Literature to Life?', *Signal Approaches to Children's Books*, 11 (May 1973), 102–7, p. 106.

[160] Nicholas Tucker, 'How Children Respond to Fiction' in *Writers, Critics and Children*, 177–89, pp. 184–5. Tucker has returned to this theme in recent years, and has modified his opinions: see for example Nicholas Tucker, 'Depressive Stories for Children', *Children's Literature in Education*, 37:3 (September 2006), 199–210.

is the depression I would want to protect emergent minds from, rather than the promiscuity.[161]

Despite such criticisms, the awarding of the Carnegie Medal to Ivan Southall's bleak and depressive *Josh* indicates that the growing acceptance of realism in children's literature allowed for a wider emotional range than had been accepted in children's literature prior to the 1960s. The shift from a view of childhood as innocent and protected to one which acknowledged more ambiguous and troubling possibilities extended perceptions of what children's literature could and should do.

Literature and the Child Critic: Measures of Quality

The shift towards more realism in children's books reflects an attempt to engage with 'real' childhoods. Librarians and activists such as Janet Hill, Elaine Moss and Leila Berg worked directly with child readers, and the growing use of the vernacular in children's books was part of a move towards a more egalitarian view of literary quality. These attempts to reach a broader demographic of child readers and to engage with their experiences not only produced new kinds of children's literature, but also led to an increasing critical engagement with the kind of material which children chose for themselves.

The new critical interest in children's literature which began to emerge in the 1950s was focused on those texts which critics perceived to be 'good' children's literature. Although surveys of children's literature such as Margery Fisher's *Intent on Reading* and John Rowe Townsend's *Written for Children* engaged critically with the material discussed, they also served as recommendations for the kind of books children 'should' be reading rather than responding to the material that children did read. The characterisation of childhood as precious and vulnerable tended to heighten the perception that children's reading material should be carefully chosen; Margery Fisher argued that 'we must help the child to choose his books so that the ineffaceable impressions will be worth while'.[162] As a consequence, many authors who enjoyed wide popularity among children were effaced from the critical discourse about children's literature; Sheila Ray points out that despite the overwhelming commercial success of Enid Blyton, Blyton's books received little critical attention.[163] When Blyton was referenced by early critics, it was typically as an example of the kind of children's literature which should be avoided: Margery Fisher's disparaging observation that 'Enid Blyton and others think that children are taxed too much if they are confronted with so

---

[161] Myles McDowell, 'Fiction for Children and Adults: Some Essential Differences' in *Writers, Critics and Children*, 140–56, p. 153. Originally published in *Children's Literature in Education*, 10 (March 1973).

[162] Margery Fisher, *Intent upon Reading*, pp. 9–10.

[163] Sheila Ray, *The Blyton Phenomenon: The Controversy Surrounding the World's Most Successful Children's Writer* (London: Andre Deutsch, 1982).

much as a polysyllable' is a characteristic example.[164] Other reading material for children, such as the highly successful *Doctor Who* novelisations produced by Target Books, were similarly absent from critical discussions of children's literature. One striking instance of neglect was the lack of attention paid to comics and magazines; although the potential moral impact of so-called 'horror comics' received widespread attention during the 1950s, culminating in the passage of the Children and Young Persons (Harmful Publications) Act in 1955, the children's literature criticism of the time shows little recognition of the fact that comics formed a significant part of children's reading.[165]

Towards the end of the 1960s, critical approaches to children's literature began to shift, and the child-centred ethos which characterised attempts to reach a demographic of child readers who had hitherto been excluded from children's literature helped to generate critical interest in the kinds of books children chose for themselves. Wallace Hildick, whose experiences as a teacher had led him to attempt to produce literature which could engage the 'reluctant' and disenfranchised reader, included analyses of both Enid Blyton and the comic book form in his examination of technique and content in children's literature.[166] While Hildick does not challenge the perception of these texts as low in quality, his attempt to analyse their techniques and appeal demonstrates a desire to engage with popular as well as 'quality' material and a greater respect for the preferences of child readers. The legitimacy of popular reading material for children was more forcibly asserted by author Peter Dickinson at the Exeter conference on children's literature in 1970, where he asserted:

> Nobody who has not spent a whole sunny afternoon under his bed rereading a pile of comics left over from the previous holidays has any real idea of the meaning of intellectual freedom.[167]

Dickinson argued that attempts to provide children only with the 'best' reading were misguided, and that children needed the opportunity to discover books for themselves, to share a sense of community in their reading, and to enjoy a sense of security when they needed it. Nevertheless, his more detailed 'defence of rubbish',

---

[164] Margery Fisher, *Intent upon Reading*, p. 28.

[165] Martin Barker, *A Haunt of Fear: The Strange History of the British Horror Comics Campaign* (Jackson, MS; London: University Press of Mississippi, 1992); Martin Barker, 'Getting a Conviction: Or, How the British Horror Comics Campaign Only Just Succeeded' in *Pulp Demons: International Dimensions of the Postwar Anti-Comics Campaign*, ed. John A. Lent (London: Associated University Presses, 1999), 69–92.
The general terms of the 1955 Act had implications for children's literature as a whole, since it was aimed at protecting children from obscenity and did not specify particular media. However, as Barker argues, the language of the Act was designed to target graphical media in particular.

[166] Wallace Hildick, *Children and Fiction*, pp. 76–108.

[167] Peter Dickinson, 'A Defence of Rubbish' in *Writers, Critics and Children*, 73–6, p. 73.

published in response to the controversy aroused by his remarks at the Exeter conference, is predicated on the belief that much children's reading material was just that: 'reading matter which contain[s] to the adult eye no visible value, either educational or aesthetic'.[168] Whereas recent children's literature criticism has defended the legitimacy of popular reading material on literary grounds, Dickinson's comments exemplify concerns about literacy:

> The question remains of the children whose diet appears to consist solely of rubbish. Obviously, as far as possible, they should be slightly weaned. But not totally weaned. And besides, if they did not have this diet they would not be reading at all, and in a verbal culture I think it is better that the child should read something than read nothing. And perhaps, long after the child is out of the hands of parents or teachers, the habit of reading – even the habit of reading rubbish – may somehow evoke a tendency to read things which are not rubbish.[169]

The belief that young readers' taste for 'rubbish' might be a route to more desirable forms of reading reflects the shift towards engaging with the reality of childhood experience rather than the idealised child. Although adult judgements of children's reading material were still privileged over those of the child, Dickinson's 'defence of rubbish' shows a move towards a construction of quality which was more closely concerned with the experience of the child reader.

A more child-centred approach to assessing the quality of children's books was not universally welcomed by children's literature critics. In a seminal article on 'The Irrelevance of Children to the Children's Book Reviewer', the critic and bibliographer Brian Alderson argued that using children's responses to texts as a critical tool was unsatisfactory: 'The adage "we needs must love the highest when we see it" has always seemed to me of doubtful application and it is at its most doubtful applied to children when they are left to themselves among books'.[170] A set of objective critical standards was essential, Alderson argued, if reading were to assume its proper role in children's lives:

> From the tone of reviews in the popular press our aim would appear to be not much more than that of keeping the children quiet for half an hour or fitting them out to be competent participants in a bureaucratic society. But once one assigns to reading the vital role, which I believe that it has, of making children more perceptive and more aware of the possibilities of language, then it becomes necessary to hold fast to qualitative judgements formed upon the basis of adult experience.[171]

---

[168] Peter Dickinson, 'A Defence of Rubbish', p. 74.

[169] Peter Dickinson, 'A Defence of Rubbish', p. 76.

[170] Brian Alderson, 'The Irrelevance of Children to the Children's Book Reviewer' in *Children's Literature: The Development of Criticism*, ed. by Peter Hunt (London: Routledge, 1990), 53–5, p. 54.

[171] Brian Alderson, 'The Irrelevance of Children to the Children's Book Reviewer', p. 55.

Alderson's argument reflects the broader division between those concerned with the social and ideological aspects of children's literature – the group John Rowe Townsend termed the 'child people' – and those who wished to focus on the literary and aesthetic elements of children's books. As Alderson's concern with the 'vital role' of reading indicates, however, an emphasis on the specifically literary aspects of children's literature did not entail a disregard for its effects on children themselves. On the contrary, Alderson's work reflects a belief that children's literature was important enough to require a formal critical approach.

The tension between responding to the needs and preferences of real children and maintaining particular literary ideals remained a central element of the debate over quality during the 1960s and 1970s. This child-centred approach was also important to children's publishers of the period: the responses of real child readers were an important consideration in the editorial work of both Kaye Webb and Aidan Chambers. However, as Peter Dickinson's approach to 'rubbish' indicates, a fundamental belief in the need to provide children with literature which was not only enjoyable but also of 'educational or aesthetic' value remained a dominant theme throughout the period.

Conclusion: A Golden Age of Debate

The 1960s and 1970s saw a diverse range of critical and literary approaches to children's literature which generated a sense of excitement and possibility. Although it is possible in retrospect to identify some clear themes across the period, these ideas emerged as part of a much more complex and contested discourse. The sense of a second golden age, therefore, was generated by the variety and vigour of debate about children's literature rather than by a consensus about the best books to offer children. Many of the titles which were awarded prizes during the period and which have continued to be regarded as benchmarks for quality emerged in response to changing ideas about the form and function of children's literature: as this chapter has shown, Alan Garner's *The Owl Service*, Robert Westall's *The Machine Gunners* and Gene Kemp's *The Turbulent Term of Tyke Tiler* reflect innovations in style and content which were highly contested at the time they were published.

Central to the debate about children's literature was the changing perception of children and society. The construction of childhood as a representation of innocence and hope in a post-war world helped to produce an intense social focus on childhood, education and children's literature. One result of this focus, however, was a growing awareness of the gulf between this ideal vision of childhood and the real lives of many children. Investment in schools and libraries, and a broader social concern with offering all children access to literature and education, helped to focus attention upon the needs of a broader demographic of children. Attempts to create a literature which catered for children from working-class and ethnic minority backgrounds, and for a wider age range of young readers, produced a shift towards more realism in children's literature, broadening the parameters for the kind of content and language perceived as suitable for children. Simultaneously, the growing ideological consciousness which characterised British society during the 1960s and 1970s was becoming evident in approaches to children's literature. The social and ideological impact of children's literature was interrogated in relation to issues of gender, race and class.

The unifying theme in children's literature throughout the 1960s and 1970s was a profound belief in its importance to children's lives and the consequent need to provide children with the best possible reading material. The diverse discourses surrounding children's literature, however, produced a variety of different and often conflicting definitions of what was 'best'. The work of Kaye Webb at Puffin Books and Aidan Chambers at Topliner Macmillan demonstrates that children's publishers were neither indifferent to nor separate from these diverse discourses. On the contrary, children's editors engaged directly with new ideas about the form and purpose of children's literature. In making decisions about the publication and marketing of children's books, they were able to affect the degree to which new ideas about children's literature were reflected in the books available to children; Chapters 2 and 3 demonstrate the ways in which these figures contributed to the making of modern children's literature.

Chapter 2
Kaye Webb and Puffin Books

A key factor in creating the sense that the 1960s and 1970s were a 'golden age of children's literature' was the flourishing nature of children's publishing. At the centre of this flourishing activity was Puffin Books, under the innovative and charismatic leadership of editor Kaye Webb. The Puffin list under Kaye Webb reflected many of the key aspects of the 'golden age'; the widespread perception that Puffin offered 'the best in children's books' gave the imprint central importance in defining ideals of 'quality' in children's literature.

Puffin Books, the children's imprint of paperback publisher Penguin, was already well-established by the beginning of the 1960s. Founded in 1939, Puffin was the first children's paperback imprint, and by 1961 it still almost completely monopolised the children's paperback market. This monopoly in part reflected a widespread perception that the market for children's paperbacks was strictly limited: the scepticism which had greeted Allen Lane's launch of Penguin in 1939 was even more acute in the children's market, which was dominated by hardback library editions.[1] By the end of the 1970s, children's paperbacks had become widely accepted, and Puffin no longer enjoyed this unique position in the marketplace. The period did not, however, represent one in which Puffin was 'left behind'. On the contrary, the years 1961 to 1979 were a distinct and significant period in the development of Puffin itself; rather than being overtaken by the developments in children's publishing, the imprint played a key role in forming them.

The formative influence of Puffin during the 1960s and 1970s owes much to its editor, Kaye Webb, whose career at Puffin spans both decades. She joined the company in 1961 as 'Outside Editor' and remained in control of Puffin until 1979, when she relinquished her editorial role but retained a position as an advisor and company director. Under her editorship, the imprint grew from a small (though well-respected) endeavour – in 1960, under its first editor Eleanor Graham, Puffin published only 12 titles on its story book list – to a well-promoted and active list which not only maintained a high publishing output but also encompassed a children's book club and magazine and an international presence.[2] All these

---

[1]   Penguin Books, *Fifty Penguin Years* (Harmondsworth: Penguin, 1985), pp. 13–16.

[2]   'So whereas in 1960 Puffins were being published at the rate of 24 a year, in 1977 we produced 127 new titles.'

Kaye Webb, 'A Red Letter Day for Children (or the Rewarding Road to the 1000th Puffin)', typescript draft of article, c. 1977, Kaye Webb Collection, Seven Stories, the National Centre for Children's Books, KW/07/01/05/09/03.

This chapter makes extensive use of archival material from the Kaye Webb Collection, Seven Stories, the National Centre for Children's Books, Newcastle, abbreviated in all

developments were directly instigated by Kaye Webb, and the breadth of her influence over the imprint is such that an analysis of Puffin in this period is de facto an analysis of Webb herself.

Despite the key importance of Puffin Books and Kaye Webb to the history of British children's literature, the imprint has received little scholarly attention. Many of the books which appeared on the Puffin list have been the subject of academic research in their own right, but apart from a special edition of *Signal Approaches to Children's Books* published in 1972 – which necessarily focused on the early years of Puffin – the only examination of the imprint's history to date is Sally Gritten's slim volume *The Story of Puffin Books* (1992). The acquisition in 2005 of Kaye Webb's personal archive by Seven Stories, the National Centre for Children's Books, and the availability of newly accessible material from the Penguin Archive at the University of Bristol has made it possible to investigate the activities of the imprint and the editorial ethos of Kaye Webb and to assess the significant impact of Puffin in creating an ideal of 'quality' children's literature during the 1960s and 1970s.

A Job for the Wife: Puffin and Kaye Webb

The activities of children's publishers play a significant role in determining cultural responses to childhood and children's literature. Children's editors and publishers actively engage in the discourse around children's literature, both through their publishing decisions and more directly. Furthermore, the attitudes of publishers to their children's imprints are indicative of the broader cultural perception of childhood: the establishment of children's imprints in the 1950s can be directly connected with the post-war desire to educate and instil appropriate values in a disrupted society.[3] However, this altruistic aspect worked to make children's imprints less significant in a commercial sense: up until the 1960s children's imprints were largely neglected within their parent companies. Both these trends were evident in Puffin; however, Kaye Webb's tenure as editor had an important impact on perceptions of children's publishing both within Penguin and in the British publishing industry as a whole.

At the beginning of the 1960s an ethos of 'quality' publishing was already a fundamental part of Puffin's brand identity. Allen Lane had founded Puffin's

---

subsequent citations to SS, and from the Penguin Archive, Bristol, abbreviated hereafter to UoB. Reference numbers relate to individual items in the Kaye Webb Collection. At the time of access the Penguin Archive was not yet fully catalogued; the fullest possible location details have therefore been given to aid future research.

Where the material cited is a draft of published material, the name of the publication in which it appeared will be given if known.

[3]   Kimberley Reynolds, 'Publishing Practices and the Practicalities of Publishing' in *Children's Book Publishing in Britain Since 1945*, ed. by Kimberley Reynolds and Nicholas Tucker (Aldershot: Scolar Press, 1998), 20–41, p. 26.

parent company in 1939 on the basis of a belief in the existence of 'a vast reading public for intelligent books at a low price'.[4] While Allen Lane's approach to Penguin reveals an astute business sensibility, there is also a strong public service ethos inherent in his desire to make 'intelligent' books more affordable: like Lord Reith's BBC, Penguin sought to 'educate, inform and entertain' the masses.[5] The same ethos is evident in the early Puffins: editor Noel Carrington launched the imprint in 1940 with four Puffin picture books intended to provide children with information about key aspects of wartime life. Puffin story books, launched the following year under the editorship of Eleanor Graham, aimed to provide 'the best of the new work being done for children'.[6] By the time Kaye Webb took over the list in 1961, it was widely regarded as offering precisely that: she reflected that 'its standards were set securely and firmly by Eleanor Graham with the help of Margaret Clark (now at the Bodley Head), and it would have taken a much more intrepid person than myself to dare to lower them'.[7] Kaye Webb therefore inherited an ethos in which high standards were defined by more than commercial success; this ethos remained a central aspect of Puffin under her editorship.

Like the majority of children's publishing imprints in the post-war period (and indeed to date), Puffin was largely female dominated. Noel Carrington's tenure as editor of the Puffin picture book list was short: it was the editorships of Eleanor Graham and Kaye Webb – both of whom remained in post for 20 years – which defined Puffin. The female-dominated nature of Puffin – both editors also presided over a largely female staff – is characteristic of children's publishing during this period: with one or two exceptions, notably Patrick Hardy at Viking/Kestrel and Anthony Kamm at Brockhampton Books, the most prominent children's editors were women. The majority were also appointed without any formal training or experience: only Grace Hogarth at Longman and Marni Hodgkin at Macmillan, who had received their training in the United States, had been trained as specialist children's editors. Kimberley Reynolds characterises this trend as arising out of publishers' 'lack of respect for children's books', arguing that 'because the editing of children's books was thought of as effectively unskilled and certainly inferior work, very few established figures (invariably men) were interested in the task of creating and managing children's lists'.[8] Kaye Webb's account of her own appointment to Puffin is extremely suggestive of the attitude that children's publishing was 'a nice little job for a woman' rather than a serious concern:

---

[4] Steve Hare, *Penguin Portrait: Allen Lane and the Penguin Editors, 1935–1970* (London: Penguin, 1995), p. 53.

[5] Bob Franklin, *British Television Policy: A Reader* (London: Routledge, 2001), p. 9.

[6] Eleanor Graham, quoted in Brian Alderson, 'Puff puff Puffin along: Brian Alderson on the publication of the thousandth Puffin', *The Times Educational Supplement* (No. 3272), 10 March 1978, p. 1.

[7] Kaye Webb, 'A Red Letter Day for Children (or the Rewarding Road to the 1000th Puffin)', typescript draft of article, c. 1997, SS, KW/07/01/05/09/03.

[8] Kimberley Reynolds, 'Publishing Practices and the Practicalities of Publishing', p. 27.

Tony Godwin [Chief Editor at Penguin] just rang me up and asked me to do it. I don't really know why he did. I had been editing a magazine called *Young Elizabethan* and I suppose it was that. I didn't really know anything about children's literature, I just knew about editing. And I think really my husband wanted to get me out of the house into a job, because otherwise I don't really know why Tony thought of me.[9]

This account suggests that Penguin treated appointments at Puffin in an essentially ad hoc manner; however, it belies the fact that Kaye Webb had an association with Penguin in her own right. Archival material relating to Webb's autobiography indicates that she had enjoyed a long friendship with Allen Lane and that he had encouraged her to work for Penguin on several occasions prior to her appointment at Puffin, indicating that she was perceived as a good fit for the company rather than simply a suitable person to work on the children's list.[10] If the connection seems more founded on personal qualities than professional experience, then this was not markedly different from hiring policy in other departments at Penguin: Jack Morpurgo characterises Allen Lane's appointments as 'promising neophyte[s]', noting that 'Versatility was at Penguin more treasured than expertise'.[11] Despite the implication that Webb was merely conveniently situated for the position, she was in fact considerably more qualified for the post than her own account suggests. By 1961 she had already had a long and varied career as a journalist and editor, not only for *Young Elizabethan*, but for a variety of other publications – most notably the well-known humorous periodical *Lilliput*, which had been a firm favourite during the war years – and for broadcast media such as *Woman's Hour*. While it was true that little of her previous experience had been focused upon children's literature, *Young Elizabethan* was a magazine for children, and her work with them had already brought her into the literary sphere; for example, through an interview with the acclaimed author Noel Streatfeild.[12] *Young Elizabethan* in fact had a significant literary component, and Webb was engaged both in commissioning pieces on children's books and in writing reviews herself. Furthermore, if her knowledge of children's literature was relatively limited, the fact that she 'knew about editing' was a not-inconsiderable asset, while

---

[9]   Kimberley Reynolds and Nicholas Tucker, 'Interview with Kaye Webb, 7 February 1995', in *Oral Archives: A Collection of Informal Conversations with Individuals Involved in Creating or Producing Children's Literature since 1945*, compiled by Kimberley Reynolds and Nicholas Tucker (London: Roehampton University, 1998), 366–88, p. 367.

[10]   Kaye Webb, 'On Being a Children's Editor', typescript draft, SS, KW/15/32, f.3.
Lane also sought Webb's advice on appointing a suitable Art Editor for Penguin, indicating his respect for her professional opinion. (Allen Lane to Kaye Webb, 3 March 1958, SS, KW/07/01/01/01.)

[11]   J.E. Morpurgo, *Allen Lane, King Penguin: A Biography* (London: Hutchison, 1979), p. 210; p. 212.

[12]   'Young Elizabethans', *Birmingham Weekly Post*, 22 April 1955, press cutting in 'Press Cuttings Album', SS, KW/16/03.

her professional experience provided her with a range of skills not necessarily available to her predecessor.

Many of the innovations which Webb brought to Puffin were based upon her previous experience in other fields: the Puffin Club, which came to define her editorship, grew directly out of her experience in magazine publishing. Furthermore, she was initially appointed as Outside Editor – a largely advisory position – with the assumption that Margaret Clark would remain as Internal Editor, an arrangement which would have allowed Webb to bring a fresh approach to the list without sacrificing the experience and expertise in children's literature which Clark had accumulated in her years working with Eleanor Graham.[13] In the event, Margaret Clark, who had expected to succeed Eleanor Graham, resigned when Webb was appointed, leaving the way open for Kaye Webb to take full control of Puffin. Deprived of this assistance, Webb was quick to acquire the knowledge of children's books which she lacked. Given the dearth of professionally trained children's editors in the British publishing industry, Webb's extensive experience as a journalist and editor arguably constituted a move towards a more professional ethos for Puffin.

In many respects Kaye Webb fitted the pattern of the 'traditional' female editor: as this chapter will show, many of the most significant and characteristic aspects of her editorship derived from a specifically feminine construction of children's editing. Nevertheless, her appointment at the start of the 1960s is indicative of the firm's interest in developing new directions for Puffin. The decision to appoint someone from outside the world of children's literature rather than maintaining the status quo by allowing Margaret Clark – an eminently capable editor – to succeed Eleanor Graham suggests a desire to bring new innovations to Puffin at a time of rapid change in children's literature.

A Golden Age: Status and Recognition in Puffin

The marginalisation of children's publishing imprints and editors during the 1950s and 1960s had a significant impact on the character of children's publishing. Children's editors were frequently overlooked within their own companies, a tendency which is certainly suggested by Kaye Webb's account of her first weeks with Puffin: she arrived at the company's offices in Harmondsworth to discover that there was no desk available for her. The suggested solution – that she should work in the office on days when there were company meetings, to which she was not invited – suggests that Puffin was not integrated into the work of the company as a whole. The fact that Webb initially had no desk of her own was in fact due to the fact that she was initially employed as an 'outside editor' – the same basis under which Eleanor Graham had worked – and thus was expected to work largely from home, while the inside editor managed day-to-day business inside the firm.

---

[13]   Kimberley Reynolds and Nicholas Tucker, 'Interview with Kaye Webb, 7 February 1995', pp. 367–8.

Use of outside editors was commonplace as a way of bringing expertise to smaller imprints, but the fact that an outside editor was considered sufficient to manage the children's section of Penguin is indicative of the fact that Puffin was seen as a minor imprint rather than a key department of the firm. Although this was understandable in the context of Puffin's low output under Eleanor Graham, who published on average about 12 titles a year, it tended to be overlooked by others in the firm even after it became a significant income source: Kaye Webb recalled, 'they were all frightfully glad about the figures, but I don't think there was anybody else who was really keen to support [the books]'.[14] In Reynolds' view, this culture of neglect brought children's editors benefits as well as disadvantages:

> Their general sense of invisibility and marginality in their own companies created both a unique sense of rapport and collaboration between children's editors and the opportunity for almost complete autonomy in the company.[15]

This high degree of autonomy was certainly an important factor in the case of Kaye Webb, who exercised almost complete control over her list. Independence was a quality valued at Penguin: Noel Carrington commented that 'Allen Lane depended much on his editors and he allowed them a large measure of freedom'.[16] Nevertheless, the degree of control Kaye Webb exerted over Puffin was almost unparalleled, especially by the 1960s, when Penguin had grown into a larger and more professionally organised firm. While Anthony Godwin advised her on her appointment, 'Any decisions you take about the purchase of material will be subject to the approval of myself or my appointed deputy', archival evidence suggests that direct interference from Godwin or Webb's other superiors at Puffin was rare and typically confined to questions of finance.[17] Meanwhile, Kaye Webb maintained a degree of control over all the books published in Puffin: even where a subeditor was directly responsible for a list, as in the case of Dorothy Wood with the teenage imprint Peacock, editorial files show that Webb remained in close contact with the editorial process (to the chagrin of some of her staff).[18] This control extended to marketing and artwork as well as the selection of the books: a memorandum of 1965 outlines the structure of responsibility for art and design at Penguin, bringing every department except Puffin under the control of a single Art and Design department, and notes 'In addition there is separate art work wholly commissioned outside, in respect of Puffins and Peacocks under the control of

---

[14]   Kaye Webb, 'Interview with Kimberley Reynolds and Nicholas Tucker, 7 February 1995', p. 381.

[15]   Kimberley Reynolds, 'Publishing Practices and the Practicalities of Publishing', p. 28.

[16]   Noel Carrington, 'The Puffin Picture Books', typescript draft, 29 March 1971, UoB, DM.1294/17.ii.

[17]   Anthony Godwin to Kaye Webb, 3 February 1961, SS, KW/07/01/01/04.

[18]   See for example the editorial file on A.P. Herbert, *The Water Gypsies*, 1973–1975, UoB, DM/1952, Box 361, ISBN 047.069 7.

Kaye Webb'.[19] Although Reynolds characterises the autonomy of children's editors as arising from the marginalisation of children's books, the truth is more complex in the case of Puffin. While the high degree of autonomy Kaye Webb enjoyed undoubtedly stemmed partly from the perception that children's books were simply not significant enough to interfere with – a perception implied in Webb's assertion that no one was 'really keen to support' Puffin – it also indicates a degree of respect for her professional opinion. An article of 1975 presents her independence at Puffin as deriving from her skill as an editor:

> That "something" [as an editor] is why her chairman Peter Calvocoressi wouldn't dream of interfering in the operation of her department.
>
> "Publishing is a gambling business," he argues, and his role is to pick good gamblers. A first-rate editor has to be almost like an independent publisher, checked by financial control; and Puffin Books certainly has a great deal of autonomy.[20]

The implication that Kaye Webb was a successful gambler is indicative of her success in improving the financial profile of Puffin: as discussed below, her skill at marketing books and identifying bestsellers was one of the defining characteristics of her work as editor. Penguin's readiness to accept that Puffin should operate 'almost like an independent publisher', however, also meant that Kaye Webb was free to impose a distinctive and personal character on the imprint: the Puffin ethos was largely synonymous with her own.

Penguin's recognition of Kaye Webb as a valuable and authoritative children's editor partly arose because of her own refusal to be marginalised within the firm. The tendency to regard children's publishing as a small-scale and relatively unimportant branch of publishing was typically reflected in the low pay awarded to children's editors.[21] Although many editors accrued formidable expertise and experience once in post, the fact that many were women with few formal qualifications helped to ensure that they were unlikely to challenge the low salaries they were awarded. This situation was exacerbated by the general perception that children's publishing offered other rewards: Eleanor Graham, Kaye Webb's predecessor at Puffin, intimated that she had been undervalued at Puffin, but was quick to qualify her criticisms, saying 'I can only be humbly grateful for the strong ways in which I have been cared for, have had deficiencies made up and blessings heaped upon me'.[22] Kaye Webb, coming from outside the world of book publishing altogether, was unprepared to acquiesce to this point of view: she remarked,

---

[19] 'AMW', memo to Executive Board, 'Art dept.', 26 May 1965, UoB, DM/1843/16.

[20] Gwen Nuttall, 'Puffin's winning gambler', *Sunday Times Business*, 6 April 1975, UoB, 'Puffin' green publicity folder.

[21] Kimberley Reynolds, 'Publishing Practices and the Practicalities of Publishing', p. 29.

[22] Eleanor Graham to Kaye Webb, c.1961, SS, KW/07/01/05/05/01.

'I couldn't believe how humble all the editors were that I met, because it was quite new to me. And it never occurred to them that they were entitled to decent offices, or more money, or much attention'.[23] Webb's own career, by contrast, had been conducted within the largely male-dominated world of magazine publishing, and she had been precipitated into a position as de facto editor of *Lilliput* when the majority of the magazine's staff had been called up for wartime service. The fact that she was swiftly ousted from this position of seniority at the end of the war undoubtedly contributed to her determination to secure a salary and working conditions commensurate with her duties at Puffin. The fact that by 1961 Webb was effectively a single mother provided an additional spur to fight for the best possible working conditions.

Archival evidence indicates that pay and working conditions were a persistent concern for Kaye Webb. Although outside editors were not unusual, she was keen to secure a position for herself which enabled her to work more closely and visibly within the company, and the first year of her employment saw a series of renegotiations of her salary based on the changed nature of her role after the departure of Margaret Clark left her with sole responsibility for Puffin.[24] Several years later she negotiated for a pay rise, arguing successfully that it should be backdated to the beginning of the year: 'More particularly since, with the increasing success of the Puffin Club, I have actually – admittedly of my own volition – doubled the amount of work that I have undertaken to do for the firm when my contract was first signed'.[25] It is striking that Webb did not exonerate Penguin of the responsibility to increase her salary because she had augmented her own workload: on the contrary, this letter indicates her sense of her own worth and the worth of the work she was doing. This is also evident in her negotiations for an assistant to cover some of the work which would have been done by Margaret Clark, who she insisted should be paid more than a secretarial wage, writing to Senior Editor Tony Godwin that 'with most bright girls the salary might be a drawback', and ultimately employing Linda Villiers at a salary of £750 a year.[26] It is difficult to determine how far Kaye Webb's salary was commensurate with those of male colleagues at the same level, since salaries varied across the company; however, her notes indicate that she was initially offered £1500 per annum for assuming sole responsibility for Puffin. This was the same salary awarded to Frank Rudman during a provisional term as Editor of Fiction – a much larger department than Puffin – although a letter of 1965 indicates that the firm were willing to pay as much as £4000 per annum for a good Fiction Editor.[27] The variance of the

---

23   Kimberley Reynolds and Nicholas Tucker, 'Interview with Kaye Webb, 7 February 1995', p. 366.

24   Kaye Webb, 'Brief Record of K.W.'s Employment with Penguins', typescript notes, n.d., SS, KW/07/01/03/01.

25   Kaye Webb to C. Dolley, 1970, SS, KW/07/01/01/12.

26   Kaye Webb to Tony Godwin, 1961, SS, KW/07/01/01/03.

27   H.F. Paroissien to Eunice Frost, 23 June 1965, UoB, Frost Papers 19, DM/1843/16.

salaries on offer even for the same position suggests that the amounts awarded were predicated upon the experience and requirements of individuals; while Kaye Webb was initially offered a modest salary, Penguin's willingness to award her successive pay increases suggests that this was due to expediency rather than a general sense that Puffin was not worth a bigger investment. Webb's readiness to negotiate a better salary positioned her within the broader culture of Penguin, establishing Puffin as not only notionally but literally worthy of investment. This was of more than personal significance: it helped to position children's literature as a legitimate and important publishing sector on a par with literature for adults.

By 1966, Kaye Webb's profile within Penguin was sufficiently high for her to be invited to join the board of directors, a position which further ensured that Puffin would be well-represented within the company as a whole. The surge of cultural interest in childhood and children's literature which occurred during the 1960s undoubtedly made it easier for Kaye Webb to claim this status; however, by ensuring that Penguin – one of the largest and best-known publishing houses – gave recognition to its children's imprint, she helped to set a precedent for children's publishing as a whole.

P'super Puffins: Publicity and Prestige

Kaye Webb's prominence within Penguin and the respect she received as an editor were closely connected with her financial success at Puffin. Restrictions on paper supplies during and immediately after the Second World War had enforced a relatively low output during the early years of Puffin, but even by the late 1950s Eleanor Graham maintained a small list, never exceeding more than 24 new Puffin storybook titles in a year.[28] By contrast, Kaye Webb dramatically expanded the list – by 1965 she had already doubled the number of new titles published annually – and achieved unprecedentedly high sales. Her skill at marketing and selling children's books made Puffin into an important element of Penguin's financial success and helped to promote children's books in Britain as a whole.

Kaye Webb's background in magazine publishing had a significant impact on her approach to children's publishing. Eleanor Graham's Puffin list had been presented as a small personal library, designed to grow gradually. By contrast, Kaye Webb approached paperback publishing as essentially ephemeral, writing to author Noel Streatfeild, 'I think paper-backs should be looked at rather like a magazine: they can buy and read and then if they fall in love with the book they can get themselves a perma[nent copy]'.[29] This viewpoint informed a vastly different attitude to publishing: Kaye Webb sought to publish a large number of new titles each year, offering children a greater range of choice. This was a radical

---

[28] Penguin Books, *Complete Catalogue of the Publications of Penguin Books* (Harmondsworth: Penguin, 1970).

[29] Kaye Webb to Noel Streatfeild, 26 July 1961, UoB, DM1107 / PS 157. The end of the sentence is illegible.

approach in the context of an economic model based on large print runs and slow sales, which made the introduction of new titles more financially risky (a situation which was to change in the 1970s when high warehousing costs made shorter print-runs more economical than storing books). Webb recalled that 'the constant problem was how many books you could do in a year, and one was always fighting for that […] If a really good book came along you couldn't bear it if it wasn't on the list'.[30] She steadily increased the number of books published by Puffin: by 1968 she had increased the annual output of Puffin storybooks, the main list, to 55 new titles, more than double the highest annual output under Eleanor Graham. In addition, she launched a host of new lists: Peacock (1961) catered for adolescent readers, while Young Puffins (1961) and Picture Puffins (1968) were specifically for younger children.[31] As a result, children enjoyed a greater variety in their reading material, while Puffin enjoyed an expansion in their market. The result was a massive increase in sales: from 669,482 books in 1960, to 1,786,058 in 1965, a rise of more than 160 per cent.[32]

The commercial success which supported Kaye Webb's expansion of the Puffin list can be partially attributed to the changing market for children's books. The growing interest in childhood and children's literature, combined with the economic prosperity of the early 1960s, helped to create a much bigger market for children's literature. The dramatic expansion of Puffin, however, owed much to Kaye Webb's talent for promoting and selling the books. Unlike hardback publishers, Puffin was largely unable to benefit from the lucrative library market, which accounted for at least 70 per cent of sales. As a paperback imprint, it relied instead upon the market for private book ownership, which had traditionally been very small. A central aspect of Kaye Webb's editorship was her determination to raise the profile of Puffin Books. She commented that when she first became editor 'the books did not have very appealing covers and nobody was doing much to get them known' and archival evidence shows her determination to remedy this situation and gain more shelf space for Puffins.[33] A memo from a member of the marketing department to Kaye Webb, dated 1975, notes a number of changes agreed with the children's book department of Selfridges in response to Webb's insistence on more prominent displays for Puffins, and notes 'within Selfridges Puffins have twice as much space as any other Paperback Imprint within the store'.[34] In order to achieve more prominent displays, Webb embraced the use of shelf headers, cardboard 'dump bins' and other promotional materials. During her

[30]   Kimberley Reynolds and Nicholas Tucker, 'Interview with Kaye Webb, 7 February 1995'.

[31]   Kaye Webb, 'History of Puffin Books', typescript, 1972, SS, KW/07/04/08/02.

[32]   'Total Sales – to end of March 1966', typescript, c. 1966, UoB, Folder: 'Misc Puffin History (incl Kaye Webb)', DM1294/17.ii.

[33]   Kaye Webb, 'On Being a Children's Editor', typescript draft, SS, KW/15/32, f.2.

[34]   Ian Savage, memo to Kaye Webb, 25 November 1975, UoB, Folder: Puffin Annual No 2, Memos & Correspondence with non-contributors, DM/1952 box 529.

first years at Puffin she hit upon the idea of advertising the books through a marketing jingle, and secured the agreement of W.H. Smith to play a jingle if she could produce one. Webb duly did so, recording it with the aid of a family friend, and the 'Puffin Song' was played in W.H. Smith stores across the United Kingdom.[35] These initiatives not only served to promote the Puffin brand, but also raised the profile of children's books in general.

Kaye Webb's focus on marketing books more effectively was also reflected in the close attention she paid to book covers. Illustrated covers had already been a feature of the Puffin list under Eleanor Graham, but under Kaye Webb they became a key focus. Colourful, wraparound artwork by artists such as Antony Maitland made jackets more eye-catching and appealing. Webb also took advantage of the publicity afforded by television and film adaptations, producing TV tie-in editions of books such as Alan Garner's *The Owl Service* (1967).[36] The importance Webb attached to the choice of cover art is reflected in the degree of personal attention she afforded jacket decisions: editorial files show that even when another editor was responsible for the majority of editorial decisions on a book the jacket design was usually approved by Webb. Frequently, she even offered specific advice to artists: during the publication of Ian Serailler's *The Silver Sword* (1956), she wrote to C. Walter Hodges:

> I hate to niggle, but while the rest of the cover is absolutely fine, I'm afraid I don't like the boy's face. I don't know exactly what it is but he seems to me to look rather unpleasant. Before you start trying anything new would you consider using a bit of white paint and taking out some of the shadows under his eyes or the shading from the sides? I'm not technically expert but there's something making him look unattractive as a hero and I'm sure it's only a matter of lightening it up.[37]

Kaye Webb's close attention to the visual appeal of children's books helped to encourage high sales for Puffin, but it was also consonant with the more child-centred ethos of the 1960s and the cultural emphasis on reading for pleasure. Activists such as Leila Berg, who were concerned to broaden the demographic of young readers, frequently emphasised the importance of books which looked attractive to young readers; as Chapter 3 will show, this belief also strongly informed the work of Aidan Chambers. Kaye Webb's exciting and appealing Puffin covers played a key role in demonstrating that it was possible to appeal directly to children – and to improve sales by doing so.

One of Kaye Webb's most distinctive and innovative strategies for raising the profile of Puffin books and children's literature was the Puffin Club. Launched in 1967, the Puffin Club was a children's book club which charged a small fee for membership. In return for their membership fee, members received a year's

[35]   Kaye Webb, 'On Being a Children's Editor', typescript draft, SS, KW/15/32, f.4.
[36]   See editorial file for Alan Garner, *The Owl Service*, UoB, DM/1107/PK66.
[37]   Kaye Webb to C. Walter Hodges, 20 August 1964, UoB, DM/1107/PS146.

subscription to the quarterly magazine, *Puffin Post*, along with a membership pack which included a badge, notepaper and sundry other Puffin-emblazoned items. In keeping with the Cold War ethos of the time, Club members were provided with a secret codebook which could be used to decode messages published in the *Puffin Post* or distributed in Puffin books, and could recognise each other by exchanging the code words 'Sniffup' and 'Spotera' (from 'Puffins are tops'). All these elements made the Puffin Club an ideal means of forming brand loyalty: Club members, known as 'Puffineers', were encouraged to identify directly with the brand. The Club also provided a basis for advertising, both directly – advertisements for new Puffin titles appeared in the *Puffin Post* – and through activities and events which generated news coverage. These events generated publicity not only in children's literature circles, but also in more mainstream media: events such as the annual Puffin Exhibition, which attracted over 1,000 young readers, attracted attention which would never have been inspired by a simple book launch. The Puffin Club was more than a marketing tool, but its success in advertising should not be discounted. By generating excitement about and loyalty to Puffin the Club benefited children's literature as a whole.

The Puffin Club benefited not only from Kaye Webb's keen understanding of marketing, but also her ability to garner assistance from a variety of quarters. Webb's time working on *Lilliput* magazine – which published work by many of the most prominent figures of the day – and her marriage to artist Ronald Searle had given her a wide social circle which included many celebrities.[38] Archival holdings of her personal correspondence include letters from actors such as James Mason and Alec Guinness and prominent poets including Laurie Lee and John Betjeman, along with many figures from the world of children's literature.[39] Webb capitalised on this network of prominent friends, frequently enlisting them to write for the *Puffin Post* or attend Puffin Club events. Laurie Lee wrote the second verse of the Puffin Song, 'There's Nuffin Like a Puffin'.[40] The first issue of the *Puffin Post* included contributions from actress Joyce Grenfell, journalist Malcolm Muggeridge and playwright Christopher Fry, while Yehudi Menuhin agreed to become the Club's president.[41] A magazine article of 1972 reported:

---

[38]   Webb's appointment at Puffin coincided with the breakdown of her marriage to Searle, a factor which undoubtedly contributed to the intensity of her focus on Puffin. Valerie Grove discusses the impact of the separation and subsequent divorce on Webb's career in *So Much to Tell* (Harmondsworth: Viking, 2010), pp. 147–61.

[39]   The fame of some of Webb's correspondents was such that when Sothebys prepared her papers for auction, they divided a substantial proportion of letters into a separate collection, with the intention of auctioning it apart from the rest of the material. This material now appears as the 'Names' series, SS, KW/01/03.

[40]   Kaye Webb, 'On Being a Children's Editor', typescript draft, SS, KW/15/32, f.4.

[41]   *Puffin Post*, 1:1 (Spring 1967).

Correspondence between Kaye Webb and Yehudi Menuhin from the period 1975–1995 comments on his involvement with the Puffin Club as well as documenting some personal matters. SS, KW/01/03/086.

Her demands and energy extend to her authors, who are involved to a degree that would be unimaginable with any other publisher. They do things for her which Sir George Weidenfeld or William Collins might tremble to ask. [Webb commented] 'I remember once we had an author hunt – we hid real authors at a harvest tea. I put Leon Garfield near a bull and he didn't like it at all, and I know there was someone on top of a haystack.'[42]

The 'amateur' status of children's publishing was an important factor in enabling Webb to request assistance which could not have been obtained in the more professional context of adult publishing. Webb's position as a woman in a sector of publishing widely regarded as of little financial significance enabled her to present favours for Puffin as essentially personal and altruistic, rather than as business transactions. Although Webb's own personal magnetism made a significant contribution, her willingness to foreground the altruistic and amateur aspects of children's publishing was a key factor in her success at involving others in Puffin.

The commercial success of the Puffin list had a dramatic effect on the children's publishing industry. At the beginning of the 1960s, Puffin enjoyed almost a complete monopoly of the children's paperback market, but Webb's success encouraged other firms to enter the field, and by the end of the 1960s a growing number of hardback publishers had their own children's paperback lists. This made the market increasingly difficult for Puffin itself, not only because of the growth in competition, but also because it became increasingly difficult to secure paperback rights from other firms:

Well, as people woke up to the fact that you could sell good paperbacks […] the really worrying thing was when they hung onto their own rights and wouldn't let you have them. Now what really was very damaging for us was when they took the rights back.[43]

Penguin did secure a supply of titles for Puffin by launching its own children's hardback list, Kestrel, following the takeover of Hutchinson Books. However, Puffin lost a number of key titles to their original hardback publishers, including J.R.R. Tolkien's *The Hobbit*, which remained in Puffin for only two years before being reclaimed by Allen & Unwin. The increasing challenges faced by Puffin reflect Kaye Webb's success in proving that children's paperbacks were a lucrative and worthwhile branch of publishing. The growing paperback market had an important and positive effect at a time when educationalists and social activists

---

[42]   Lesley Garner, 'The Queen of Puffinland' in Nova (August 1972), clipping in 'Press Cuttings for Puffins' scrapbook, SS, KW/16/06.

Sir George Weidenfeld was the founder of the publishing firm Weidenfeld and Nicolson; William Collins was founder of the eponymous publishing firm.

[43]   Kimberley Reynolds and Nicholas Tucker, 'Interview with Kaye Webb, 7 February 1995', p. 375.

were emphasising the importance of book ownership: Kaye Webb's Puffins helped to demonstrate that buying children's books need no longer be confined to the rich.

An emphasis on marketing and promotion of children's books was one of the most distinctive aspects of Kaye Webb's work as Puffin editor. The shift towards a greater volume of titles allowed a greater variety into the Puffin list and dramatically expanded the imprint's commercial potential. Her commercial impact was not merely significant to Puffin's profits. By demonstrating that children's paperback publishing could be lucrative, Kaye Webb helped to fuel the expansion in children's publishing which was such a distinctive aspect of the 'golden age' of the 1960s and 1970s. This helped to make book ownership into a more everyday experience – Webb aimed to ensure that children could 'count on two new Puffins a month' – and offered working-class children the opportunity to build their own libraries.[44] Furthermore, the excitement generated around Puffin books helped generate excitement about children's books, raising the profile of children's literature in general. In establishing children's literature as a lucrative, exciting sector of publishing which deserved to be considered on a par with literature for adults, Kaye Webb made a significant contribution to the trends that made the 1960s and 1970s a 'golden age' of children's literature.

Puffin for the Best in Children's Books

The commercial success of Puffin Books could not have been achieved solely through effective marketing. While Kaye Webb's understanding of the importance of promoting the books on the list undoubtedly played a major part in the success of Puffin during the 1960s and 1970s, of even greater importance was her ability to recognise books which held popular appeal. The success of her Puffin Originals – titles which made their debut on the Puffin list having never been published in hardback – demonstrates her gift for spotting books with bestseller potential. Clive King's *Stig of the Dump* (1963) had been rejected by a host of other publishers before it found its way to Puffin. Webb recalled:

> I remember reading it in bed, and I was so excited. I remember putting it down and thinking – I actually had the hairs on my arms standing up! And I thought, 'That's the perfect book', because I was very conscious that there weren't any right books for young boys. [...] It seemed to me you could say, 'Here, you'll enjoy this, no matter what'.[45]

Webb's instinct was good: since its publication as a Puffin Original, *Stig of the Dump* has remained continually in print. The same gift for recognising a bestseller resulted in Webb's acceptance of a long, complex fantasy based on

---

[44]   Kaye Webb to Noel Streatfeild, 26 July 1961, UoB, DM1107 / PS 157.

[45]   Kimberley Reynolds and Nicholas Tucker, 'Interview with Kaye Webb, 7 February 1995', pp. 377–8.

the lives of rabbits and filled with classical allusions: *Watership Down* (1972) became a national phenomenon, topping the bestseller lists and winning both the Carnegie and the Guardian awards. Like *Stig of the Dump, Watership Down* had received a number of rejections before it reached Kaye Webb; her enthusiasm for the book encouraged publisher Rex Collings to move forward with the hardback edition, and the paperback edition was to become a top seller for both Puffin and Penguin.[46] Kaye Webb's ability to recognise the potential of the book even before the hardback went to press is indicative of her acumen in choosing books which would genuinely appeal to children, even when – as in the case of *Watership Down* – the length or complexity of the texts made them appear unlikely candidates for such a role.

The commercial success of Puffin demonstrates both Kaye Webb's gift for marketing and her ability to select books with a broad appeal. The significance of Puffin Books to the children's literature world of the 1960s and 1970s was not, however, limited to its dominance of the paperback market; the imprint was widely regarded as an imprimatur of quality. Frank Eyre, writing in 1972, stated:

> 'Best selling' unhappily is not always synonymous with 'best' but with Puffins it was and no titles were included solely because they had sold well. Every book included represented a value judgement by the editor and that was the great strength of the series.[47]

The success of *Watership Down* is a striking example of the way in which Puffin achieved both commercial success and cultural status: in addition to receiving both the Carnegie and the Guardian awards for children's literature, on its American publication it was nominated for the Mythopoeic Award for fantasy literature.[48] Although the book attracted criticism for its realism – its portrayal of the natural lives of rabbits does not omit sex or bloodshed – and for the use of the phrase 'piss off', which provoked controversy among parents, this did not inhibit its commercial or critical success.

The strength of Puffin's reputation was such that it can be said to have defined contemporary perceptions of quality in children's literature. Inclusion on the Puffin list constituted a confirmation of an author's worth: Kaye Webb recollected that 'Every author if they possibly could wanted to be Puffin […] it just meant

---

[46] Kimberley Reynolds and Nicholas Tucker, 'Interview with Kaye Webb, 7 February 1995', p. 379; Joan Bridgmann, 'Richard Adams at Eighty', *Contemporary Review*, 277:1615 (2000), 108–12, p. 108; 'List of 100 Best-selling Puffins', typescript, n.d., SS, KW/07/04/08/24, f.3.

[47] Frank Eyre, *British Children's Books in the Twentieth Century* (London: Longman, 1971), p. 33.

[48] Although the Carnegie and Guardian Awards were made to the first edition of the book, published by Rex Collings, Kaye Webb's role in encouraging Rex Collings to publish the book, and her early acceptance of it for the Puffin list, demonstrates that she had recognised its potential before it became an award winner.

that you had been picked as the best people'.[49] This attitude is evident in author Nicholas Fisk's letter to Kaye Webb on her retirement:

> It was the Puffin list that made me realize that children's books could be as good as you could make them – that an attempt to put real horsepower behind the typewriting might be welcomed. It was the Kaye Webb 'fluence, permeating the whole field, that was so liberating and encouraging. Whatever the Scene is today, most probably you set it. Certainly you did for me.[50]

As both Nicholas Fisk and Frank Eyre's accounts imply, quality in Puffin was closely associated with Kaye Webb's editorial skills. The fact that Webb's name appeared on the flyleaf of all Puffin books – a custom inherited from her predecessor – and her ability to communicate directly with readers through the Puffin Club and *Puffin Post* helped to ensure that this conflation of Puffin values and editorial values existed among the general public as well as among writers and critics who encountered Webb directly. Kimberley Reynolds comments that children's editors of this period 'relied on their own tastes and experiences' to determine what was 'best' for children; in the case of Kaye Webb, the perception that the Puffin list reflected her personal value judgements was a key aspect of Puffin's reputation for quality.[51] This is aptly reflected by one response to the news of Webb's retirement: one of Webb's friends overheard a bookseller exclaim: 'I wonder if her successor will have her integrity. I always knew I should be safe ordering from her list. I didn't feel I had to read every book'.[52] The same association between quality and safety is evident in Webb's own descriptions of the list: she commented, 'I always tell parents they can turn their children loose with Puffins because they are made with butter and eggs. They can't possibly be harmful'.[53]

Puffin's reputation for reliable quality was a key element of its commercial success during this period. The idea that parents could safely 'turn their children loose' with Puffin was an essential component of Kaye Webb's strategy of modelling paperback publishing on the high output of magazine publishing: since Webb stood in loco parentis, it was possible for parents to buy books for their children on a regular basis without reading them first.[54] As Nicholas Fisk's account shows,

---

[49]   Kimberley Reynolds and Nicholas Tucker, 'Interview with Kaye Webb, 7 February 1995', p. 388.

[50]   Nicholas Fisk to Kaye Webb, 12th November 1979, SS, KW/07/06/11.

[51]   Kimberley Reynolds, 'Publishing Practices and the Practicalities of Publishing', p. 30.

[52]   Reported in a letter from Eileen Moloney to Kaye Webb, c. 1979, SS, KW/01/04/073/01.

[53]   Kaye Webb, quoted in Linda Howe Beck, 'Puffin Books "Made with Butter and Eggs"', unidentified newspaper clipping in 'Press Cuttings for Puffins' scrapbook, n.d., SS, KW/16/06.

[54]   As the controversy evoked by the inclusion of a swearword in *Watership Down* suggests, this strategy had costs as well as benefits; the challenges inherent in including more controversial material in Puffin are addressed below.

Puffin's reputation for quality also helped Kaye Webb secure the best authors: although the establishment of more paperback imprints during the 1960s and 1970s made it more difficult to secure paperback rights, the prestige associated with Puffin ensured that she continued to have a high chance of securing the titles she wanted.

Prizes and Popularity: The Construction of Quality in Puffin

Puffin's reputation for offering 'the best in children's books' and the degree to which the Puffin brand was associated with Kaye Webb ensured that her personal construction of quality played a major role in establishing contemporary perceptions of what was best for children. The personal nature of Kaye Webb's editorship was reflected not only in the degree to which others associated her with the Puffin brand, but also in her editorial approach. While scholarly approaches to children's literature were becoming more prevalent during the 1960s and 1970s, she stressed the intuitive and personal aspects of her editorial work. Reflecting on her strategy for selecting books, she commented:

> I should also say that my choice is very idiosyncratic, and I don't take any form of scholarly approach. I'm afraid I don't even evaluate grammatical style or vocabulary, at least not consciously. I simply endeavour to respond to them as if I were a child with one half of my mind, and with the other half as if I were a parent hoping that my child would find the kind of enlightenment, the stretching of the imagination and the awareness of the world that I would want them to receive having finished a book.[55]

Although a 'scholarly' approach may not have been central to Webb's editing technique, on the basis of archival evidence the impression conveyed here of a largely instinctive approach to editing is slightly disingenuous. In fact, the scope of her working library – now held at Seven Stories, the National Centre for Children's Books – indicates that she did attempt to remain abreast of contemporary scholarly discourse about children's literature: her personal collection included critical texts such as *The Cool Web* and Edward Blishen's *The Thorny Paradise* (1975), Harvey Darton's landmark historical survey *Children's Books in England* and Dorothy Butler's account of bibliotherapy in *Cushla and Her Books* (1979). In a letter to John Rowe Townsend she reported, 'I have been reading your book WRITTEN FOR CHILDREN with great enjoyment', and it is clear from archival evidence and contemporary interviews that she placed a high importance on remaining well-informed about contemporary criticism.[56] Furthermore, it is evident

---

[55] Kaye Webb, Speech notes, typescript draft, c. 1986, Seven Stories, the National Centre for Children's Books, KW/07/04/08/17. It is probable that the speech was intended to coincide with the publication of *I Like This Story*, a collection of extracts from Puffin books selected and introduced by Kaye Webb. *I Like This Story: A Taste of Fifty Favourites*, ed. Kaye Webb (Harmondsworth: Puffin, 1986).

[56] Kaye Webb to John Rowe Townsend, 22 March 1966, UoB, DM/1107/PS299.

that she not only read but also engaged with the contemporary critical debate: notes for one speech refer to the work of psychologists Bruno Bettelheim and K. Chukovsky, drawing on their defences of fantasy literature.[57] Her emphasis on the 'idiosyncratic' nature of her approach to children's books therefore constitutes a construction of herself as editor which discounts the professional and scholarly aspects of her practice in favour of a more intuitive model. This is significant not only in biographical terms, but also because of the parameters it establishes for quality in children's books. Women were often seen as particularly suited to editing children's books because of their presumed connection to children; Webb's assertion that she approached books from the perspectives of children and parents, and the degree to which she was personally associated with standards at Puffin, are indicative of this attitude.[58] By prioritising the intuitive and personal aspects of publishing, Webb was participating in a 'feminising' of children's literature in which the nurturing and safe qualities of both editor and books were important. This approach was strongly in harmony with Paul Hazard's construction of childhood and children's literature, which rejected reason in favour of a more liberated and imaginative model of childhood. Puffin books, Webb implied, were good on an instinctive and intrinsic level, rather than because of the degree to which they conformed to particular criteria.

Despite Webb's emphasis on the intuitive aspects of her editorial work, in practice she did seek to sustain a particular model of quality. This rested partly upon Puffin's existing reputation for quality: Webb frequently emphasised her desire to continue the standards established by Eleanor Graham and Margaret Clark, commenting:

> The books they chose for the Puffin list were selected not only for their appeal to children and their literary excellence, but the skills and honesty with which they offered what Edward Blishen has called, 'a proper expectation of life'.[59]

This passage reveals the three elements which were central to the Puffin construction of 'quality' children's literature. The idea of pleasure in literature is placed at the forefront, a fact which reflects the focus on imaginative enjoyment which was a feature of children's literature criticism from the post-war era until the mid-1960s. Literary excellence is a more amorphous concept, and one which was the focus of considerable contention during the 1960s and 1970s, as Chapter 1 has shown. Its presence on the Puffin list is most easily identified in individual texts, for example the work of writers such as William Mayne, Alan Garner and Philippa Pearce, whose writing is characterised by linguistic sophistication and

---

[57]   Kaye Webb, 'Notes For Speech', typescript draft, n.d., Seven Stories, the National Centre for Children's Books, KW/07/04/08/12.

[58]   Kimberley Reynolds, 'Publishing Practices and the Practicalities of Publishing', p. 30.

[59]   Kaye Webb, 'A Red Letter Day for Children (or the Rewarding Road to the 1000th Puffin)', typescript draft of article, c. 1997, SS, KW/07/01/05/09/03.

nuanced stylistic and narrative modes. The final element Webb identifies – 'a proper expectation of life' – was also subject to significant debate during the 1960s and 1970s. It reflects a belief in literature as a socialising and educating force, but without specifying what kind of expectations should be inculcated in child readers. This very lack of specificity suggests a degree of traditionalism in Webb's editorial choices: as suggested in Chapter 1, the emphasis in the early 1960s on the numinous in literature stemmed from an acceptance of dominant ideologies which tended to obscure the inherent didacticism of some texts. This interpretation is complicated, however, by an examination of the books Webb selected for the Puffin list: as this chapter will show, she was by no means resistant to the moves to challenge implicit ideologies in the 1960s and 1970s.

The commercial success of the Puffin list under Kaye Webb indicates her business acumen in selecting titles which would 'appeal to children'; as the above passage suggests, however, popularity with child readers was not the only criterion. On the contrary, Webb's determination to maintain her predecessor's policy of offering children 'butter and eggs – not candyfloss' suggests a desire to exclude material which was of immediate appeal to children but was perceived to lack 'nourishment'. She recalled:

> When I first joined Puffin, Allen Lane asked me if I would publish Enid Blyton, and I said, 'No'. She was an amusing and lively writer, but her books were undemanding, and there were too many of them.[60]

The exclusion of Enid Blyton from the Puffin list is an important indication of how a certain definition of 'quality' was prioritised over the potential for high sales: Blyton remained one of the most popular writers for children throughout the 1960s and 1970s. It is important to note, however, that excluding Blyton also had important implications for the Puffin brand: since she was widely regarded as poor quality, introducing her books onto the list would have threatened Puffin's reputation for offering 'the best in children's books' even if Kaye Webb had regarded her as a quality writer. Furthermore, her repudiation of Blyton was largely academic, since the author was already published by Armada. It is notable that Kaye Webb did publish Roald Dahl – another writer who garnered immense popular appeal but little critical acclaim – although she stated that 'It was a terribly difficult thing to decide. [...] I hadn't liked any of [Roald Dahl's books] much, but they were alright'.[61] Despite her ambivalence about Dahl's books, he was one of her most popular and heavily promoted writers: an unpublished chapter of *Charlie and the Chocolate Factory* was printed in the *Puffin Post* to raise interest in the

---

[60] Kaye Webb, 'SIDELIGHTS: Kaye Webb Revised text, September 1991', typescript draft of article, September 1991, KW/15/32, f.8. A handwritten note suggests that this was intended for *Children's Literature*; however, it does not appear in the ChLA journal of that name.

[61] Kimberley Reynolds and Nicholas Tucker, 'Interview with Kaye Webb, 7 February 1995', p. 377.

Puffin edition of the book, and Dahl frequently took part in Puffin Club events. While Kaye Webb's rejection of Enid Blyton demonstrates that she was not ruled by populism, it is clear that popular appeal was a factor when selecting titles for the Puffin list. In the case of Roald Dahl, his appeal was perhaps too great to dismiss: by 1983, seven of the books in Puffin's 100 bestsellers were Dahl titles.[62] Having fostered Dahl's early career, Webb's dislike of some of his later titles was overmatched by their popularity.

Kaye Webb's desire to include titles of 'literary excellence' in Puffin is reflected in the large number of prize-winning books she selected for the list. Although literary excellence was (and remains) contentious and difficult to define – a fact reflected in the debate surrounding literary prizes – book awards did represent an external guide to quality children's literature. The high proportion of prize-winning books in Puffin suggests that Kaye Webb actively sought them for the list: she published 10 of the titles awarded the Carnegie Medal during her editorship, along with an additional 11 Carnegie winners dating from before 1961. American Newbery Medal winners were also well-represented on Webb's list, a fact which speaks even more strongly of a motivation for quality: whereas the publication of Carnegie Medal winner may have been motivated partly by the additional publicity and prestige afforded by the award, the relative obscurity of the Newbery Medal amongst the British public limited its value as a promotional tool.

Literary excellence in Puffin was further represented in the style and language of the books published. Kaye Webb commented that children should be offered more than 'Post Office Prose', and a corresponding sophistication is evident in many of the books which she published.[63] The opening passage of Lucy M. Boston's Carnegie winner *A Stranger at Green Knowe*, published in Puffin in 1977, is characteristically demanding:

> Imagine a tropical forest so vast that you could roam in it all your life without ever finding out there was anything else. Imagine it so dense that even if a man flew over it for hours, his aeroplane bumping on the rolling uplifts of heat, he would see nothing but the tops of trees from horizon to horizon. It is in such a forest that this story must begin. It is a far flight, both in distance and in imagination, from the dewy meadows and long history of Green Knowe to this primeval and almost immortal forest in the Congo. The journey however can be made, but not in a hurry.[64]

Both the pacing and the vocabulary of this passage demand a fluent reader; the use of words like 'primeval' certainly makes few concessions to the pre-adolescent reader at whom the book is aimed. The book makes further demands of its readers by opening the action at a far remove from the main action of the narrative: the child

---

[62]   'List of 100 Best-selling Puffins', typescript, n.d., SS, KW/07/04/08/24.

[63]   Kaye Webb, Notes for a speech on children's reading, n.d., SS, KW/07/04/08/13.

[64]   Lucy M. Boston, *A Stranger at Green Knowe* (Hemingford Grey: Oldknow Books, 2003), p. 11.

protagonist, Ping, is not introduced until Chapter 2, and the action does not move
to the eponymous Green Knowe – already familiar to readers of the other books
in the series – until Chapter 3. The book demands a committed and experienced
reader capable of enjoying context and description as well as narrative action.
A similar focus on language and description is evident in the works of William
Mayne. The opening passage of his supernatural story *Earthfasts* (1966) luxuriates
in language and description:

> It was the half past eight dusk of a day at the end of summer, the time when the
> sun goes down full before man sleeps and is up again full before he wakes. It
> was a warm night. The setting sun pulled a coverlet of cloud over the dales as it
> went down behind Walker Fell.
>
> There were hazel nuts green and fast in their leafy cups in Haw Bank, the wood
> below Garebrough. The nuts were still bitter with unripe milk. Blackberries
> hung on their barbed vines at the edge of the wood, and the warm weather
> bruised them into ripeness. Their readiness comes from the surrounding air, but
> the ripeness of nuts springs from the root of the tree.[65]

Mayne is sparing in his use of demanding words, but the slow pace and lyrical
style of the passage require an attentive reader and an appreciation for language.
This sophistication of language and style was a characteristic feature of the
'quality' books on the Puffin list; books like *Earthfasts* and *A Stranger at Green
Knowe* reflected Kaye Webb's conviction that 'If we don't see to it that [children]
have a vocabulary which they can really use to express themselves we may look
forward to a time when our lovely language is forgotten [...] but we can do it'.[66]

Kaye Webb frequently emphasised the importance of developing a 'balanced
list' in Puffin, and the breadth and variety of the list under her editorship
demonstrates that her definition of literary quality was decidedly broad. Perhaps
the most characteristic titles on the list, however, and certainly those closest to
Webb's own heart, were the fantasy novels. Kaye Webb's contribution to the
second golden age of children's literature is therefore closely associated with
fantasy literature, which formed an important part of 'the best in Puffin books'.

Childhood and Imagination: Fantasy in Puffin

As explored in Chapter 1, a construction of childhood as uniquely imaginative and
free of adult rationality was a strong theme in children's literature and criticism in
the post-war period. This emphasis on imaginative liberty was found most strongly
in the work of the French comparative critic Paul Hazard; critics such as Margery
Fisher, Mary Thwaite and Eleanor Cameron followed Hazard in emphasising
fantasy and fairy tale as a key genre in children's literature. Born in 1914, Kaye

---

[65]　William Mayne, *Earthfasts* (London: Puffin, 1969), p. 9.
[66]　Kaye Webb, Notes for a speech on children's reading, n.d., SS, KW/07/04/08/13.

Webb was part of the wartime generation among which these ideas found strongest expression, and she can be closely identified with this critical school.

Paul Hazard's notion of a 'republic of childhood' which was both distinct from and superior to the adult world contributed to a widespread critical emphasis on the importance of 'entering the child's world' when writing or reading children's literature. Kaye Webb's insistence that she did not 'take any form of scholarly approach' when evaluating books for the Puffin list reflects this belief in seeing children's literature from the child's perspective. Responding to an article by critic Margaret Meek, which emphasised the value of a formal approach to evaluating children's books, Webb stressed the importance of her ability to recall her experience of childhood reading. The passage is worth quoting at length for the depth of insight it affords into Webb's perception of children's literature:

> Night time adventures. which start with dreams and secret fears and roving imaginations, as suddenly focussed into someone else's adventures and flights of fancy. And oh the marvellous Safety of it. Here I was between covers, wiping out the day's anxieties and disappointments, [word deleted] demands, failures or even more rarely triumphs excitements and happiness... were Someone Else's Ideas and Adventures and Flights of Fancy and they were all resolved they'd go on till the[y] finished and all would end well and right would triumph "Katie Would Live It Down" Henry Esmond would (my reading was very catholic)
>
> And I was the privileged but safe and only secondarily involved person and the marvel that there would be more tomorrow, and that this one would still always be there.
>
> Well then, but I'm taking ages to say it, by some alchemy I've stayed like that. or had until recently. I was uncritical accepting, ready to be wooed and won child.. and it was the child in me which felt dissatisfied with thin language and dishonest manipulations of plot and people [sic].[67]

This passage is strongly reminiscent of assertions by Eleanor Cameron and Margery Fisher that children's literature requires adults to re-experience 'the true aura of childhood' and 're-enter the child's world'.[68] It is notable that Kaye Webb emphasises not the objective criteria by which books might be judged – 'thin language and dishonest manipulation of plot and people' – but the instinctive childlike ability to identify these characteristics. Children's reading is presented as intensely experiential, literally 'wiping out' the real world and replacing it with imagination and fantasy.

The construction of childhood as essentially removed from adult experience and characterised by imaginative liberty was closely linked to an emphasis on

---

[67]   Kaye Webb, typescript draft of speech, c. 1980, SS, KW/07/04/08/31, ff. 2–3.

[68]   Eleanor Cameron, *The Green and Burning Tree: On the Writing and Enjoyment of Children's Books* (Boston, Toronto: Little, Brown, 1969), p. 14. Margery Fisher, *Intent upon Reading: A Critical Appraisal of Modern Children's Fiction* (Leicester: Brockhampton Press, 1961), p. 14.

the importance of fantasy literature. This emphasis is clearly evident on the Puffin list, where fantasy novels were a strong presence at every level, from the anthropomorphism of Michael Bond's *Paddington Bear* stories and Rumer Godden's doll stories, to the high fantasy of C.S. Lewis, J.R.R. Tolkien and Susan Cooper. The prevalence of fantasy can be partly ascribed to the dominance of the genre in British children's literature as a whole during the 1950s and 1960s; however, Kaye Webb's fantasy list stands out even in this context. She was instrumental in the publication of a number of fantasy titles: her enthusiasm encouraged Rex Collings to publish *Watership Down*, she won first British publication rights to Ursula Le Guin's *A Wizard of Earthsea* (1968) and her first Puffin original was Clive King's *Stig of the Dump* (1963).[69] *Stig of the Dump*, one of the first books Webb selected for the Puffin list, shows many of the features characteristic of Hazard's construction of childhood and imagination. On one level, the book is a celebration of the kind of imaginative play which transforms elements of ordinary life. When Barney goes exploring in the local dump, his imagination transforms the everyday rubbish: 'Was that the steering wheel of a ship? The tail of an aeroplane?'[70] His discovery of a caveman – Stig – amongst the rubbish initially appears to be part of the same imaginings; when he announces his new friendship to his family, his sister remarks '"Stig's just a pretend friend, isn't he, Barney"'.[71] However, as in Pauline Clarke's *Twelve and the Genii* (also published in Puffin), what at first appears to be a very intensely realised game gradually takes on more and more reality. Stig is real enough to intimidate the local bullies, to disrupt the hunt and to chase off a pair of silver thieves. Although the book always leaves open the possibility that Stig is no more than an aspect of Barney's imagination, it presents that imaginative experience as equally vivid and important as the more prosaic aspects of life. The influence of Hazard's republic of childhood is also evident in the way in which Barney's experience – whether real or imaginary – provides a transhistorical link. Although Barney and Stig do not share a common language, they are connected by an essential childness which allows them to work together as equals; at the end of the book, this connection with Stig transports Barney and his sister Lou back in time to share in the building of a Neolithic stone circle.

The interplay of fantasy and history found in *Stig of the Dump* is also present in the work of another key Puffin author: Lucy M. Boston. Centred around the eponymous manor house, Boston's Green Knowe series (1954–1976) offers perhaps the most fully realised portrayal of Hazard's imaginative and liberated

---

[69] Webb wrote to a fan of Ursula Le Guin: 'It is, as you may know, a book which I regard with a great deal of affection since I was the means of introducing it to England via Puffin (although it has now been snatched by Penguins and printed as a trilogy.)' Kaye Webb to Michael Powell, 1981, SS, KW/01/03/101/02.

Stig of the Dump had been rejected by a number of publishers before Webb accepted the book, bringing it out as a paperback original. Both titles are still in print today.

[70] Clive King, *Stig of the Dump* (Harmondsworth: Puffin, 1987), p. 8.

[71] Clive King, *Stig of the Dump*, p. 16.

'republic of childhood'. The first two books, *The Children of Green Knowe* (1954) and *The Chimneys of Green Knowe* (1958) are constructed around a frame narrative in which Grandmother Oldknow tells stories of the house and its history to her grandson, Tolly. Between each story, Tolly experiences his own adventures, but as in *Stig*, the barrier between imagination and reality is unclear. In the first book, this uncertainty is made explicit:

> Tolly was glad that Mrs Oldknow seemed not at all surprised by the hide-and-seek [with the ghost children]. He was not quite sure whether she thought that he and she were playing a game together pretending that there were other children, or whether she thought, as he did, that the children were really there.[72]

In engaging fully with Tolly's imaginative experience of the house, Grandmother Oldknow models the 'entry into the child's world' which Hazard, Fisher and others argued was an essential component of children's literature. Entry into this imaginative state allows Tolly – and to a lesser extent Grandmother Oldknow – to interact with children from across all periods of the house's history: a transhistorical 'republic of childhood'. In the final book, *The Stones of Green Knowe* (1976), Grandmother Oldknow's engagement with this imaginative fantasy is so complete that she is able to literally return to childhood:

> The curtain was parted yet again, and this time a tall slim girl came in. She was the same age as Toby and just as beautiful, with long shining hair. She hesitated just inside the circle, like someone who is lonely.
>
> [...] Tolly laughed and ran across to her.
>
> 'I know you,' he said, taking her hand. 'I'd know you anywhere, any time. You're my grandmother. There's only one of you.'[73]

This literal return to childhood is part of the unique gift which Green Knowe offers its inhabitants: Lucy Boston follows Paul Hazard in presenting childhood as intrinsically valuable. Throughout the series, child characters repeatedly repel evil from the house: in the most sinister of the books, *An Enemy at Green Knowe* (1964), it is Ping and Tolly's ready engagement with the fantastic that allows them to recognise and defeat the true character of Dr. Melanie Powers – not merely a professor of the occult, but a witch. Although by the final book in the series the realities of the modern world are intruding upon Green Knowe, its hope for preservation lies with the children and their instinctive connection with what is valuable. The series' presence on the Puffin list is indicative of Kaye Webb's sympathy with the post-war ethos which shaped Paul Hazard's construction of childhood.

---

[72] Lucy M. Boston, *The Children of Green Knowe* (Harmondsworth: Puffin, 1975), p. 49.

[73] Lucy M. Boston, *The Stones of Green Knowe* (Hemingford Grey: Oldknow Books, 2003), pp. 109–10.

The 'return to childhood' is a strong theme in the fantasy books of Kaye Webb's Puffin list, but another brand of fantasy entirely is present in the form of books such as *Watership Down*, *A Wizard of Earthsea* and *The Owl Service*, in which the fantastical is used to explore the progression into independent adulthood rather than employed to evoke the experience of childhood. As discussed in Chapter 1, Alan Garner uses the supernatural elements in *The Owl Service* to explore powerful themes of sexual jealousy. In *A Wizard of Earthsea*, Ursula Le Guin explores the full responsibility of adulthood through her wizard hero Ged: the terrible mistake he makes through his overweening adolescent pride literally shadows him throughout his life, a reflection of the darkest aspects of his character. Theorists such as Kornei Chukovsky and Bruno Bettelheim argued for imaginative literature as a means of allowing children to explore such complex and threatening psychological issues in a safe context; Webb's description of how her childhood reading operated to give her adventures in which she was a 'privileged but safe and only secondarily involved person' is consonant with this perspective. She argued that fantasy could explore things which realism could not, commenting, 'children ought to be told – that the world is frightening, beautiful, fantastic, and that they can journey as far or fast as they want to in their imagination'.[74]

The strong presence of fantasy on the Puffin list helped to strengthen the perception that fantasy was an integral part of 'quality' children's literature. Although she maintained a diverse list, the construction of childhood as intrinsically linked with fantasy and imagination was an integral aspect of Kaye Webb's own outlook. As this chapter will show, she sought to foster imagination not only through the books she published, but also through her work with the Puffin Club. The perception that the 'golden age' of the 1960s and 1970s was in large part a golden age of fantasy owes much to the strength of fantasy on the Puffin list.

Puffin Books: Providing a Proper Expectation of Life

Kaye Webb's emphasis on fantasy and pleasure in children's literature, and her determination to maintain a reputation for quality in Puffin books which encompassed many authors who were regarded as essentially 'literary' and sophisticated, suggests that she was closely allied to the school of criticism which John Rowe Townsend characterised as 'book people': one essentially concerned with literary merit rather than the social and political impact of children's books.[75] As shown in Chapter 1, however, Peter Hollindale's charge that such a division represents an oversimplification is well-founded, and critics such as Margery

---

[74] Kaye Webb, 'Australian Broadcasting Commission: Guest of Honour: Kaye Webb', broadcast transcript, 11 July 1971, SS, KW/07/01/04/03/12, p. 3.

[75] John Rowe Townsend, 'Standards of Criticism in Children's Literature', in *Children's Literature: The Development of Criticism*, ed by Peter Hunt (London: Routledge, 1990), 57–70, p. 63.

Fisher, Eleanor Cameron and Mary Thwaite, who emphasised the literary rather than social aspects of literature, nevertheless placed a strong value on the educational and socialising powers of children's books.[76] The same concern was an integral aspect of Kaye Webb's approach as a Puffin editor; while many of her literary preferences owed much to the post-war ethos of theorists such as Paul Hazard, her approach to the functions of children's literature is characteristic of the trends of the second golden age.

Reflecting on the motivations of other children's editors among her contemporaries, Kaye Webb characterised herself as unusually concerned with children as individuals, saying of other women in children's literature: 'I think they were just interested in the books! [...] I'm soppy about children.'[77] In a speech given in an Australian broadcast, Webb elaborated at length on her view of childhood and the role of the children's editor, emphasising the extent to which she was concerned with the whole child:

> I happen to have a job I love very much which has brought me close to the kind of people I love best, that's children. Although the job itself is to do with buying and finding and giving children the right books to read, it seemed to me that what had happened is, that I'd also got very passionately involved with the way children are handled from the time that they're born. I don't believe that many adult people realise what a profound effect they have on children from the day that they're born and how deeply they can influence the way their lives go and their characters and their understanding.[78]

This passage demonstrates the extent to which Kaye Webb was concerned with child development in a broad socialising and moral sense. Her conception of childhood places heavy emphasis upon the innocence and impressionability of children, a feature which is evident throughout Webb's work. She frequently criticised what she saw as the unthinking tendency of adults to impose particular roles upon children, for example by characterising them as 'shy' or 'clumsy', arguing that children relied upon adults to form a sense of self:

> What I'm after urging is we must keep remembering that young children are innocent, unfledged. They don't know about themselves. [...] They don't know what they are, how they stand in relation to other people. It's a sort of waking dream they live in, when all is to be learnt and discovered [...] every word, everything that happens that they hear or experience makes its mark for ever and ever. They are waiting to be told.[79]

---

[76]   Peter Hollindale, *Ideology and the Children's Book* (Stroud: Signal, 1988), p. 5.

[77]   Kimberley Reynolds and Nicholas Tucker, 'Interview with Kaye Webb, 7 February 1995', p. 385.

[78]   Kaye Webb, 'Australian Broadcasting Commission: Guest of Honour: Kaye Webb', broadcast transcript, 11 July 1971, SS, KW/07/01/04/03/12, p. 1.

[79]   Kaye Webb, 'NOT IN FRONT OF THE CHILDREN (Pas devant les Enfants)', typescript draft, probably for a radio broadcast, SS, KW/07/04/08/20, pp. 2–3.

Kaye Webb's emphasis on the importance of providing children with 'a proper expectation of life' reflects the degree to which she regarded the social impact of literature as an integral component of literary quality. As Chapter 1 has shown, the fantasy literature of the 1950s and early 1960s was far from lacking in moral and social messages, despite an emphasis on literary rather than social values. There are prominent social and moral themes in the fantasy selected by Kaye Webb for the Puffin list: it is notable that *A Wizard of Earthsea*, which received its first UK publication in Puffin, is deeply concerned with themes of equality and balance which were closely connected to political movements in the 1960s.

Although, as this chapter has argued, fantasy literature was one of the most significant genres on the Puffin list, this did not mean that Puffin was disconnected from the move towards more socially conscious literature which characterised the 1960s and 1970s. On the contrary, many of the most prominent works of social realism published during this period appeared in Puffin. Kaye Webb was quick to publish John Rowe Townsend's groundbreaking novel *Gumble's Yard* (1961), which appeared in Puffin in 1967. Robert Westall's *The Machine Gunners* (1975) and Bernard Ashley's *The Trouble with Donovan Croft* (1974) also appeared in Puffin: as discussed in Chapter 1, titles like these were at the forefront of the move towards socially conscious literature in this period. Similarly, Kaye Webb was directly involved in the selection of Jan Mark's *Thunder and Lightnings* (1976) for the Guardian Award, which was administered by Puffin's sister company Kestrel.[80] Part of Puffin's success under Kaye Webb was undoubtedly due to her ability to keep pace with such developments in children's literature.

The moral and social values of Puffin Books were recognised by many of Kaye Webb's contemporaries. Illustrator Richard Kennedy praised her for the ethos behind the imprint:

> Puffin Books have become a not inadequate substitute for the Bible & Shakespeare since they contain a dynamic force, a human inspiration, not of the same power but on the same dimension.
>
> In collecting the authors you have you have created a gigantic spiral carrying children upwards inspiring them to be better human beings not in the way Victorian children's authors attempted, but on a broad emotional spectrum. They constitute one of the great cultural movements of recent years.[81]

Kennedy's comments position Puffin in the quasi-religious position which critics such as Eleanor Cameron characterised as central to the best children's literature. The high sales of Puffin Books illustrate Kaye Webb's ability to select books which appealed to children; the praise she elicited from her contemporaries in the world of children's literature demonstrates the extent to which this was combined with a genuine concern with the ethical and social impact of reading.

---

[80]   Philippa Pearce, 'Competition Winners', *Guardian*, 16 July 1975, p. 16.
[81]   Richard Kennedy to Kaye Webb, n.d., SS, KW/01/02/43/17.

Protecting Childhood: 'Adult-eration' and Censorship

The inclusion of titles such as *The Trouble with Donovan Croft* and *The Machine Gunners* in the Puffin list involved a move towards more 'controversial' content. As Chapter 1 has shown, the move towards more social realism during the 1960s and 1970s – both in the books themselves, and in the number of realist books available – introduced themes such as racism, disability and sexuality, along with a move towards more colloquial language and swearing. The Puffin list reflected many of these new trends; however, archival evidence suggests that the shift towards more adult content was a point of conflict both for Kaye Webb personally, and for the list as a whole.

Kaye Webb's view of children as 'innocent, unfledged' and essentially malleable beings made her acutely concerned with the potential for books to negatively affect their child readers. Like social commentators such as Neil Postman, Webb was concerned by the impact that changes in society had on childhood, perceiving a shift towards the 'adult-eration' of childhood:

> One thing my 5 years taught me. [word deleted] It's as dangerous to <u>over</u> rate c's sophistication as to <u>under</u>rate it. It's we adults who often 'force the pace'. T.V. compels them to take part in an adult world. We are less reticent than our parents and grandparents about discussing adult problems. The adult world is nudging at them far too often and early. They often say they like grownup books, or in advance of their age because 'being grown up' 'advanced' is represented as desirable so they keep running. But they need childhood, a time to put down proper roots and [deleted: 'find a strong'] to grow from.[82]

The desire to provide children with books which would not 'force the pace' was reflected in Kaye Webb's establishment of a number of different Puffin imprints, separated by the intended age of the readers. In particular, the establishment of the Peacock imprint for adolescent readers provided a venue for material considered too adult for younger Puffin readers. Webb also showed little compunction in rejecting books which she considered unsuitable for publication in Puffin:

> I wouldn't do 'Go Ask Alice' because most of my books are read up to the age of 12, and I thought the language in it was so awful and I couldn't risk it. It makes me mad when teachers want to be thought modern and 'in' and they don't care what's happening to the children. All my staff loved 'Go Ask Alice' and pressured me to publish it. I took it home and read it three times and I

---

[82]   Kaye Webb, 'Eleanor Farjeon Award', typescript draft for acceptance speech, 1970, SS, KW/11/01/01.

Elaine Moss coined the term 'adult-eration' in a 1974 discussion on the subject 'Are children's books becoming too sophisticated?'. Elaine Moss, 'The Adult-eration of Children's Books' in *Part of the Pattern: A Personal Journey Through the World of Children's Books, 1960–1985*, 113–8.

thought maybe I'm getting old and prim and I must be careful. But I'd rather be thought to be a prissy old woman and try to safeguard them when I really think something is false.[83]

Go Ask Alice (1971) was an anonymous American book purporting to be the real life diary of a teenage girl, chronicling her drug use and subsequent descent into prostitution and death.[84] The book was characteristic of the move towards topical social realism which was a strong feature of attempts to cater for the 'reluctant' teenage reader; Kaye Webb's criticism of the title in the face of her (younger) staff's praise is indicative of her resistance to the vogue for 'issue' novels.

A key element of Kaye Webb's desire to protect child readers was her desire to avoid the inclusion of 'awful language' in Puffin titles. The move towards more social realism in children's books brought with it more non-standard English, including more swearwords. This trend created tension in Puffin, where Kaye Webb had made the quality of language a fundamental aspect of her editorial policy. Some of the swearwords in Robert Westall's Carnegie Medal-winner *The Machine Gunners*, published uncut in its hardback edition, were edited out in the Puffin edition following concerns about the possibility that the obscenities would inhibit sales to school book clubs.[85] Nevertheless, Webb recognised the need for Puffin's standards to evolve with the times, commenting of *The Machine Gunners*:

> I left a few of them [the obscenities] in but not many. I mean, we did cut it down, but it was such a strong story, wasn't it? [...] it was very difficult because one had to acknowledge that this was happening and that writers were deliberately conveying what they wanted to convey.[86]

Webb's recognition of the need to publish some books which challenged her personal boundaries is reflected in the diversity of the Puffin list. Despite her concerns about the 'adult-eration' of children's literature, she included a significant number of books with potentially controversial themes. Rosa Guy's *The Friends* (1973), published in Puffin in 1977, covers themes of poverty, racism, domestic abuse and death. The hard-hitting nature of the book is evident in a scene in which Phyllissia, the protagonist, is forced to eat by her father, after a period of grief-induced fasting:

---

[83] Kaye Webb, quoted in Judith Higgins, 'Publishing Children's Paperbacks: A Talk With Puffin's Kaye Webb' in *Publishers Weekly*, February 24, 1975, Clipping in 'Puffin' scrapbook, SS, KW/16/03.

[84] Kaye Webb's reference to *Go Ask Alice* as 'false' is striking in light of the fact that the book is now widely accepted to be a work of fiction.

[85] Kaye Webb to Robert Westall, 10 January 1975, Robert Westall Collection, Seven Stories, the National Centre for Children's Books, RW/14/01/20 ff. 1–2.

[86] Kimberley Reynolds and Nicholas Tucker, 'Interview with Kaye Webb, 7 February 1995', p. 374.

Then, picking me up from the bed, he carried me down the hall to the kitchen, put me on a chair, pushed it up to the table, placed the tray of food in front of me, unbuckled his belt, and said, 'Now eat!'

I had no choice. I picked up the fork. Too heavy, my hands too weak, it clattered to the table. Ruby rushed to pick it up. Taking some food from the plate she tried to feed me. The belt came down across her back.

'No!' I felt the pain. 'No!'[87]

The presence of such titles on the list demonstrates Kaye Webb's willingness to push the boundaries when she considered authors to be 'conveying what they wanted to convey' rather than writing in an attempt to be 'modern and "in"'.

Puffin's reputation for publishing 'the best in children's books' made the tensions surrounding more explicit and realist content in children's literature particularly acute for Kaye Webb. Although Puffin's status as a 'quality' imprint conferred a degree of respectability on books which appeared on its lists, a significant component of Puffin's reputation for quality rested upon the perception that the books would not contain anything 'harmful'. Kaye Webb recalled:

I think we set this high standard and the whole idea was that you could trust a Puffin. I can remember meeting the Duchess of Kent. She said, 'I don't know what I'd have done without Puffin', she said, 'I felt so safe'.[88]

The perception that Puffin represented a 'safe' arena in which parents did not need to supervise their children meant that the imprint was particularly vulnerable to accusations of publishing 'unsuitable' material. The expectation that Puffin would provide books of a consistently high standard frequently resulted in strong reactions when readers felt this expectation had not been met, as a letter from an 18-year-old reader of Arthur Calder-Marshall's *The Fair to Middling* (1959) demonstrates:

I have been shocked out of my acceptance of Puffin books by one of them, 'The Fair to Middling' by Arthur Calder-Marshall, PS 175.

I cannot think this is suitable for any child. C.S. Lewis surely went as far as it is advisable to go with children in his allegories, all of which we know and love. This absolutely horrible, warped book is, to my mind, wholly unsuitable for any child.[89]

Far from being a realist, adult-oriented novel, *The Fair to Middling* is a religious allegory in which a group of orphans are cured of their various disabilities, only

---

[87]   Rosa Guy, *The Friends* (Harmondsworth: Puffin, 1994), p. 140.

[88]   Kimberley Reynolds and Nicholas Tucker, 'Interview with Kaye Webb, 7 February 1995', p. 374.

[89]   Kathleen Marley to Kaye Webb, 17 September 1964, UoB, DM1107 / PS175.

to find that this does not necessarily improve their lives. Although the concept is certainly problematic, the reader's visceral reaction to the book is indicative of the difficulty Kaye Webb faced in retaining the trust of her readership while maintaining the quality of the Puffin list.

A certain amount of censorship was undoubtedly part of Kaye Webb's construction of quality in the Puffin list. Although Puffin under her editorship kept pace with broad movements in children's literature, including books with potentially controversial themes and language in the list, Webb remained uncomfortable with the broader move towards more 'adult' themes and language in children's books. One of the ways in which she attempted to negotiate this tension was in the establishment of a teenage list: Peacock. As this chapter will show, however, some of the same tensions were present in the development of Peacock.

The Changing Age of the Child Reader: Peacock Books

The shift in the perceived age demographic of child readers formed one of the key changes in perceptions of children's literature during the 1960s and 1970s. As discussed in Chapter 1, the growing demand for books which could cater to the new teenage market disrupted the critical views which had prevailed up until the early 1960s. These new readers did not fit comfortably into the construction of childhood as an essentially innocent and protected space: the desire to reflect the lives of older and more socially diverse readers created demands for more social realism and more explicit language and themes in children's literature. This trend posed a challenge to the reputation for safety and trustworthiness which was an inherent part of Kaye Webb's construction of quality at Puffin; nevertheless, Puffin was one of the first to respond to the need for books to supply the new demographic of adolescent readers. The Peacock imprint was launched with Enid Bagnold's *National Velvet* (1935) in 1962, under the slogan 'Peacocks, for Older Boys and Girls'.[90] As the first dedicated imprint for adolescent readers, Peacock represented a first attempt to shape the new genre of teenage literature.

Margery Fisher, writing in 1961, had argued that older children and teenagers would be best served by a judicious selection of adult titles, rather than literature written especially for them. A similar philosophy is evident in the selection of titles for Peacock, which Kaye Webb characterised as a way to 'bridge the gap between Puffin and Penguin'.[91] A large percentage of the titles were drawn from the existing canon of adult literature, and in some cases had been drawn from Penguin's own adult lists: seven of the first 20 Peacocks had previously been published in Penguin. Kaye Webb's notes on ideas for the Peacock list make it clear that the primary focus of the imprint was as an introduction to the broader canon of literature:

---

[90] 'Now Peacocks join the Penguin and Puffin family', *Smiths Trade News*, c. 1962, clipping in 'Press Cuttings for Puffins' scrapbook, SS, KW/16/06.

[91] 'Now Peacocks join the Penguin and Puffin Family'.

Existing books, and or existing Penguins might do, two editions with diff. cover.

Known authors.. Conrad, Wodehouse to stay in Penguin because children can be told names (n.b. even hold in Peacock back list [i.e. list in the back of the book of suggested further reads]).[92]

The idea of listing appropriate Penguin titles in the back of Peacock books suggests that the list was initially intended to function essentially as a reading guide, directing children towards further reading in the way which might be expected of an interested and knowledgeable adult reader. Margery Fisher had suggested that 'genre' literature was a particularly appropriate way into adult literature for young readers, and this viewpoint was reflected in the type of authors chosen for Peacock: P.G. Wodehouse, C.S. Forester, Georgette Heyer and John Buchan were all represented amongst the early titles.[93]

Although the Peacock list was undoubtedly designed to ease young readers into the realms of adult literature, it did include a significant proportion of material aimed directly at adolescent readers. Some of Kaye Webb's characteristic flair at selecting successful books is discernible in these titles: Beverly Cleary's *Fifteen* (1956), which appeared in Peacock in 1962, was widely hailed as the model of an ideal teenage novel. The book was directly concerned with specifically adolescent concerns, chronicling the story of a young girl's first romance and culminating in her first kiss. The book was warmly received by the demographic of adolescent readers who had received most attention from advocates of a specialist teenage literature: Aidan Chambers commented that it 'works its sway almost inevitably on the majority of reluctant readers among the girls'.[94] Dodie Smith's novel *I Capture the Castle* (1948) was another success for the list and was reprinted several times: the book is still in print today. Webb also secured Alan Garner's striking novel *The Owl Service* for Peacock, having previously published his works for younger readers in Puffin. The reception of the novel in the *Guardian* is suggestive of the need for a specialist list such as Peacock:

Is it really a book for children? There's room for argument, but such arguments tend to be barren and semantic. Certainly "The Owl Service" is not for young

---

[92]   Kaye Webb, 'Puffin notes in diary form', March 15th 1962, SS, KW/07/01/03/04.

[93]   P.G. Wodehouse, *Very Good, Jeeves!* (1965); John Buchan, *The Three Hostages* (1963), *Greenmantle* (1964) and *The House of the Four Winds* (1966); C.S. Forester, *Hornblower Goes to Sea* (1963) and Georgette Heyer, *Devil's Cub* (1963) were among the adult titles selected for Peacock. With the exception of *Hornblower Goes to Sea*, all these titles had previously been published as Penguins: the Penguin catalogue of 1970 lists their original Penguin numbers along with the Peacock details. (Penguin operated an in-house book numbering system which numbered books consecutively as they were added to the Penguin lists. Each imprint had its own number sequence, with the imprint denoted by a prefix – PS for Puffin, PK for Peacock. The system was discontinued after the introduction of Standard Book Numbers (SBNs) in the early 1970s.)

[94]   Aidan Chambers, *The Reluctant Reader* (London: The Pergamon Press, 1969), p. 46.

children: if it's especially "for" anyone it's for adolescents. It's a novel that will impress adults, too. With it Garner adds a new dimension to his work.[95]

The Peacock list offered a venue for books like *The Owl Service*, which sat uncomfortably on the children's lists. The account of author Lynne Reid Banks suggests that the imprint was regarded as a good model for teenage literature:

> I came upon them [Peacocks] ten years ago, when I was first asked to write a book for teenagers, which turned out to be One More River. I hadn't realised that there were such things as books specially written for teenagers, so I asked for samples, and was sent two: I Am David by Anna Home [sic], and The Endless Steppe by Esther Hautzig.

> I read these with an increasing sense of wonder, delight and admiration, more by far than for many an adult title. Both these novels do to perfection what all novels, for any age-group, should do: enlarge the reader's capacity for feeling and understanding, as well as rivet him to the story and characters.[96]

Lynne Reid Banks' account suggests that some of the same reputation for quality which characterised Puffin was also associated with Peacock. Nevertheless, the list encountered a number of problems in offering books written especially for teenagers. The predominance of adult titles among early Peacocks was an inevitable consequence of the relative novelty of the genre: as Chapter 1 has shown, in 1962 teenage literature was only just beginning to emerge in Britain. Books which were written for adolescents not infrequently inspired hostility in critics. One review in *The Spectator* commented:

> Two books now republished in Penguin Books' new series for older children, Peacock Books, illustrate rather than quite overcome the difficulties in such a venture. It's valuable to have attention drawn to those books which conveniently bridge the gap between childhood and adult reading. Roy Fuller's *With My Little Eye* only differs from a detective story in that the hero is an adolescent, and a pretty conventional public-school boy at that. I can't help thinking that if you can read this you can read Simenon, with a good deal more profit and interest.[97]

This tension was perhaps an inevitable consequence of the desire for Peacock to lead readers quickly into the adult lists. The relative sophistication of many of the titles on the Puffin list was calculated to produce a fluent and accomplished reader, and in aiming to provide a bridge between Puffin and Penguin the Peacock list was calculated to reach exactly such a reader. The eponymous heroine of Jane

---

[95] 'The Guardian Award: "Both Real and Magical"', *Guardian*, Friday March 29, 1968, p. 14, photocopied press clipping, UoB, DM/1107/PK66.

[96] Lynne Reid Banks, c. 1979, 'Puffin scrapbook', UoB, DM1952/File 742.

[97] Anonymous review of Peacock, *Spectator*, 7 June 1963, press cutting, UoB, DM1107/PK05.

Gardam's *Bilgewater* (1976) employs a host of literary references, constructing an elaborate Tennysonian fantasy around her newly acquired friend before concluding:

> A narrative must be what everyone is thinking and nobody dares to say. I present you therefore with my obedience to Thomas Hardy, my attempt at naked truth, the thoughts I really thought, the fantasy I really had.

> Though it's not somehow as good as *Ulysses*.[98]

Bilgewater herself is precisely the kind of 'bookish' adolescent the novel is calculated to please: the kind of reader who might be expected to have emerged from a childhood of reading the more complex and sophisticated titles on the Puffin list.

The redundancy of a list which catered to the fluent and committed adolescent reader who – as the review in *The Spectator* noted – were likely to be capable of venturing into adult literature perhaps accounts for the relative lack of success of Peacock. The series' sales were much smaller than its sister list – in 1968 Peacocks sold 84,442 titles, compared to Puffin Storybooks' 1,324,406 – and by the 1970s it had fallen into stagnation, publishing only a few new titles a year.[99] Whereas the concept of a separate list for adolescent readers had been innovatory in 1962, by the mid-1970s developments in the teenage market had outpaced those in Peacock. Correspondingly, the list was relaunched in 1977, with Dorothy Wood assuming primary editorial responsibility. This in itself was significant, since Kaye Webb had retained a high degree of control over the various imprints of Puffin. The relaunched list more consciously sought to include books written especially for teenagers, rather than curating suitable adult content. Dorothy Wood stated:

> We are extending the age range to 15/17 year-olds and want to make it an exciting list to catch the more uncommitted reader, and at the same time provide an introduction to the wide range of books on the Peacock list.[100]

The desire to 'catch the more uncommitted reader' reflected the general trend in thinking about teenage literature: the reformulation of Peacock on these lines

---

[98]   Jane Gardam, *Bilgewater* (Harmondsworth: Peacock, 1979), p. 57.

[99]   'Penguin Books Limited: Net Sales and Trading Profit for the Year Ending 31 December 1968', UoB, DM/1843/16; Dave Gregory, 'A Bibliography of Penguin Books: Part 1: Peacock Series', typescript copy, SS, KW/01/04/047/011.

[100]   Dorothy Wood to Diana Mackey, Michael Joseph Ltd, 17 February 1976, UoB, DM 1952/047.0964.

Dave Gregory, in his overview of the Peacock series, asserts that the 1977 relaunch took place under the editorship of Tony Lacey. However, editorial files from throughout the 1970s suggest that Dorothy Wood played a significant role in developing the relaunched list. Kaye Webb retained ultimate control of the list, and editorial files show that she remained actively involved. (Dave Gregory, 'A Bibliography of Penguin Books: Part 1: Peacock Series', typescript copy, SS, KW/01/04/047/011.)

suggests that in this area Penguin and Puffin were responding to changes in British children's literature, rather than leading them.

One of the key opportunities inherent in Kaye Webb's establishment of a teenage imprint was the possibility of exploring more adult themes without impinging upon the innocence of Puffin's child readers. As this chapter has shown, the perception that Puffin was a 'safe' list made Kaye Webb particularly sensitive to accusations of inappropriate content. The intended age range of the Peacock list, which was aimed at readers from the age of about 14, made it possible to include themes of a more controversial nature. The list included a number of novels dealing with relationships and sexuality, including Françoise Sagan's *Bonjour Tristesse* (1954) and Charles Webb's *The Graduate* (1963) – both written for an adult audience – and John Rowe Townsend's *Goodnight, Prof, Love* (1973). In practice, however, the fact that Peacocks were aimed at older readers did not protect the list from criticisms about content. Editorial files for the series show that it was frequently challenged by readers concerned at the adult nature of the titles on the list. A.P. Herbert's novel *The Water Gypsies* (1930) provoked one such complaint:

> Peacock books are intended for people of twelve years of age and upwards and this includes a very vulnerable age group of older children to whom you have a responsibility. Although this book was first published forty-five years ago and although sex acts are not described in detail, it was obviously written for adults. [...] We are surprised that Penguin Books, who normally appear to have a sense of responsibility towards their young reading public, have allowed 'The Water Gypsies' to be published as a Peacock and are of the opinion that it should be reclassified as literature for adults only.[101]

The question of appropriate levels of content in Peacock remained a difficult one throughout the lifetime of the imprint. The predominance of older novels in the early list – like *The Water Gypsies*, many titles dated from the 1930s or even earlier – suggests an attempt by Kaye Webb to provide adolescent readers with books which addressed adult concerns without including explicit depictions of sex. The early titles contained little of the topicality which was a primary feature of the emerging genre of teenage literature. The reformulation of the imprint in 1977 involved a move towards more topical and more explicit titles, but the changes in British societal mores over this period did not protect Peacock from criticism over content. Barry Hine's *The Blinder* (1966), published in Peacock in 1977, represented a considerably more daring approach to teenage literature than had been evident in the early years of the Peacock list. Originally published for adults, the book gives an explicit account of the sporting and sexual exploits of a first-division footballer. The book was criticised in the press by the Newcastle M.P. Sir William Elliott, who characterised the book as 'pornography', provoking a number of letters of complaint to Penguin from members of the public.[102]

---

[101] Mr and Mrs J.C. Orr to Kaye Webb, 5 April 1975, UoB, DM/1952/047.069 7.

[102] Jenny McKay, 'M.P. slams sexy books for kids', *Sunday Sun*, 13 November 1977, press cutting, UoB, DM 1952/047.0964.

One teacher commented: 'Many adults have become accustomed to relying on the Peacock imprint as a guarantee of a good read for a young person [...] but 'The Blinder' is a cuckoo in the Peacock's nest'.[103] On Kaye Webb's instructions, the novel was subsequently dropped from Peacock and restored to the Penguin fiction list: she commented 'It simply isn't worth losing good-will from influential people for the sake of a few sales'.[104] The incident illustrates the tension between the reputation for quality and safety which Kaye Webb had developed in Puffin, and the desire to include more daring material in Peacock: the firm's reputation for quality created constraints as well as benefits.

One of the significant challenges in producing a teenage list during the 1960s and 1970s was the question of how to position it in the market. Some of Kaye Webb's talent for marketing is evident in the cover choices for Peacock. The cover as well as the content of Beverly Cleary's *Fifteen* was striking, utilising a full face photograph of a young girl rather than the more typical illustration. Photographic covers were employed on a number of Peacocks, including Alan Garner's *The Owl Service*, which used a still from the television adaptation of the book, and Brian Glanville's sporting anthology *A Bad Lot* (1977). As Chapter 3 will show, Aidan Chambers characterised this strategy as one of the most effective aspects of Peacock, adopting it for his own teenage imprint Topliner. Despite such innovations, however, branding and promotion proved one of the most significant challenges for Peacock. Webb herself identified the difficulty of creating a separate brand identity as a problem:

> I had always felt that the kind of books we did in Peacocks were a better transition from Puffins to adult reading than any specially written series for teenagers could possibly be, but we only did well with individual books, not the whole series because, as you rightly supposed, they were muddled in with the Puffins and only a certain type of child would take the trouble to look for them; I couldn't persuade the booksellers to give them a special shelf to themselves. That, of course, was in 1962, or whatever it was. Nowadays they are much more aware of the demands of teenagers.[105]

The difficulty in distinguishing between Puffin and Peacock titles also presented additional challenges in terms of the kinds of content which could be presented in Peacock. While an association with Puffin was obviously desirable from the point of view of encouraging readers to maintain their brand loyalty as they grew older, the perception that Peacocks were intended for the same readership as Puffin was undesirable both in terms of attracting adolescent readers, and because of the likelihood that it would encourage younger readers to access more adult material. The similarity of Peacock to Puffin contributed to the controversy which erupted over *The Blinder*, which one parent observed was 'totally unsuited to the young

---

[103] Peter A. Lane to Kaye Webb, 24 March 1978, UoB, DM 1952/047.0964.

[104] Kaye Webb, memo to John Rolfe, 31 March 1978, UoB, DM 1952/047.0964.

[105] Kaye Webb to Dave Gregory, 1988, SS, KW/01/04/047.

children most likely to be attracted by its cover design', which employed the same kind of full-cover watercolour illustration which Webb has used to effect in Puffin.[106]

The Peacock list attained neither the prominence nor the high reputation enjoyed by Puffin. The difficulties encountered in establishing the list emerged primarily out of the new and rapidly changing status of teenage literature: as Chapter 3 will show, the difficulties in branding and targeting the appropriate audience were not unique to Puffin. More fundamentally, however, Peacock suffered from a lack of the inspiration which was so evident in Kaye Webb's work on Puffins. While she had responded with energy to the challenges inherent in promoting and developing children's literature, she lacked enthusiasm for a specialist literature for adolescents. In the 1990s, when teenage literature had become established in the market, she commented:

> I think it's ridiculous. I mean, I don't think it's necessary, really, because if you're half-way reading, you're going to read adult books. This teenage thing is absolutely frightful.[107]

In a difficult market for teenage literature, Peacock was never supported by the enthusiasm or innovation which characterised Kaye Webb's work on Puffin as a whole. Furthermore, the bias towards the fluent and enthusiastic reader which characterised the Puffin reputation for quality tended to work against success in Peacock, since the teenage market of the 1960s and 1970s was focused towards the 'reluctant' reader, as in Aidan Chambers' Topliner series. Although Peacock was undoubtedly important in making the first steps towards establishing teenage literature as a distinct category in its own right, the overall impact of the list was limited: the imprint was dropped in 1979, to be replaced by Puffin Plus.

Making Them Readers: The Puffin Club and Puffin Post

The limited cultural impact of Peacock is in stark contrast to the dramatic impact of the Puffin Club, which was undoubtedly the most unique and distinctive of Kaye Webb's initiatives as Puffin editor. As discussed earlier in this chapter, the concept of a fan club tied to the Puffin brand had significant marketing benefits, encouraging children to identify directly with the Puffin brand and affording many possibilities for advertising and promotion. The underlying ethos of the Club, however, was not based upon making children into consumers of Puffin books, but was focused on making children readers.

In the early years of Puffin, Eleanor Graham had presented the imprint as a means of creating readers who would ultimately transition into adult readers of Penguin books.[108] Kaye Webb presented the Puffin Club to Allen Lane as another

---

[106] John Griffin to Kaye Webb, 12 September 1977, UoB, DM 1952/047.0964.

[107] Kimberley Reynolds and Nicholas Tucker, 'Interview with Kaye Webb, 7 February 1995', p. 387.

[108] Kimberley Reynolds and Nicholas Tucker, 'Interview with Kaye Webb, 7 February 1995', p. 372.

means of achieving this, promising that it would 'make children into readers'.[109] Penguin directors were initially resistant to the Club, however, fearing it would be 'too expensive to run and only a limited number of children would join'.[110] Webb was able to convince them of the business value of the scheme, chiefly through the warm response the proposal elicited from sales reps attending the 1963 Penguin Sales Conference, but it is clear from the various accounts Webb gave of the Club that the marketing potential of the Club was secondary in her mind to the opportunities it offered for a genuine connection with readers. Indeed, some of her own private comments on the subject indicate that the business case for the Club was somewhat spurious: one page of notes observes 'It obviously is not commercially sensible', but identifies the Club as a way to 'catch [children's] imaginations, help them want the best'.[111] While the concept of 'making children into readers' had obvious commercial benefits, the ways in which it was manifested through the Puffin Club were more complex than a simple desire to capture the market for Penguin. On the contrary, the Club's emphasis on creating active, engaged and discerning readers was calculated to produce a group of readers who were too sophisticated to be governed simply by brand loyalty.

The sense of exclusivity the Puffin Club generated through strategies such as the use of secret codes and passwords between members, branded merchandise and reader contributions to the *Puffin Post* were all effective means of creating brand loyalty, but also functioned on a more fundamental level to build a sense of community. Membership of the Puffin Club functioned as a means of building friendships among children. One Club member wrote:

> I have mainly written to you to say thank you! As I have made a best freind [sic] through your Club.
>
> I was on a bus when this boy got on and sat next to me. I noticed he was wearing a Puffin badge so, like a true Puffineer, I said Sniffup, he replied Spotera and from then on we have been the best of freinds [sic].[112]

The Puffin Club and the *Puffin Post* also served to build a genuine connection between child readers and members of staff at Puffin. Archival evidence shows a high volume of correspondence from readers, relating not only to Puffin titles and features in the *Puffin Post*, but also to more personal matters such as the birth of a new baby to one of the Puffin Club staff. Such interaction was a primary aim of the Club rather than a side effect: Kaye Webb stated that the founding of the Puffin Club was 'an act of love to get us closer to the children. It was obvious from

---

[109] Puffin Books, 'The History of Puffin', *Puffin Books* (2010), <http://www.puffin. co.uk/static/aboutpuffin/historyofpuffin/> [accessed 20/01/10].

[110] Kaye Webb, 'On Being a Children's Book Editor', final version of typescript article for *School Bookshop News*, n.d., SS, KW/11/03/35.f.5.

[111] Kaye Webb. 'Getting to Children', typescript notes, n.d., SS, KW/07/04/08/12d.

[112] Michael Willox to Puffin Staff, n.d, SS, KW/07/04/01/04/09.

their letters that a lot of them wanted guidance – and not just about reading'.[113] In creating a sense of community around the Puffin Club, Kaye Webb helped to create a social structure for books. This endeavour was central to her view of literature: having grown up in a home which appreciated literature, she was keen to create the same kind of discourse around books for all children:

'I am absolutely convinced,' she says, 'that there is only one real way to make a child a joyful, life-long, irredeemable reader, with all the wealth of the written world at his command, and that is to *share* books with him not only in his earliest days, but right through his school career. Books can be one of the best bonds of family interest lasting right into adult life. [114]

Webb emphasised the way in which her own upbringing had helped to make her into a critical and enthusiastic reader, stating:

I shall always be grateful to my mother for the way she shared books with us, encouraged us to talk about them, made the good things in them fun that we all enjoyed together and understood so much better because we shared. She taught us, too, another enormously important thing – to discuss books, and learn to criticise as well as enjoy, to discriminate and know why a book succeeded or failed, its weak points and its strong ones.'[115]

By creating opportunities for interactions with other readers, the Puffin Club was designed to provide just such an environment for children. This was bolstered by the range of opportunities the Club put in place for children to communicate with one another, including a pen pal network, the Puffin excursions, and the forum provided by the *Puffin Post*, which published children's letters and creative work. Reading has typically been regarded as a 'solitary vice': in the Puffin Club it became a community activity. Furthermore, in aiming to encourage children to discriminate and identify the weak points in the books they read, the Club was modelling a form of reading which ran counter to the aim of simply creating consumers.

The efforts of the Puffin Club to make children into active and engaged readers are most clearly evident in the *Puffin Post*, which formed the main focus for the club's ongoing activities. Kaye Webb's professional experience as a journalist was of key importance in this area: as an experienced magazine editor she was able to draw on her time on the children's magazine *Young Elizabethan* as well as those on the adult variety magazine *Lilliput*. The *Puffin Post* offered children a mixture of non-fiction articles, puzzles, stories and poems, and artwork, enriched by contributions from writers such as Dylan Thomas, Walter de la Mare, Joan

---

[113] Gwen Nuttall, 'Puffin's winning gambler', *Sunday Times Business*, 6 April 1975, UoB, 'Puffin' green publicity folder.

[114] Kaye Webb, quoted in Gladys Williams, 'Queen of the Puffins: Kaye Webb' in *Books and Bookmen*, magazine clipping, [n.d, c. 1969], SS, KW/16/03.

[115] Kaye Webb, quoted in Gladys Williams, 'Queen of the Puffins: Kaye Webb' in *Books and Bookmen*, magazine clipping, [n.d, c. 1969], SS, KW/16/03.

Aiken and Alan Garner. Perhaps more important than any of these, however, was the material provided by the child readers themselves. The *Puffin Post* ran regular competitions to encourage its readers to write and draw for the magazine. The competitions were not designed simply to give children a sense of ownership, but focused upon encouraging genuine creativity and participation. When initial submissions to the magazine seemed not to be fulfilling these aims, Webb and her staff sought strategies for encouraging children to be more creative:

> We really got worried because we felt that half the stuff the children [sent] was school-inspired: the best essay, something that had got high marks, and wasn't necessarily spontaneous. So we invented Odway [...] What we were trying to make children see, was that it is the idea that mattered.[116]

Odway the dog, a recurring character in the *Puffin Post* designed by Jill MacDonald, stimulated readers' creativity through 'thinks' bubbles in which he mused on a variety of topics, including 'earth', 'clouds' and even 'the ampersand'. His speech was written in an elaborate cod-Elizabethan style which reflects both the playfulness and what John Rowe Townsend termed the 'junior eggheadedness' of the magazine. Children were invited to submit material responding to Odway's 'thinks'; this ranged from illustrations, stories and poems to one-word responses and jokes, often quite sophisticated in nature.

The freeform nature of Odway invited a critical and creative approach which was designed to make children engage more subtly and more honestly with words. Making children active participants in a forum which carried writing by well-respected literary authors helped to give children ownership of such writing, encouraging more engagement in reading. Crucially, the Puffin Club rejected an overtly educational approach – as her account of the creation of Odway demonstrates, Webb actively discouraged children from remaining within the boundaries set for them in an academic context – and focused on making the entire act of reading pleasurable.

The aims and strategies of the Puffin Club were characteristic of approaches to children's literature and reading in Britain during the 1960s and 1970s. As Chapter 1 has shown, successive education reports had emphasised the importance of an approach to literature which engaged young readers, while librarians and activists such as Elaine Moss, Janet Hill and Leila Berg developed strategies for directly engaging children. In this context, the Puffin Club stands out for its popularity, prominence and initiative: by 1972, 100,000 members had enrolled. Its cultural importance was widely recognised: Kaye Webb was awarded the Eleanor Farjeon Award in 1969 for the contribution the Club had made to British children's literature:

> The change in attitudes towards children literature in the past twenty years has been said by Brian Jackson, Director of ACE [Advisory Centre for Education], to be most clearly evidenced by the Puffin Club, 'which has marked and assisted the changeover from books as gifts to books children buy for themselves'. It is here, in her tireless efforts to make books part of everyday life for thousands

---

[116] Kaye Webb, 'Draft talk on Odway', n.d., SS, KW/07/04/03/01.

of children, that Kaye Webb's main achievement lies. The Puffin Club was started in 1967 as a means of publicising Penguin's children's paperback list, but through Kaye Webb's energy and drive, which go far beyond the demands of a publisher's recognised function, the Club is now the instigator of an enormous range of activities up and down the country which, whilst ranging from picnics to poetry, are all centred on books or related to books in such a way that the reading and owning of books is seen as a source of excitement and pleasure by the children themselves.[117]

The Puffin Club's success in fostering a sense of excitement about reading was a significant part of its achievement. Publisher Julia McRae congratulated Kaye Webb on the award, commenting:

> [Y]ou are the only one of us who really reaches out to a child and makes a book an exciting, alive and vigorous thing. The Puffin Club is the best thing to happen in years and it is a tribute to your genius that it is so huge a success.[118]

Writing later, after the Puffin Club had been disbanded, the critic and reviewer Brian Alderson spoke of 'the free enjoyment so evident in those old Posts'.[119] Such testimonies suggest that Kaye Webb had successfully put into practice the theory advocated by Paul Hazard and others, that reading should be a source of liberating enjoyment for children.

Kaye Webb's attempt to offer a 'reading community' through the Puffin Club represents an attempt to address the social inequalities identified by Leila Berg and others as presenting the most significant barriers to working-class literacy. Nevertheless, on retiring from Puffin, Kaye Webb reflected, 'I feel I've failed in one particular direction, although I've opened up Puffins in the Club, in a way, we've still not really tackled head-on the problem of getting to the generally under-privileged children'.[120] Although a limited number of more working-class children became members, the Puffin Club remained predominately middle class. An article of 1972 noted:

> Fiona MacCarthy once observed that Puffin readers were the *Guardian* readers and *New Statesmen* competition entrants of the future, and the only blot on the Puffin Club's horizon is the awareness that they are very middle class. They'd dearly love not to be, but attempts to draw in other children have been only half successful. A children's theatre morning in Camberwell tried to mix up regular club members with working-class children and they all enjoyed it, but the Puffin Club children afterwards confessed to Kaye Webb that really they liked it better when they were all on their own.[121]

---

[117] 'CHILDREN'S BOOK CIRCLE ELEANOR FARJEON AWARD: Winner of the 1969 Award: Kaye Webb', press release, 1970, SS, KW/11/01/06.

[118] Julia MacRae to Kaye Webb, February 1970, SS, KW/11/01/16.

[119] Brian Alderson to Kaye Webb, 1988, SS, KW/11/01/16.

[120] Kaye Webb to Julia MacRae, 1978, SS, KW/07/01/05/07.

[121] Lesley Garner, 'The Queen of Puffinland' in *Nova*, August 1972, magazine clipping, SS, KW/16/03.

The middle-class dominance of the Club was perhaps inevitable, since membership relied on children being exposed to the Club – typically through reading a Puffin – and having the motivation and money to become members. At a cost of five shillings in 1967 – the average cost of a Puffin book was 3 shillings and sixpence – membership was not exorbitant, but nor was it insignificant. Archival evidence shows that Kaye Webb sought to keep the Club more affordable by subsidising membership; however, the need to charge any fee at all inevitably imposed some restrictions on the Club.[122]

Despite the egalitarian aims of the Puffin Club, the ethos of quality in the *Puffin Post* was perhaps inherently biased towards the middle-class child. As Leila Berg had persuasively argued, children from 'bookish' families – typically the middle classes – enjoyed significant advantages in developing literacy. Although the community aspect of the Puffin Club was designed to offer some of the same advantages to all children, the *Puffin Post* itself demanded a high level of literacy and confidence with text. John Rowe Townsend characterised the *Puffin Post* as 'junior egghead stuff', although he added in its defence, 'I like junior eggheads myself, and I think they should be encouraged to persist in their eggheadedness'.[123] Undoubtedly this 'junior eggheadedness' was part of the Puffin Club's appeal, but it also tended to exclude precisely the demographic which received the most attention from educationalists and social activists during the 1960s: the predominately working-class 'reluctant readers'.

The Puffin Club did have some limitations as a strategy for reaching disadvantaged children, but its shortcomings were far outweighed by its successes. In attempting to engage directly with child readers and foster creativity and imagination it is characteristic of the 'golden age' of the 1960s and 1970s: the Club's prominence and success undoubtedly helped to foster this ethos in British children's literature. The 'junior eggheadedness' of the Club, however, is more characteristic of the public service ideals of the period immediately post-war: fundamental to the Club was the notion that offering children the opportunity to experience 'quality' in the form of complex and literary material was an essential means of helping them develop the ability to appreciate such material. The Puffin Club therefore represents a highly successful combination of Kaye Webb's instinct for marketing and engaging with children, and her commitment to the tradition of quality established at Puffin under Eleanor Graham.

Principles before Profit: Puffin as 'Public Service Publisher'

The combination of marketing acumen and altruism present in Kaye Webb's creation of the Puffin Club characterises a tension which ran through her work at Puffin. Her success at marketing and expanding Puffin had helped to establish children's books as an important sector of the market, but the perception of

---

[122] Kaye Webb, 'Puffin Books - Marketing Plan 1967', 1967, UoB, DM/1879/23/5.

[123] John Rowe Townsend, 'Operation Junior Egghead', *Guardian*, 3 April 1989. Clipping in 'Press Cuttings for Puffins', scrapbook, SS, KW/16/06.

children's publishing as potentially lucrative was potentially at odds with the altruistic motives which Kimberley Reynolds characterises as an important force in children's publishing in the 1950s.[124] Certainly the idea of using high selling titles as a means of supporting worthwhile but less popular books became increasingly difficult to maintain in the more straitened publishing climate of the 1970s, and Webb was increasingly forced to justify her decisions to the company on financial grounds. In an article written in the 1980s, she commented on the increasingly profit-driven nature of children's publishing:

> Now it seems to me that children's publishing (not its literature) has simply become a business and has entered a state of unconcerned greediness, perhaps rather like the children we imagine we are catering for. In fact, children are now thought of, and catered for, not as children but as consumers.[125]

Webb's criticism of the business-oriented nature of children's publishing is ironic given her own role in establishing it as more professional and more lucrative, and she acknowledged that the lack of emphasis on profit during her own years as Puffin editor was a luxury which arose partly from the relatively buoyant nature of children's publishing. Nevertheless, her distaste for the idea of children as consumers highlights the fact that the socially-focused aspects of Puffin were a key aspect of her own ethos.

The concept of 'public service publishing' was an important element of Penguin's ethos as a whole. Allen Lane's initiative of providing 'cheap editions of good-quality contemporary writing' was irrefutably a brilliant business concept, but also had a significant public service element, making the ownership of quality literature no longer the sole preserve of the rich.[126] The establishment of Puffin extended the same courtesy to the child reader: Kaye Webb commented that 'Allen Lane was for the first time making available a regular supply of genuinely low-priced books – the first Puffin cost one shilling – therefore making it possible for children to choose for themselves what they wanted to read instead of having to accept what grown-ups decided would be right for them.'[127] Webb's combination of marketing genius and social conscience was fundamentally in tune with Allen Lane's outlook. Jack Morpurgo argues that her period as editor saw Puffin become more closely aligned with Penguin philosophy, with the support of Allen Lane:

> Puffins, he would say, were the persuaders, the educators, the means to establish the firm's corps of future Penguin readers; it was he who defended the series most vociferously against the attacks of his more seemingly hard-headed colleagues

---

[124] Kimberley Reynolds, 'Publishing Practices and the Practicalities of Publishing', p. 26.

[125] Kaye Webb, 'The Children's Market Grows Up', typescript draft of article for *The Bookseller*, c. 1980s, SS, KW/07/04/08/19.

[126] Penguin Books, *Fifty Penguin Years*, p. 13.

[127] Kaye Webb, 'Paperback Buyer', typescript draft of article for *Paperback Buyer*, c. 1978, SS, KW/07/01/05/09/03.

when they complained about Puffin losses, and it was he who accepted with good grace Kaye Webb's plea that the price of Puffins be kept low when all other Penguin prices were rising rapidly.[128]

Kaye Webb frequently emphasised the importance of Lane's 'swings and roundabouts' ethos to Puffin: with bestsellers such as *Watership Down* to 'carry Puffin along', she justified the inclusion of titles which she saw as poor sellers but important for their literary qualities. Following the death of Allen Lane in 1970, Webb continued this ethos. Penguin director Charles Clark, who had worked with the company from its early days, articulated this on his move to Hutchinson Publishing in 1972:

> It's critical that as the last publisher on the books board, you hang onto the role of Penguins as a publisher with all that the word means as an attitude to words, language and that 'connectedness' to society that is unique to Penguins – of which the Puffin list and Puffin Club is, in my view, the outstanding champion.
>
> [...] I have tried to build up at Penguin Education that publishing is about producing good books that sell well & produce enough profit to enable you to carry on producing more good books.[129]

The tone of Clark's letter indicates that Penguin as a whole had begun to move away from the notion of 'public service publishing', but it remained a fundamental aspect of Kaye Webb's ethos at Puffin. Archival evidence shows that she consistently fought to keep the cost of Puffins low; as this chapter has shown, the quality rather than the marketability of the books she published remained her primary concern. Although her determination to raise the profile of children's literature and to encourage more book ownership had important commercial implications, it was underpinned by a genuine belief in the value of giving books to children. She wrote in her autobiography, 'If I could meet a friendly Genie with unlimited powers who was prepared to put himself at my disposal I would command him to give every child in the country three books of their own choosing'; a wish which was to be partially fulfilled in the 1990s with the establishment of national book scheme Bookstart.[130]

Kaye Webb's ability to focus on quality rather than profit margins was supported by the buoyancy of the children's market in the first half of her tenure at Puffin. The more challenging market of the 1970s made such an attitude more difficult to support, but, this strengthened rather than diminished Kaye Webb's commitment to public service publishing:

---

[128] J.E. Morpurgo, *Allen Lane, King Penguin: A Biography*, p. 311.

[129] Charles Clark to Kaye Webb, c. 1972, SS, KW/07/01/05/02/01.

[130] Kaye Webb, 'A Beggar's Knock', draft of Kaye Webb's autobiography transcribed in Charles Kennedy's hand, c. 1988, SS, KW/01/02/43/19.

I have one solution, but I have been hesitant to offer it because it sounds so political. But somebody has to say it – and the Bullock report gives me support. Children's literature is an inherent part of children's development, of making the next generation not only worthy of inheriting the world, but also able to improve it. And for that reason I truly believe that the publishing of children's literature ought not to be something which is done for profit.[131]

This statement seems almost unbelievable in the context of Webb's immense success at generating profits in Puffin, but it reflects the benefits Webb had accrued from beginning her career in a context in which children's lists were typically required only to break even. Although Kaye Webb's editorship of Puffin was characterised by her remarkable gift for marketing books, this was ultimately based on a sincere belief in the importance of reaching more children with books rather than in a purely commercial outlook. This attitude was to become increasingly threatened in the publishing world during the 1980s and early 1990s, when close profit margins helped to produce a more commercially focused industry.

Kaye Webb: A Maker of Modern Children's Literature

The public service ethos which characterised Kaye Webb's work as editor of Puffin was a central ingredient in her contribution to the 'golden age' of children's literature in the 1960s and 1970s. Her belief that childhood was an important and formative period during which children should be offered 'butter and eggs – not candyfloss' helped to shape a list which was almost universally regarded as representing the best in children's literature. The high reputation of Puffin, along with Webb's skill at marketing and promotion, helped to publicise the work of many authors and illustrators who remain in print today. At the same time, however, some of the tensions evident in Webb's own work highlight broader issues in the children's publishing industry.

Kaye Webb's success in expanding the Puffin list had a significant impact on children's publishing as a whole. In proving that children's paperback publishing could be both exciting and lucrative, she helped to inspire the dramatic expansion in children's publishing which characterised the 1960s and 1970s. This expansion helped to support the development of a more diverse and exciting children's literature in Britain. At the same time, however, it created increasing tensions between a model of children's publishing which had been largely shaped by altruistic motives, and one which was subject to the vagaries of market forces. Ironically, then, Webb helped to create the more profit-driven market which she was ultimately to decry. Nevertheless, in maintaining a reputation for quality publishing at the same time as she expanded the output of Puffin and adopted more modern marketing techniques, Kaye Webb demonstrated that a focus on literary quality need not be incompatible with high sales.

---

[131] Kaye Webb, 'On Being a Children's Book Editor', typescript draft of an article for *School Bookshop News*, c. 1975, SS, KW/11/03/35.

In many respects, Webb successfully combined the altruism of 1950s children's publishing with the business acumen necessary in a changing marketplace. Her intuitive approach to selecting books certainly helped to produce a list which was both well-regarded by critics and parents, and popular with children. If the perception of the Puffin list as 'safe' created constraints in terms of content, these were largely in accordance with Webb's own impulses. Where her sympathies were not engaged, as in the case of Peacock, her intuition served her less well.

Significant as the Puffin list itself was, it is Kaye Webb's creation of the Puffin Club which most defines her contribution to the second golden age. While the Club – like Puffin as a whole – never entirely overcame its bias towards middle-class members and values, it made children's books more exciting and accessible to thousands of children. In visibly celebrating the work of authors and illustrators, and creating links with child readers, she fuelled the sense of excitement and creativity which characterised the era. The Puffin Club is the most visible demonstration of a model of children's publishing which was concerned neither with a small elite, nor with profit margins, but with genuine engagement in the social and cultural life of the country. Kaye Webb's commitment to quality rather than profit, and her passionate belief in the social importance of children's literature, fundamentally characterised the 'second golden age'.

Chapter 3
Aidan Chambers and Topliner

One of the characteristic features of the 'golden age' of the 1960s and 1970s was the increasingly varied nature of children's publishing. The support provided by high levels of social funding, which created guaranteed markets in libraries and schools, and the commercial success achieved by existing children's publishers such as Puffin created an attractive prospect for publishers entering the children's market during the 1960s. These high levels of investment did not continue into the 1970s, but the pressure of competing in a diminishing market encouraged publishers to diversify their lists, targeting smaller imprints at specific demographics. At the same time, the diverse discourse around children's literature explored in Chapter 1 encouraged the establishment of new children's lists which reflected new ideologies about children and reading. Topliner, an imprint for the 'reluctant' adolescent reader, is representative of this trend. Founded and edited by the critic, educationalist and writer Aidan Chambers, the imprint also reflects the intersection of disciplines which characterised children's literature during the 1960s and 1970s. While it has now largely disappeared from memory, the activities of Topliner and other imprints like it played an important role in the making of modern children's literature.

The buoyancy of the education market during the 1960s offered obvious opportunities for educational publishers. Schools were adopting new curricula and new models of teaching, creating a demand not only for books to stock school libraries but also for new books for use in the classroom. Furthermore, many of those advocating for new types of literature were teachers and educationalists, meaning that schools were an obvious target audience for specialist imprints. Macmillan Education was one of the most active publishers, launching a number of significant imprints, including Leila Berg's *Nippers* reading scheme, and Topliner.

Established in 1968, Topliner was only the second paperback imprint aimed specifically at adolescent readers – Kaye Webb having led the way with the Peacock list – and was one of only a handful of publishing imprints catering for this group at all.[1] Although it was an imprint of Macmillan Education, its remit was never solely educational; on the contrary, Aidan Chambers consistently sought to secure a foothold in the commercial market. The ethos of the list differed significantly, however, from its nearest competitor, Peacock: whereas Kaye Webb's commitment to offering 'the best books for children' was predicated upon a notion of quality as essential and universal, Aidan Chambers' focus on the reluctant adolescent reader in the Topliner list reflected a more socially-focused and culturally specific

---

[1] Brockhampton Press targeted readers over the age of 10 with their Black Knight series, launched in 1967, while Bodley Head launched Bodley Head Books for New Adults in 1968, but the concept of specialist publishing for young adults was much slower to become established in Britain than in North America or Scandinavia.

construction of quality which paid as much attention to the reader as to the book. Aidan Chambers' work as editor of Topliner can therefore be broadly characterised as aligning him with the group John Rowe Townsend characterised as 'child people' rather than with the aesthetic and literary concerns of the 'book people'. Although in practice Chambers' approach was more complex than this label suggests and, paradoxically, his own writing for young adults is highly literary in nature, the potential social and commercial impact of the books published in Topliner was at least as important an editorial consideration as their literary qualities. As this chapter will show, the difficulty of reconciling the literary and the social aspects of reading formed a key tension in Aidan Chambers' work at Topliner.

Like Puffin, Topliner was closely associated with its editor: Aidan Chambers conceived the idea of a publishing imprint aimed at reluctant adolescents and edited the imprint for 12 of the 14 years it was in existence. Whereas Kaye Webb was an editor and publisher whose activities extended into the social and educational aspects of literature, Aidan Chambers' editorial role grew out of his work as an educationalist, author and critic. Topliner therefore constitutes a particularly clear example of the ways in which developments in these areas affected children's publishing during the 1960s and 1970s: Chambers' critical and creative writing can be directly related to his ethos as editor of Topliner. Chambers himself provides an interesting contrast to Kaye Webb: whereas Webb was part of the same generation who had dominated children's publishing in the 1950s, Chambers was part of the new post-war generation who had benefitted from the educational investments and social mobility of the post-war years, and who were beginning to criticise the status quo in both publishing and education. He thus exemplifies some of the new ideologies and attitudes which this new generation brought to children's publishing.

Although Topliner did not enjoy either the dominance or the longevity of Puffin, it exemplifies many of the key trends in publishing for children and young people during this period and was influential in shaping the emerging genre of teenage literature. The recent acquisition of the Chambers Archive by Aberystwyth University has allowed an extended investigation of the imprint: the archive, which documents the entire working lives of Aidan and Nancy Chambers, includes extensive correspondence dating from the period of his editorship, along with business records relating to Topliner[2]. In addition, Aidan Chambers has published extensively on literature for children and adolescents throughout his career. By analysing archival evidence of Chambers' work as editor of Topliner in the light of his published works, and of his own reflections given in a 2009 interview, it is possible to build a clear picture of the Topliner imprint and the ways in which it reflected changing trends in the children's publishing of the 1960s and 1970s.

---

[2] Nancy Chambers, née Lockwood, is a significant figure in British children's literature in her own right, notably for her work as editor of Signal Responses to Children's Literature and its parent company Thimble Press. The Chambers Archive represents a valuable resource for future research on her contribution to the field.

Aidan Chambers: Literature and Education

Aidan Chambers' career in children's literature exemplifies the trend towards interdisciplinarity which, as noted in Chapter 1, was a key feature of the second golden age of British children's literature. Kaye Webb is notable for her consuming devotion to Puffin Books; by contrast, Chambers is significant for his contribution to an impressively wide range of endeavours. Although today he is best known as an author of literature for adolescents – he won the Carnegie Medal in 1999 for *Postcards From No Man's Land* (1999), the fifth in his Dance Sequence of young adult novels – his career has spanned almost every field in children's literature.[3] Beginning his career in 1957 as a secondary-school teacher, his experiences as a teacher-librarian in the early 1960s quickly led him to engage with contemporary debates about children's literature and education. His critical engagement with children's literature is reflected in a continuous output of reviews and critical articles in publications including *The Times Literary Supplement*, *The Horn Book Magazine* and *Signal Responses to Children's Books*, which was founded by Chambers and his wife Nancy. In the field of children's publishing, he was responsible not only for Topliner, but also for two of Macmillan's other educational imprints – Club 75 and Rockets – and for an imprint specialising in works in translation, Turton and Chambers, which he launched in partnership with Australians Rayma and David Turton. Chambers has also exerted an influence on the fields of children's literature and education through his work as a teacher-trainer and lecturer; he continues to work in these fields today, and between 2003 and 2006 served as Honorary President of the School Library Association.[4] As in the case of other multi-disciplinary figures such as John Rowe Townsend and Wallace Hildick, there are strong intersections between Chambers' work in different areas: Topliner is a particularly effective example of the ways in which children's publishing was influenced by developments in other arenas during the 1960s and 1970s.

One of the most formative influences of Aidan Chambers' career was his experience as a teacher-librarian, which played a significant role in shaping his editorial and critical work. As a young teacher charged with the task of establishing a new school library, he began to question the relevance of both the literature and the teaching methods to which the vast majority of young readers were exposed. These

---

[3]   The Dance Sequence is a series of six novels, begun in 1978 with *Breaktime* and completed in 2005 with *This is All: The Pillow Book of Cordelia Kenn*. Chambers himself identified the books as a single series, which he termed the Dance Sequence, although the name was not included in editions of the books until relatively recently. (Aidan Chambers, 'The Dance Sequence', *Aidan Chambers*, <http://www.aidanchambers.co.uk/sequence.htm> [accessed 06/01/10]).

The Dance Sequence and the impact of Chambers' literary work has been addressed in two recent critical works: Betty Greenway, *Aidan Chambers: Master Literary Choreographer* (Lanham, MD: Scarecrow Press, 2006) and Nancy Chambers (ed.), *Reading the Novels of Aidan Chambers: Seven Essays* (Stroud: Thimble Press, 2009).

[4]   Alec Williams, 'Afterwords: An Interview With Aidan Chambers', *The School Librarian*, 54:4 (2006), 168.

concerns are a recurrent theme in his critical work, notably in his 1968 monograph *The Reluctant Reader*, which outlined many of the ideas which were fundamental to Chambers' work at Topliner. Chambers' early fiction was also closely tied to his experiences as a teacher: his first two published works, *Johnny Salter* (1966) and *Cycle Smash* (1967), were plays written for the students at his school. During the same period he began to seek opportunities to put his ideas into practice in the wider world, investigating the possibility of establishing a specialist publishing imprint for the kind of literature he had identified as successful with his adolescent students. This aim was ultimately realised in the Topliner series. The imprint therefore grew directly out of Aidan Chambers' practical and theoretical work on children's literature: whereas Kaye Webb had inherited a particular tradition of 'quality' publishing from her predecessors at Puffin, he was building upon contemporary developments in education to create a new model of publishing for young people.

Launching a List: New Possibilities in Publishing

Aidan Chambers was directly responsible for the founding of the Topliner list. As a librarian and teacher, he had sought strategies to encourage his adolescent students to read and engage with books, but he quickly came to believe that there was a dearth of suitable reading material. His attempts to remedy the lack through his own writing were hampered by the difficulty of finding a publishing venue, and he became increasingly convinced that a new kind of publishing endeavour was needed, arguing: 'Only the publisher, with his capital and most of the other reins in his hand, can possibly bring about the redirection that is needed'.[5] In the mid-1960s he contacted Joan Tate, author of a series of educational books which he felt fulfilled many of the criteria for a successful series for adolescent readers, and together they developed a proposal for the kind of list they envisaged.[6] They approached a number of publishers with the idea, and discussed these plans with Heinemann – who had published work by both Chambers and Tate – and with Kaye Webb, who was exploring new directions for Peacock.[7] Despite initial interest from

---

[5]   Aidan Chambers, *The Reluctant Reader* (London: Pergamon Press, 1969), p. 136.

[6]   Aidan Chambers, Interview with Lucy Pearson, 27 April 2009 (Appendix).

[7]   Correspondence with author Josephine Kamm describes the proposed scheme at Heinemann, and explains its failure. Aidan Chambers to Josephine Kamm, 4 June 1966 and 11 December 1966, Chambers Collection, University of Aberystwyth, Box 110/111 01, Folder: Josephine Kamm.

This chapter makes extensive use of archival material from the Chambers Collection, University of Aberystwyth, which will be abbreviated in all subsequent citations to UoA, and from the Penguin Archive, University of Bristol, hereafter abbreviated to UoB. At the time of access these collections were only partially catalogued; the fullest possible location details have therefore been given to aid future research.

Where the material cited is a draft of published material, the name of the publication in which it appeared will be given if known.

both publishers, neither came to fruition, but Chambers' ideas attracted the interest of Michael Wace, editor of Macmillan Education, who invited him to establish an imprint with Macmillan.[8] The result was Topliner, aimed directly at the reluctant adolescent reader. Catering primarily to the education market, Topliner remained active from its establishment in 1968 until the beginning of the 1980s, when the list was discontinued. Aidan Chambers acted as General Editor for almost the entirety of this period: his resignation in 1979 helped to precipitate the closure of the list.

Aidan Chambers' conviction that the problems he had encountered as a teacher and librarian required a publishing solution arose partly out of practical considerations: new kinds of books for young people could only be made available if publishers were willing to publish and distribute them. However, his belief in the potential power of publishing also reflected his own experiences as a reader, in particular his experiences of Penguin and Puffin books, which had played a formative role in his development as a reader. The first book he owned was *Worzel Gummidge* (1936), the first title on Eleanor Graham's Puffin Storybook list. In adolescence he graduated to the Penguin list and began to build his own library, purchasing a new Penguin every week. In essence, therefore, he embodied many of the qualities which Allen Lane had envisaged in a Penguin reader: working class by birth, he took advantage of the cheap paperback prices to expand his horizons. Penguin books represented more than an affordable way to build a home library, however:

> For in those days one somehow came to believe that anything published by Penguin was not only worth reading but ought to be read. I trusted the list completely as I trusted Jim [his inspirational teacher], knowing that both would take me where I couldn't take myself, that they had my interests at heart and knew what I wanted to know. I loved Penguin books, their size, their look, their feel, their typography. They were elegant, democratic, unthreateningly attractive, affordable. I was proud of them and proud to own them.[9]

Chambers' account of the role Penguin books had played in his life is indicative of the possibilities he saw in publishing. Publishing imprints could do more than simply make books available: they could also represent a guide for the reader and provide a point of contact and recognition for those who might otherwise be excluded by the literary canon. The example set by Penguin was an important influence on Chambers' concept of a new teenage imprint: one of his earliest proposals for the project explicitly states, 'What Penguins did for adult readers is, in fact, just what is suggested we should do for the submerged sixty per cent of teenage readers'.[10] While Topliner was focused specifically on

---

[8]   Aidan Chambers, Interview with Lucy Pearson, 27 April 2009.

[9]   Aidan Chambers, 'Pick Up a Penguin' in *Reading Talk* (Stroud: Thimble Press, 1995), 99–112, p. 112.

[10] Aidan Chambers, 'Suggestions for a Reading Library for early teenage (13–16 years) of average and below average ability in Secondary Modern and Comprehensive Schools', November 1965, UoA, Box 110/111 01, Folder: Series publicity, f. 4.

the reluctant reader, therefore, it is important to note that it was never envisaged purely as a remedial list. On the contrary, Aidan Chambers aimed to develop a list with the kind of democratic and unthreatening qualities which he associated with Penguin, and with the same power to take readers beyond where they could go themselves.

Some of the key features of the Topliner list were directly modelled upon Penguin. One of the most important elements was the choice of the paperback format, which Chambers had found successful with his reluctant students:

> We [Chambers and Joan Tate] believed it had to be coming from the commercial publishers, but that it had to be in paperback. And there was the problem, because paperback publishing was not then like it is now, and people were not original in paperback. So Topliner was unusual: it was one of the first to do this. [...] There were paperbacks within educational publishing, but they were educational books. They looked it: they had comprehension questions in them, that kind of thing. They were terrible looking. They were one of the reasons the kids weren't reading.[11]

Chambers' recognition of the appeal of the paperback format was astute in the context of a publishing industry which still placed more value on hardback titles. Although Penguin and Puffin had demonstrated that paperback publishing could be both lucrative and respectable, Penguin was still first and foremost a reprint list. By contrast, Aidan Chambers' belief in the greater appeal of the paperback format led him to sidestep hardback publishing altogether: since the requirement for a new kind of book meant that it would be necessary to commission original titles, he argued, then it was better for them to appear as paperback originals. The novelty of this proposal was a major reason for the failure of the proposed list at Heinemann, who were ultimately unwilling to risk a list of paperback originals.[12] Macmillan accepted the proposed paperback format, establishing a partnership with Pan Books for commercial distribution. The paperback format succeeded, but the commercial returns were too low: Pan dissolved the partnership after only a year, leaving Topliner confined to sales through schools.[13] The growth of school bookshops, however, made the schools market more significant: in the context of an increasing emphasis on book ownership as well as literacy, the affordability of paperback books made it an ideal format. Shrinking budgets in the 1970s diminished the market for children's books as a whole, but bolstered the demand for paperbacks: whereas schools had once been reluctant to buy flimsier paperback copies of texts for classroom use, the low cost of paperbacks offered a way of obtaining more variety for the same amount of money. In this context the imprint

---

[11]   Aidan Chambers, Interview with Lucy Pearson, 27 April 2009.

[12]   Aidan Chambers, Interview with Lucy Pearson, 27 April 2009; Aidan Chambers to Josephine Kamm, 11 December 1966, UoA, Box 1110/111 01, Folder: Josephine Kamm.

[13]   Aidan Chambers to Irma Chilton, 5 August 1967, UoA, Box 110/111 02, Folder: Irma Chilton; Aidan Chambers to Irma Chilton, 13 September 1969, UoA, Box 110/111 02.

prospered: at the height of its success Topliner sold over 450,000 titles a year, and by the end of the 1970s it had spawned copycat competition from other teenage paperback lists.[14] Despite the relatively niche appeal of the original Topliner list, it was successful enough to diversify into a cluster of more sophisticated and demanding series, Topliner Redstars, and a hardback imprint, Topliner Trident.

Although Aidan Chambers' vision for a teenage imprint emerged from his own experiences of Penguin, it differed significantly from that of Kaye Webb: the failure of the Peacock list to live up to the possibilities he envisaged was one motivating factor in the creation of a new list. Webb envisaged Peacock primarily as a list of adult titles of interest to adolescent readers, and she met Chambers' attempts to pursue his vision of a new kind of teenage publishing within Penguin with little enthusiasm. Despite an initial interest in appointing Aidan Chambers as editor for the Peacock list – which by 1968 was already beginning to show signs of struggling – Webb rejected Chambers' proposal for a new direction for the list, citing the difficulty of 'starting again' with Peacock at a time when Puffin were already engaged in launching a new series.[15] She was certainly capable of resisting objections within Penguin when she was committed to a project: her reluctance to champion the scheme reflects the difference between her vision and Aidan Chambers' proposed model.[16] Whereas Kaye Webb had developed a teenage list aimed at the fluent and committed reader, Chambers was focusing on the 'reluctant' demographic, emphasising the social and educational components of literature.

The Reluctant Reader: Targeting a New Demographic

One of the key issues Aidan Chambers had encountered as a teacher and librarian was the problem of 'reluctant readers': students who could read but largely chose not to. His experience with his own students convinced him that this demographic –

---

[14] Sales figures for all Topliner titles in the years 1971–1977 show that in 1975, the most successful year, 54 titles were in print and 473,307 books sold. 'Topliner sales', sales ledger, 1971–1977, UoA, Box 110/111 02, Folder: Topliner: In-Hand Materials.

No figures are currently available for Peacock's sales in the same year, but records from 1968, when Topliner was launched, show that Peacock sold only 84,442 titles. It seems that Topliner enjoyed a significant level of success, therefore, despite the difficulties posed by the lack of a commercial distributor. ('Penguin Books Limited: Net Sales and Trading Profit for the Year Ending 31 December 1968', UoB, DM/1843/16.)

[15] Aidan Chambers, 'Peacock Books', typescript editorial proposal. Enclosure with letter, Aidan Chambers to Kaye Webb, 5 January, 1968, UoA, Box 155, Folder: Penguin – Puffin, f. 1; Kaye Webb to Aidan Chambers, 10 January 1968, UoA, Box 155, Folder: Penguin – Puffin.

Webb's new series of Puffin Picture Books was launched in 1968.

[16] Aidan Chambers asserts that Kaye Webb's reluctance to accept his proposal was deepened by the incompatibility between their personalities, commenting that Webb found him insufficiently pliable. (Aidan Chambers, Interview with Lucy Pearson, 27 April 2009.)

the 'submerged sixty per cent' – was reluctant because young people's needs were not being met by the literature on offer to them. In *The Reluctant Reader*, which brought together much of the thinking which had underpinned his work during the 1960s, he argued, 'A good deal of the material we provide in "children's lists", fondly imagining it right for "them", is far off target'.[17] Chambers' own writing and editorial work during this period was focused on remedying this situation.

The idea that reluctant adolescent readers needed special attention did not emerge solely from Aidan Chambers' own experiences in teaching; it was also evident in the broader discourse surrounding education during the 1960s. As Chapter 1 has shown, successive education reports focused attention on the importance of developing literacy across the population. Chambers was directly influenced by the Newsom Report (1963), which focused upon the needs of underachieving secondary-modern students. An early proposal for the Topliner list states:

> The Newsom Young are the least academic 13 to 17 year olds, for the most part still at school, and compulsorily so until 16 soon. They are 60% of the population in that age range.

> They become physically adult and socially free during these years, but remain emotionally and mentally immature. They need a special creative literature.[18]

Aidan Chambers concurred with the authors of the Newsom Report that this demographic represented untapped potential which was poorly served both by the existing education system and by children's publishing. His call for 'a special creative literature' is analogous to the Newsom Report's advocacy of new teaching methods, an initiative Chambers also supported in *The Reluctant Reader* and in his subsequent critical writing.[19] Whereas Kaye Webb emphasised the intuitive aspects of her editorial ethos, therefore, Aidan Chambers' work at Topliner was founded upon a specific educational philosophy.

The idea of a 'special creative literature' for adolescent readers was central to Aidan Chambers' proposed new model of publishing. He explicitly challenged Kaye Webb's policy of selecting a large proportion of Peacock titles from the adult lists, stating in his proposal for a redesign of Peacock:

> Often reprints from adult titles are possible, but it is undoubtedly true that there is an increasing need for books to be written with such people in mind (not 'for' them, note). [...] What one is, in fact, saying are the same things that were said

---

17   Aidan Chambers, *The Reluctant Reader*, p. 63.

18   Aidan Chambers, 'THE NEWSOM YOUNG REED BOOKS: a new and growing market', typescript proposal for a teenage publishing imprint, August 1966. UoA, Box 110/111 01, Folder: Series Publicity.

19   Aidan Chambers has continued to seek strategies for successful teaching of literacy skills throughout his career: he explores methods for teachers and librarians to help children engage with books and reading in *The Reading Environment* (1991) and *Tell Me: Children, Reading and Talk* (Stroud: Thimble Press, 1993).

about Children's books years ago, and now need saying about 'teenage' books. Thus just as PUFFINS are so successful because they contain many books written by writers of worth and quality with children in mind, it is conceivable that teenage books could grow in the same way.[20]

The concept of a literature written with adolescents in mind ran counter to the prevalent view of teenage literature during the 1960s. Kaye Webb's policy at Peacock conformed with the approach of critics such as Margery Fisher, who argued that a judicious selection of adult literature was the best means of catering for the developing tastes of adolescent readers and moving them seamlessly into the full range of literature. Aidan Chambers criticised this approach for excluding those readers who most needed a specialist literature, arguing that 'bookish children, which Peacocks supplied, have left children's books and gone without much effort to adult books'.[21] By contrast, the 'emotionally and mentally immature' adolescents who comprised the 'submerged sixty per cent' were neither intellectually nor emotionally ready for the demands of books written for adults:

> Teenage books as a bridge between children's and adult literature was the initial impelling idea between Topliners and the beginning of my accidentally acquired career as an editor. As one Topliner reader wrote, explaining why he liked them, 'It is a big step up from Blyton to Dostoevsky'. If you haven't made it by the time you are twelve you need help.[22]

The concept of a bridge from Blyton to Dostoevsky has an inherent class dimension. As established in Chapter 2, Kaye Webb's Peacock list was catering not for readers of Enid Blyton but for children already familiar with the kind of complex literary works found in the Puffin list: the step from William Mayne to Dostoevsky is considerably smaller. Webb's commitment to 'the best in children's books' was predicated on an ideal of quality as objective and universal, but the difficulty she faced in reaching children from working-class backgrounds is suggestive of the limitations of this approach. Leila Berg had identified the degree to which children who did not enjoy the advantages of a bookish home were deterred from reading; for those who had not overcome this disadvantage by adolescence the problem was compounded. Aidan Chambers' assertion that adolescent readers needed a specialist literature reflects a more socially focused view of quality which considered the experiences of readers as well as the literary aspects of the books.

---

[20] Aidan Chambers, 'Peacock Books', typescript editorial proposal. Enclosure with letter, Aidan Chambers to Kaye Webb, 5 January, 1968, UoA, Box 155, Folder: Penguin – Puffin, f. 1.

[21] Aidan Chambers, *The Reluctant Reader*, p. 138.

[22] Aidan Chambers, 'Alive and Flourishing: A Personal View of Teenage Literature', in *Booktalk: Occasional writing on Literature and Children* (Stroud: Thimble Press, 1995), 84–91, p. 87.

Quality Literature: A New Model

The identification of Topliner as a bridge 'from Blyton to Dostoevsky' implicitly positions the list as a transition from the low-brow and populist to the high-brow and literary; the discourse of quality in children's literature during the 1960s and 1970s typically excluded the popular and commercially successful works of Enid Blyton. Aidan Chambers presented the problem of the reluctant reader as essentially a problem of quality, arguing that adolescents who were reluctant to read the literature offered to them in the school environment typically consumed a wide range of popular reading material. Popular fiction by authors such as Enid Blyton and Ian Fleming, newspapers, periodicals on hobbies such as football and fishing and magazines such as *Jackie, Petticoat* and *Honey* – aimed explicitly at teenagers – all found a ready audience among adolescent readers. '[W]hen we say they read "nothing"', he observed, 'we really intend to say that they read nothing we care to recognise as profitable, healthy or wise'.[23] The Topliner list was therefore not aimed simply at encouraging adolescents to read *something*, but at encouraging them to read the *right* material.

In seeking to create a list which could help readers make the transition from the kind of popular reading which they voluntarily consumed in their leisure time to more overtly literary material, Aidan Chambers was participating in some of the dominant constructions of quality evident in the publishing and criticism of the 1960s. His analysis of the reasons for teenagers' preference for populist reading material is strikingly reminiscent of Kaye Webb's 'butter and eggs' analogy:

> It is like poor food and foul air.
>
> We go on eating poor food because we don't know there is better, or because we were not brought up with the taste for better. We breathe foul air because we have created the foul air, and often because the foul air stretches over such an area of the land that the effort of reaching the fresh air is too demanding. In the end we notice neither the poor food nor the foul air, and may even talk as if we prefer them.[24]

The characterisation of teenagers' reading as analogous to 'poor food and foul air' maintains the division between 'quality' and populist literature which was evident in Kaye Webb's rejection of Enid Blyton for the Puffin list. However, whereas Kaye Webb's work at Puffin was predicated on the belief that giving children access to quality literature was the most important means of weaning them off the 'candyfloss' of less wholesome literature, Aidan Chambers regarded this approach as insufficient. Reluctant readers, he argued, were hampered by the effort involved in appreciating more demanding work. Overcoming this difficulty required a different publishing response, which Chambers aimed to provide in Topliner.

---

[23]   Aidan Chambers, *The Reluctant Reader*, p. 20.
[24]   Aidan Chambers, *The Reluctant Reader*, p. 40.

A key element of Aidan Chambers' ethos as editor of Topliner was the belief that much of the 'quality' literature offered to adolescent readers actually worked to exclude them. This belief was partly based upon belief in the need to reflect the diverse lives of child readers, in line with the growing cultural discourse of the 1960s and 1970s. However, Chambers was also critical of the 'quality' values which prevailed in the world of children's literature: his criticism of the 'bookish' Peacock list reflects his perception that the literary values of publishers like Puffin often worked to exclude the very readers they were intended to benefit. He explicitly challenged some of the dominant ideas about literary quality, arguing that the children's book world was dominated by a small clique of critical arbiters with elitist ideals. In 1966, he wrote to publisher Anthea Joseph, at Michael Joseph Ltd.:

> I shudder when I think of the folk like Eleanor Graham who rule the children's book world. They are probably delightful folk, but they have ideas about what the young like that are based on knowledge of a certain few. And, I suppose, on their own ideas as children.[25]

Chambers was particularly critical of the standard for quality established by the Carnegie Medal, characterising the winning books as typically 'intellectual, sophisticated, over-written, unremarkable for anything in the slightest "questionable" in thought, word or deed', whose lack of appeal to most children adequately accounted for the phenomenon of the reluctant reader.[26] These criticisms challenged the construction of quality which Kaye Webb had established at Puffin, which was predicated on an idea of quality which would allow parents to provide children with books secure in the knowledge they contained nothing 'questionable'. The implication that 'questionable' material might be a desirable aspect of the best children's literature destabilised the idea of a single, universally accepted construction of quality; as discussed below, 'questionable' books were certainly included in Topliner.

Aidan Chambers challenged the belief that children should always be provided with 'the best' in literary reading. Whatever the virtues of such books, he argued, it was both unfair and unrealistic to hold children's literature to this literary standard:

> There are too many 'educationalists' – as well as parents, maiden aunts librarians and teachers – who always seem to suggest that kids should be reading Dickens or Scott or Ransome or Sutcliffe [sic] while they themselves hide behind their thrillers and third rate biographies. It is precisely this intellectual dishonesty, this double standard that has misled us in children's writing into thinking like Eleanor Graham about 'beautifully produced books of good quality'.[27]

---

[25] Aidan Chambers to Anthea Joseph, 6 May 1966, UoA, Box 110/111 01, Folder: Michael Joseph Ltd. Correspondence.

[26] Aidan Chambers, *The Reluctant Reader*, p. 67.

[27] Aidan Chambers to Barbara Bell, 10 May 1966, UoA, Box 156, Folder: Barbara Bell correspondence, recto.

By adhering to this construction of quality, Chambers argued, children's publishers were creating a gulf between literary reading and the kind of reading that young people actually enjoyed. The Topliner list was therefore predicated on an alternative notion of quality which encompassed its readers' more populist tastes. The importance of books which children enjoyed reading was central to Kaye Webb's editorial ethos; nevertheless, she did consciously exclude material which was popular with child readers if it did not fall within the parameters within which she defined 'quality' literature. By contrast, as this chapter will show, in Topliner Aidan Chambers sought to develop a list which was founded upon the tastes and preferences of its adolescent readers.

As Chambers had pointed out, then as now, many adults enjoyed reading 'thrillers and third rate biographies' rather more than they enjoyed Dickens or Dostoevsky, and teenage 'reluctant' readers were often avid readers of magazines and 'pulp' fiction. He shared Peter Dickinson's belief that reading 'rubbish' like this was not in itself problematic; however, like most of those active in children's literature during this period, Chambers rejected the notion that it was important only that young people should read *something*. Like Peter Dickinson, he presented 'rubbish' reading as a potential grounding for more quality literature. The stark division between 'quality' and 'rubbish', however, presented a barrier to such a transition:

> Reluctant readers know what they like and they find it in the popular magazines. The magazines merely deepen their reluctance to read more solid work. But also the solid work available seems to have little common ground with the fiction they know they like. This is not just a gap, it is a cultural failure.[28]

In order to remedy this perceived cultural failure, Chambers turned to the literature which was typically condemned as 'rubbish'. As a teacher-librarian, he had sought to assist readers in making the transition from popular reading to more demanding fare by allowing students from so-called 'backward' classes to stock the school library with their own favourite reading materials. The inclusion of this familiar material on the shelves formed a basis for developing readers' confidence before they were encouraged to move outwards to the other books in the library.[29] The success of the scheme encouraged Chambers to apply a similar philosophy to Topliner: since teenage magazines were sufficiently appealing not only to be *read* by teenagers, but also to be *bought* by them, he looked to them as a model for a new kind of literature, soliciting a number of books from successful magazine writers. Vicky Martin, whose story 'The Break' he had cited in *The Reluctant Reader* as an example of the 'directness and truthfulness' magazine writers had to offer in writing for teenagers, contributed *September Song* (1969) to the early Topliner list. Philippa Adams, with *Hitch on the Way* (1976) and *Nine Months* (1977), and Maureen Stewart, with *Orange Wendy* (1974), were among the other

---

28 Aidan Chambers, *The Reluctant Reader*, p. 40.
29 Aidan Chambers, *The Reluctant Reader*, p. 113.

Topliner authors who had started their careers in the pages of magazines. The opening passage of *Girl in a Gondola* (1980) – by another magazine alumna, Dianne Doubtfire – illustrates the kind of ingredients which were derived from the magazine genre:

> My mother was still asleep when I woke up on that first fantastic morning in Venice. She was curled up on the other twin bed, her brown hair in rollers, a half smile on her round freckled face. [...]
>
> I looked at my watch. The bedroom shutters were closed behind the flowered curtains but a glimmer of sunlight filtered through the slats. It was twenty to seven. Twenty to six in England, I thought, loving the foreign feel of it.[30]

Aidan Chambers had identified the 'directness and truthfulness' of magazine stories and their capacity for offering the reader wish-fulfilment as key reasons for their popularity among adolescents.[31] The immediacy of Dianne Doubtfire's opening scene reflects these qualities. The reader is quickly situated within the story: in these two paragraphs we are made aware that she is in Venice, that the adventure of a foreign holiday is unusual to her and that she is probably part of a single-parent family. The excitement of the trip to Venice provides an element of wish-fulfilment which is leavened by the fact that the narrator is an 'ordinary' girl with whom the average working-class reader can identify. By the end of the chapter, only two pages later, we have also been introduced to the protagonist's tastes and hobbies, provided with more information about her family situation, and introduced to a potential love interest, who is 'olive-skinned and strikingly handsome'.[32] The economy with which Doubtfire conveys this information shows a clear debt to the short story format of the popular magazine; the fast pace of the story and the swift introduction of several points of interest – a foreign adventure, troubled family circumstances and a new love affair – are obvious strategies to engage the reluctant reader.

In commissioning magazine writers to produce Topliners, Aidan Chambers was not simply seeking to exploit the lucrative commercial potential of the magazine world, but to bridge the gap between magazines and more 'solid' material. Writing to Celia Harcourt, a prospective Topliner author, he emphasised:

> [...] the great difference between Topliners and the magazine stories is that Topliners are novels: they try to probe their themes and characters more deeply than magazine stories on the whole manage to do – or, indeed, I sometimes feel, than their editors or authors want to.[33]

---

[30] Dianne Doubtfire, *Girl in a Gondola* (London: Macmillan, 1980), p. 5.

[31] Aidan Chambers, *The Reluctant Reader*, p. 33.

[32] Dianne Doubtfire, *Girl in a Gondola*, p. 7.

[33] Aidan Chambers to Celia Harcourt, 19 January 1976, UoA, Box 42, Folder: Macmillan Correspondence 1 October 1975 – 25 March 1976.

The idea that magazine stories could provide a basis on which to build readers' ability to tackle more complex work is in keeping with Chambers' early view of teenage literature as a bridge to adult material. By seeking to adopt some of the narrative and stylistic strategies of the popular magazines, however, Chambers was also recognising the literary values of this more populist medium. In practice, Topliners did not always succeed in developing beyond the scope of magazine stories – *Girl in a Gondola* is an exciting and engaging narrative, but it cannot be said to probe its themes and characters in any depth – but in valuing the immediate appeal and accessible reading style of these works they established parameters for quality which were significantly different from those embodied in the Peacock list. The attempt to create a new kind of literature was a feature of Aidan Chambers' work at Topliner which was to become increasingly important as the series progressed.

Books for Teenagers: Creating a New Literature

The genesis of the Topliner list as a strategy for reaching the reluctant reader, and the fact that the list fell under Macmillan's educational publishing division rather than its children's or adult's fiction departments gave it a strong pedagogical focus. As Aidan Chambers' early proposals to Peacock and Macmillan indicate, however, his vision for teenage literature extended beyond the specifically educational. This belief was strengthened as the list developed:

> Very quickly, however, I came to see that teenage literature was not simply about bridging, a kind of literary remedial course. It could do, and should do, what any literature that is whole does: grow to satisfy writers and readers in increasingly multifarious ways, responding to its own history, to other arts, and to the needs of its own time. Topliner readers led me to that recognition: to the possibilities for teenage literature.[34]

While the problem of the reluctant reader had initially highlighted the needs of those adolescents who were unable or unwilling to access the full range of literature for adults, Chambers' assertion that books written for adolescents could constitute 'a literature that is whole' reflects a much broader view. If books written with teenagers in mind could 'grow to satisfy writers and readers in increasingly multifarious ways' then they could also offer something to the teenage reader who was already capable of making the step to Dostoevsky – or even satisfy the adult reader. Topliner represented a first step towards such a literature by providing a publishing venue for authors interested in writing specifically for adolescents. By publishing original novels and actively soliciting authors for the kinds of books required, Aidan Chambers played a significant part in shaping the new genre of books for adolescents; he approached his work at Topliner with the belief that he was 'creating a literature'.[35]

---

[34]   Aidan Chambers, 'Alive and Flourishing: A Personal View of Teenage Literature', p. 88.

[35]   Aidan Chambers, Interview with Lucy Pearson, 27 April 2009.

Born in 1934, 20 years after Kaye Webb, Aidan Chambers was part of a dramatically different generation. Part of the post-war generation, he had benefited from the extension of secondary education instituted by the 1944 Education Act: he attended grammar school from the age of 13 after being identified as a 'late developer'. He was thus part of the new generation for whom childhood was extended by compulsory education. Although too old to be part of the first wave of 'teenage culture' in the late 1950s – a cultural phenomenon which was in any case somewhat removed from his provincial home town Darlington – he did experience it first hand as a young secondary teacher. Crucially, he was connected to the experience of adolescence in a way that Kaye Webb's generation, which had grown up in the shadow of two world wars, were not. As the criticism discussed in Chapter 1 demonstrates, one of the key strands in the discourse surrounding children's literature in the post-war period was the characterisation of childhood as a distinctive and important time. Aidan Chambers was part of a generation which ascribed similar importance to adolescence. Speaking in 1986 about his own experience of writing for teenagers, he stated:

> [...] though I am presently enjoying the pleasures and pains associated with middle age, there is still alive inside me that state of being I experienced as a sixteen-year-old adolescent. I do not simply mean that I remember that time, and look back at it with whatever degree of nostalgia or distaste my present personality dictates. Rather I mean that adolescence still informs me, is still active in me. Just as my childhood is. And I am glad. Indeed, one of the values that distinguishes the best literature of childhood and youth is that it helps maintain and refresh those states within us. That is part of their purpose as literary forms, one of the reasons we need them, whether or not we are professionally involved. Childhood and youth are not the sole possessions of children and adolescents.[36]

The passage is crucial to an understanding of the distinctive approach Aidan Chambers brought to Topliner. Strongly reminiscent of Kaye Webb's evocation of her childhood when discussing her experience of reading books for the Puffin list, it posits adolescence not only as legitimately distinct from childhood and adulthood, but also as possessed of the same kind of inherent value which had been claimed for childhood. The idea that adolescence possessed important and distinctive qualities underpinned the view that books for teenagers could do more than present adult literature in a more easily digested format, and could constitute a literature in their own right.

The legitimate distinctiveness of the teenage years was a key part of Aidan Chambers' ethos in developing the Topliner list. Whereas existing imprints for teenagers culled titles from the children's and adult lists, Topliners were written specifically for adolescents. Many titles were commissioned by Chambers himself, while others were selected from young adult lists overseas; Paul Zindel, one of the

---

[36] Aidan Chambers, 'All of a Tremble to See His Danger', in *Reading Talk* (Stroud: Thimble Press, 2001), 29–50, p. 351.

pioneers of young adult literature in the United States, was one of several American authors published in Topliner. Early promotional blurb for the series stated:

> TOPLINERS are not children's books. They are novels written by authors of quality because they had a story to tell and which they wanted to tell for adolescents, who, perhaps like the authors themselves, find the run-of-the-mill older children's books uninspiring, 'bookish', even dull.[37]

In a period when many critics and writers were still sceptical about the existence of teenage readers as a distinct group, this clear statement that Topliners were *not* children's books is particularly striking. By contrast, Peacocks and Brockhampton's Black Knights described themselves as books for 'older children'. Only Bodley Head, in its New Adult series – launched shortly before Topliner – had unequivocally presented teenage literature as a category distinct from children's literature. The question was of importance not only in establishing the distinctive nature of books aimed at adolescent readers, but also in determining how these books should be marketed and evaluated. Attempts to develop publishing imprints for teenagers often originated in children's departments seeking to retain young readers, as at Peacock. Similarly, teenage literature was reviewed on the children's pages, not among the adult reviews. As the promotional text for Topliner suggests, however, Aidan Chambers sought to resist this trend, attempting to establish teenage books as a body of literature in its own right rather than as a branch of children's literature.

A key reason for the presentation of Topliners as young adult rather than children's books was Aidan Chambers' belief that adolescent readers were keen to escape the limitations of childhood. Growing up in a working-class environment, when he graduated from a secondary modern to a grammar school at the age of 13, he was leaving behind many contemporaries who would enter the world of work only two years later. In seeking to appeal to such readers, Chambers attempted to produce books which more closely resembled adult popular fiction than the books on the children's shelves. Like Kaye Webb, Chambers paid close attention to the design of the books; he commented on one set of jacket illustrations, 'They are much too quiet and are taking us in the direction of the older children's book style of jacket rather than in the direction that the adult paperbacks are going.'[38] The desire to follow trends in the design of adult books reflected Chambers' concern that Topliners should not be identified as children's books. Attempts to capture the appeal of popular magazines were also evident in the design of the series: many Topliner jackets were a deliberate echo of teenage magazines such as *Jackie* and *Petticoat*, using bold designs and photographs rather than illustrations. Although the majority of Kaye Webb's Peacocks had carried illustrated covers,

---

[37]   Aidan Chambers, 'Aidan – Revised blurb suggested for Topliners pamphlet', typescript draft, c. 1968, UoA, Box 110/111 01, Folder: Series publicity.

[38]   Aidan Chambers to Alyn Shipton, 19 December 1977, UoA, Box 110/111 02. Folder: House editor.

Chambers was ready to imitate Webb's successes. The jacket of Joan Tate's *Sam and Me* (1968), one of the first titles in Topliner, was strikingly similar to that used for Beverly Cleary's *Fifteen* in Peacock, which Chambers had singled out in *The Reluctant Reader* as particularly suitable for 'reluctant' teenagers. A plain background framed a close-up shot of a young girl's face, with the title and author in simple black lettering above, and the Topliner colophon discreetly displayed at the top. Later, the framing device was abandoned and jacket illustrations expanded to fill the whole cover.

The jacket of Petronella Breinburg's *Us Boys of Westcroft* (1975) is markedly similar to the teenage titles of today: an extreme close-up of a black boy takes up the whole cover, cropped so that his eyes and mouth dominate the image, while the title of the book is superimposed over his forehead. The lens of his sunglasses reflects a group of three white boys, the tallest of whom looks back with a hostile stance; the impassivity of the black boy's face suggests that he has become inured to the implied racism. The whole effect of the jacket is to suggest a hard-hitting realist narrative, which is precisely what the novel delivers. Designs like these helped to establish a distinctive identity for Topliner, which not only explored new territory in the stories themselves but also stood out on the shelves.

A key reason for Aidan Chambers' determination that books for adolescents should not be classed as part of children's literature was his belief that teenage literature needed the freedom to explore more controversial and adult themes. In according adolescence the same distinctive character which was usually associated with childhood, he established the idea that teenagers also had specific concerns and interests which needed to be addressed in the books they read. Reflecting on the books which had affected him most during his own adolescence, he commented:

> I liked them because they talked about me, or so I thought. And I took note of the extra pleasure I got from the deeper attention I gave to books which connected directly with my current state of being.[39]

The number of books which talked directly about teenage experience had been few in Chambers' youth; the changing state of British society and the degree to which experiences of adolescence in the 1960s and 1970s differed from those of previous generations had widened the gap between literature and life. Topliners were intended to bridge this gap and to engage directly with teenagers' key concerns, which Chambers identified in *The Reluctant Reader* as sex, parents, authority, work and 'the standard problems' – under which he included such heterogeneous issues as drugs, death, shyness, illegitimacy, war and race.[40] The dominance of the 'issues' novel in teenage literature, which drew criticism from figures such as Nina Bawden, was strongly evident in Topliner, which featured many books centred around specific life issues. Petronella Breinburg's *Us Boys of*

---

[39] Aidan Chambers, 'Alive and Flourishing: A Personal View of Teenage Literature', p. 86.

[40] Aidan Chambers, *The Reluctant Reader*, pp. 72–5.

Westcroft dealt with race and racism, Gunnel Beckman's *Nineteen is Too Young to Die* (1971) explored a young girl's reaction to her diagnosis with terminal leukaemia, Anna Greta Winberg's *When Someone Splits* (1978) centred around divorce and Maia Rodman's *Tuned Out* (1976) tackled the issue of drug addiction. These books led the trend in the United Kingdom for the 'problem novel', which flourished during the 1970s and 1980s. The proliferation of such titles on other publishers' lists tells its own story about the popularity of the genre with teenage readers – or at least about adult perceptions of its popularity. Although critics argued that the genre tended to produce what Joan Aiken had termed 'Filboid Studge', several of the novels published in Topliner illustrate the literary potential of books which explored more difficult issues. Despite the heavy-handed title of *Nineteen is Too Young to Die*, a title chosen especially for the Topliner edition – Macmillan simultaneously published an edition under the title *Admission to the Feast*, a direct translation of the book's original Swedish title – the novel is a sensitive and stylistically interesting exploration of a life-changing event.[41] The book is told in the form of a letter from the narrator to her best friend, moving from a stream-of-consciousness account of the girl's initial reaction to her terminal diagnosis to a more considered narrative of the events leading up to it:

> This morning, as I slithered down to the well for water, I saw for the first time this year that half non-existent, that merest shimmer of spring lilac-colour over the birch tops on the island.
>
> It smelt of thaw, wet, fresh. Soon it will be spring, hooray, hooray.
>
> What use are signs of spring to me? Signs of life. I, who am going to die.
>
> Now I've said it. Now at last the pig has got over the stile.[42]

The swing between the poetic and prosaic, the dramatic tone of the revelation 'I, who am going to die' and the use of the homely expression 'the pig has got over the stile', are effective in conveying a sense of realism. The book ends neither with a tragic deathbed scene, nor with serene acceptance of death, but with temporary composure as the narrator awaits her boyfriend, aware that if she cries 'the mascara will run and then I'll be ugly and red-eyed'.[43] The publication of novels like this helped to expand the boundaries for topics covered in books for young people; the success of Jenny Downham's *Before I Die* (2007), shortlisted for the Guardian Children's Fiction Prize in 2008, demonstrates that books on sickness and death still find a ready audience in today's teenage market. As this chapter will explore, however, the realism of some of the books on the Topliner list drew criticism when they appeared.

---

[41]   Gunnel Beckman, *Admission to the Feast* (London: Macmillan, 1971). Thanks to Anne-Li Mell for providing a literal translation of the Swedish title.

[42]   Gunnel Beckman, *Nineteen is Too Young to Die* (London: Macmillan, 1971), p. 13.

[43]   Gunnel Beckman, *Nineteen is Too Young to Die*, p. 109.

Aidan Chambers' attempt to establish books for teenagers as a literature in their own right extended not only to the design and content of the books, but also to their stylistic characteristics. Whereas Peacock and Black Knight had selected titles from the adult and children's lists which they judged to contain themes of interest to adolescents, the majority of the books published in Topliner were original novels written specially for the purpose. In 1967, Chambers approached Stuart Jackman – who wrote thrillers for the adult market – as a possible author for the new list:

> I'm anxious to find writers who have the qualities in their writing which are 'right' for these youngsters; who are professional adult authors, rather than children's authors. And this is, as you can imagine, not easy. I'm sure, judging from your novel, that you have the right qualities as a writer. I'm anxious to use adult authors because I find that children's authors, after a book or two for younger children, are rarely able to use the themes and subjects that one wants for young people's novels in any other voice than one uses for children. And this is fatal in working for kids who want to be adult, don't want to be 'talked down' to; need maturity in the imaginative work they read, and yet can't manage with ease the full adult novel.[44]

The idea that teenage novels demanded a voice distinct from that used in books for children established the possibility that they might constitute a literature with its own stylistic and literary conventions. The importance of voice as one of the defining characteristics of a literature was to become a key element of Aidan Chambers' attempt to develop a critical method for children's literature: as discussed below, his theory of the implied child reader identified the form and style of writing as a means of creating an implicit audience for a book. Topliner authors' attempts to find a voice which did not 'talk down to' teenagers frequently resulted in the literal adoption of a teenage voice: many books on the list followed more general trends in teenage literature in employing first-person narration by teenage characters. Christopher Leach's *Answering Miss Roberts* (1968), which was one of the first batch of six Topliners, is characteristic in its use of an adolescent narrator to produce a simple, direct style. The book is written as a first-person account by a young girl in an Approved School, who is responding to a request from a teacher (the titular Miss Roberts) to write about herself. The opening paragraph is direct and immediate, plunging the reader into the story:

> When we met outside the station I thought you were going to be different. I thought *Well, she's young enough* – and I liked that blue coat and the way you did your hair. You drove well, too. I've always admired people who seem to do things well.[45]

---

[44] Aidan Chambers to Stuart Jackman, 13 February 1967, UoA, Box 110/111 01, Folder: Stuart Jackman.

[45] Christopher Leach, *Answering Miss Roberts* (London: Macmillan, 1968), p. 5.

The strategies intended to appeal to the reluctant adolescent reader are clear. As in Dianne Doubtfire's *Girl in a Gondola,* the immediacy of the narrative is calculated to grab the reader from the outset, rather than risking the loss of attention which might occur during a more descriptive passage. The style, while not strikingly vernacular, is not notably 'literary', and the short sentences demand a limited amount of attention or reading fluency on the part of the reader; it is certainly different from the complex style of the Puffin titles discussed in Chapter 2. The cultural references in this passage are also designed to appeal to the presumed interests and concerns of the 'kid who wants to be adult': the implication that the teenager is misunderstood – 'I thought you were going to be different' – and the focus on clothes and on exclusively adult achievements such as expert driving have much in common with the picture of teenage life present in the pages of popular magazines like *Jackie.* All these characteristics were evident in the portrait of the reluctant teenager which Aidan Chambers had put forward in *The Reluctant Reader,* where he had argued that the success of popular magazines was due to their keen understanding of contemporary teenage concerns. The popularity of *Answering Miss Roberts* indicates that his strategy of transferring such characteristics to the Topliner list was effective: the book was one of the most popular titles on the list, maintaining sales figures of at least 5,000 a year, and achieving sales of over 15,000 in 1973.[46]

The use of a particular style and voice in Topliner helped to establish some of the characteristics for teenage literature as a whole. The direct, autobiographical style of *Answering Miss Roberts* and *Nineteen is Too Young to Die* is reminiscent of J.D. Salinger's *The Catcher in the Rye* (1951), which, although originally published for adults, had been widely read by teenagers and had contributed significantly to the development of young adult literature in the United States. First-person narrative was a characteristic feature of Topliners: Joan Tate's *Sam and Me,* Joan Aiken's *Night Fall* (1969) and John Crompton's *Up the Road and Back* (1977) all employed this device. Although the characteristic was not original to Topliner, Aidan Chambers' selections for Topliner helped to bring these trends into the UK market. The popularity of young adult titles such as Louise Rennison's Georgia Nicholson series (2004–2009) and Jacqueline Wilson's Girls series (1997–2002) demonstrates that first-person narratives are still a key feature of contemporary literature for adolescents.

Diversity in Literature: Class and Race in Topliner

Aidan Chambers' belief that existing literature for adolescents worked to exclude many teenage readers reflects the wider cultural concern with diversity in children's publishing which emerged during the 1960s and 1970s. His accusation

---

[46] Sales figures for *Answering Miss Roberts* in the period 1971–1978 were (year by year): 5,871, 6,843, 15,287, 9,975, 9,472, 6,725, 5,173, 4,941. 'Topliner sales', sales ledger, 1971–1977, UoA, Box 110/111 02, Folder: Topliner: In-Hand Materials.

that Eleanor Graham and other traditional arbiters of quality in children's literature catered only to 'a certain few' was closely allied to the criticisms of the white, middle-class hegemony in British children's publishing by figures such as Bob Dixon and Robert Leeson. In order to establish a successful literature for adolescents, Aidan Chambers argued, it was important to publish more diverse and inclusive books which reflected the lives of ordinary readers.

Aidan Chambers' work at Topliner had an inherent class dimension. The middle-class focus of the Peacock list reflected the background of Kaye Webb and her staff. By contrast, Aidan Chambers had grown up in a working-class environment which placed little emphasis on reading for pleasure. Although his background was far from deprived – his father was a skilled joiner and head of a firm of funeral directors – it was radically different from the literate and literary culture in which Kaye Webb had grown up. He recalled that 'You could count the books in our house on one hand' – a situation which was the norm in most working-class households in the post-war period.[47] Although he became a habitual reader from the age of about 10, it was the experience of reading D.H. Lawrence's *Son's and Lovers* (1913) at the age of 16 which established literature as something relevant and meaningful to his life:

> The reason is simple. This was the first time I had read a book about myself. Till then I had thought literature was about other people. Everything that Jim Osborn [his English teacher at grammar school] had revealed fell into place. Books, literature, reading were about what happened to me, and what happened to me made a kind of sense when discovered in writing that it didn't otherwise. My own life was suddenly as alive as the life on the pages that held my mind. And it was all done with words in bookprint.[48]

The appeal of *Sons and Lovers* to a boy from a Northern provincial town whose educational experience was moving him from his working-class background into a more middle-class milieu is obvious. The experience of recognising his own life in a book allowed Chambers a more personal relationship with reading: he recollects, 'I found myself, my own culture, my own kind, my own way of living and I made that equation – until you find yourself written, you don't exist, and you're not so keen to read the literature written for another kind of person'.[49] Chambers' belief that a series like Topliner could help readers make the transition 'from Blyton to Dostoevsky' reflects the effect of this experience on his own reading: the effect of relating literature to his own experience helped Chambers to appreciate the possibilities of literature as a whole, enabling him to access books which depicted ideas and emotions outside his own experience. He sought to offer adolescent readers a comparable experience through the Topliner list, publishing books which depicted a diverse range of lives. Joan Tate's *Whizz Kid* (1969) and *Clipper* (1969)

---

47   Aidan Chambers, 'Pick Up a Penguin' in *Reading Talk*, 99–113, p. 99.
48   Aidan Chambers, 'Pick Up a Penguin', p. 111.
49   Aidan Chambers, Interview with Lucy Pearson, 27 April 2009.

depicted urban British working-class life, Robert Lipsyte's *The Contender* (1967; Topliner edition 1969) explored the streets of Harlem, Reginald Maddock's *The Pit* (1966; Topliner edition 1972) dealt with life in a Northern mining community and Max Lundgren's *Summer Girl* (1976, translated from the Swedish by Joan Tate) told the story of a deprived inner-city teenager sent as a 'holiday child' to a middle-class couple in the country. Middle-class characters were not excluded from the list, and titles such as Joan Aiken's thriller *Night Fall* (1969) offered wish fulfilment stories about the lives of the wealthy upper-classes; however, the predominance of stories about working-class characters reflects Chambers' desire to cater for readers who were excluded by the middle-class literary canon.

The attempt to create a more inclusive literature in the Topliner list was not restricted to the question of class. Figures such as Rosemary Stones and Janet Hill had criticised the ethnocentric character of British children's literature; the discourse explored in Chapter 1 demonstrates that the need for more representative portrayals of Britain's non-white communities was a growing concern during the 1970s. Aidan Chambers' work at Topliner is particularly notable for his efforts to include more books by and about people of colour, and to tackle themes such as racism and cultural difference directly. The list had a conscious policy of encouraging writers of colour:

> We didn't have a lot of success: it was difficult because finding the black writers who were able to write the kind of book we were looking for was hard to come by. [...] And we didn't have a lot of contact with black teachers working in schools who were writers, or black writers who were [just] writers. But we kept on looking.[50]

Although the difficulty of finding suitable writers meant that there were relatively few writers of colour on the Topliner list, there were some notable titles. Petronella Breinburg, who had already become known for the picture book *My Brother Sean* (1973), explored racism in contemporary Britain in *Us Boys of Westcroft*. The book depicts racism as part of a broader dialogue of power which is not purely about ethnicity. The Westcroft of the title is Walter's school, where the richest and best educated students are referred to as 'lads', while the poorer and least academically accomplished students are dismissively characterised as 'boys'. Walter's allegiance to the 'boys' forms an uneasy dialogue with his ethnic identity; when a black teacher joins the school, she offers the 'boys' more respect, but their response to her forces Walter to become complicit in racism:

> Perhaps my heart thumped a bit too loud because the others were looking at me without looking, if you see what I mean. If that Da Sousa woman is black and I was black it may fall to me to take her on. Just for a joke of course. They'd expect me to do all the things she forbade me to do.[51]

---

[50]   Aidan Chambers, Interview with Lucy Pearson, 27 April 2009.

[51]   Petronella Breinburg, *Us Boys of Westcroft* (London: Macmillan, 1975), p. 83.

The difficulties Walter faces in negotiating his identity reveal a more complex picture of race in Britain than was offered by books such as Bernard Ashley's *The Trouble With Donovan Croft*: rather than condemning racism as the preserve of the ignorant and the malevolent, it presents it as embedded in the social structures of society, a message which retains relevance today. The book also broke new ground in its attempt to represent black British vernacular more authentically, although Chambers standardised much of the language because of concerns about confusing readers – a decision he was later to regret.[52] The book's uncompromising depiction of racist attitudes – including the use of the word 'nigger' and references to Irish characters as 'bloody IRA' – and the representation of violence and abuse as part of the day-to-day experience of young people made the book controversial, but also gave it a realism which made it popular among young readers. Petronella Breinburg wrote to Aidan Chambers:

> "Us boys..." – one of the schools I have visited for my data collecting is Vauxhall girls. There "Us boys..." is top of the top ten in the library. I had crowd [sic] of girls, shooting questions – why isn't there any more books like "Us boys. [sic] Why don't I write one about a black girl .... I'm afraid I had to tell the truth that I do write them but can not get them published.[53]

The limitations of Breinburg's writing provide some explanation for Chambers' reluctance to accept subsequent titles from her – reviewer Geoff Fox described *Us Boys* as 'unconvincing' – but the positive reception she encountered among readers of colour demonstrates the importance of the book.[54] Despite its flaws, *Us Boys of Westcroft* was a bold attempt to provide a realistic treatment of race in Britain.

Farrukh Dhondy's *East End At Your Feet* (1976), published a year after *Us Boys of Westcroft*, is significant not only in the context of Chambers' attempt to publish more writers of colour on the Topliner list, but also for its impact on British children's literature as a whole. A Topliner original, the book was commissioned by in-house editor Martin Pick, who was responsible for the in-house production of the list.[55] Indian-born Dhondy, who was working as a teacher, had begun to make a name as an activist and journalist, but had not published any fiction

---

[52] Aidan Chambers, Interview with Lucy Pearson, 27 April 2009.

[53] Petronella Breinburg to Aidan Chambers, 21 February 1979, UoA, Box 110/111 02, Folder: Petronella Breinburg.

[54] Geoff Fox, 'Where the Kids Are', *Times Educational Supplement*, 6 February 1976, UoA, Box 42 – Woodchester Post Office, Folder: Macmillan Correspondence 1 October 1975–25 March 1976.

Aidan Chambers identifies some of the faults in *Us Boys of Westcroft* as a result of his heavy-handed editing. Nevertheless, the book represented some of the possibilities inherent in publishing works by writers of colour rather than their apogee.

[55] Archival evidence suggests that Martin Pick was generally in sympathy with Chambers' ideas, but apart from this instance there is little evidence of his direct involvement in commissioning titles; he seems in general to have been responsible for ensuring that the list remained in line with Macmillan's general policies.

prior to being approached by Pick, who had 'heard [his] reputation as some kind of Black politico'.[56] The result was a collection of short stories portraying life in the ethnically diverse East End of London. The book received far more critical attention than the majority of Topliners; John Rowe Townsend praised its 'wry humour and sympathy, not the shrill note associated with race relations campaigners' – a somewhat dismissive comment which reveals something about the ideological context of the period – and author and critic David Rees praised the book for its honest representation of racial diversity.[57] The decision to commission a book from a 'politico' like Farrukh Dhondy indicates the socially progressive ideology which underpinned Topliner, and which was consonant with the concerns of other groups active in children's literature during the 1970s. The Children's Rights Workshop, which campaigned for the elimination of racism and sexism in children's books, awarded *East End At Your Feet* the Other Award in 1977. The book's honest and engaging depiction of British Indian lives admirably fulfilled the award's criteria for titles which showed 'the variety and richness of all those other worlds whose existence and validity were not being acknowledged in books'.[58] The stories' themes remain fresh and relevant today: 'Pushy's Pimples' revolves around a teenage girl's embarrassment over her acne, which her friend assures her can be cured if she has sex. The story uses the tension created by the question of whether Pushpa will attempt this suggested 'cure' to explore the conflict between her Indian and British identities, which are given equal weight in the narrative. From the opening words of the story, Dhondy makes the reader aware of the complexity involved in these combined identities:

> Samir and Pushpa sometimes called their father 'Daddy', and they sometimes called him '*Pitaji*' according to Indian custom. It depended on his mood. If he was angry, or lecturing them about how Indian girls and Indian boys should behave or not behave, how they could so easily spoil his good name in the town, then they said 'Yes, *Pitaji*', 'No *Pitaji*'. [...] They knew he preferred the English word, especially in front of white customers in the shop. His face would compose itself in pride when he was called 'Daddy', especially if it was Pushpa. He would ask her to get the extra bottle of milk from the fridge in back for a late and regular customer and his eyes would shine with pride when she replied in her London accent.[59]

---

[56]   Farrukh Dhondy, quoted in Pat Triggs, 'Authorgraph No. 4', *Books For Keeps*, 4 (September 1980), <http://www.booksforkeeps.co.uk/issue/4/childrens-books/articles/authorgraph/authorgraph-no4-farrukh-dhondy> [accessed 12/01/10].

[57]   John Rowe Townsend, *Written For Children: An Outline of English-language Children's Literature* (Harmondsworth: Kestrel, 1983), p. 337; David Rees, 'Skin Colour in British Children's Books', *Children's Literature in Education*, 11:2 (June 1980), 91–7.

[58]   Rosemary Stones, '13 Other Years: The Other Award 1975–1987', *Books For Keeps*, 53 (November 1988), <http://www.booksforkeeps.co.uk/issue/53/childrens-books/articles/other-articles/awards> [accessed 12/01/10].

[59]   Farrukh Dhondy, 'Pushy's Pimples' in *East End At Your Feet* (London: Macmillan, 1976), 31–45, p. 31.

The conflict between Indian custom and English ways is not simplified as a generational one: Pushpa's father is shown to share his daughter's pride in her English identity, while maintaining the desire for her to behave like an Indian girl. When his children address him as '*Pitaji*' it functions simultaneously as a mark of respect and as a rebuke – a reminder that he is being 'too Indian'. The freshness of Dhondy's writing and the skill with which he uses the short story form to engage readers epitomises the values which underpinned Topliner: the book is accessible, enjoyable and thought-provoking. The enduring appeal of *East End At Your Feet*, which is still in print today, illustrates that at least in this instance Topliner had succeeded in eliciting a viable teenage literature.

East End At Your Feet and Dhondy's second Topliner, *The Siege of Babylon* (1978), used the vernacular English of immigrant communities they portrayed, as well as words from characters' native languages, and referred to the dress and foods of these communities without explanation. In *The Siege of Babylon*, Farrukh Dhondy addressed the political implications of these features, reflecting 'Language was identity. [...] Identity was power.'[60] Aidan Chambers' editorial approach to Dhondy's work reflects his growing acceptance of this position; whereas he had made significant edits to Petronella Breinburg's non-standard English, he fought to preserve Dhondy's use of Indian vocabulary and vernacular English. Chambers rejected the suggestion that a glossary be included with *Siege of Babylon* on the grounds that the context made the meaning of unfamiliar words clear, commenting, 'there is something more than a little condescending and patronising to reader, writer and black English people in glossing language in our own tongue and used in our own society!'[61] This had important implications, both literary and political: in positioning non-standard English as part of 'our own tongue and [...] our own society', Chambers was working to legitimise the position of immigrant communities and broadening the parameters of quality in literature. The fact that a glossary was considered at all is indicative of the extent to which books like Dhondy's were breaking new ground: by championing authors like Farrukh Dhondy, Topliner made a significant contribution to a more diverse literature.

Pushing the Boundaries: Controversial Content

The portrayal of working-class and ethnic minority communities in Topliner pushed at the boundaries of children's literature both in terms of language and content. The social realism of the list entailed more adult content than had traditionally been admitted into children's literature, particularly in relation to topics such as racism, sex and drugs. This reflected the more general move towards more realistic and darker themes in children's literature during the 1960s and 1970s, but

---

[60]   Farrukh Dhondy, *The Siege of Babylon* (London: Macmillan, 1978), p. 37.
[61]   Aidan Chambers, memo to Alyn Shipton, 2 January 1978, UoA, Box 110/111 02, Folder: House editor.

it was also an integral part of Aidan Chambers' construction of teenage literature. The need for teenage literature to address content which might be considered too controversial for children was a key factor in his belief that publishers needed independent teenage departments:

> Until there is a separate publishing department which makes it clear to everyone in the professional book business that these books are meant for adolescents, will be all right for adults but not for children to read, then there is no real hope that we can achieve the artistic freedom needed.[62]

The idea that teenage publishing should be totally removed from children's publishing was a radical break with the existing publishing model, and Chambers was unsuccessful in achieving it. Topliner fell partly under the aegis of Marni Hodgkin, Macmillan's children's editor, an arrangement which has persisted in the majority of British teenage imprints. In practice, however, archival evidence reveals that Hodgkin exerted little influence over editorial decisions at Topliner, which was an imprint of Macmillan Education rather than an offshoot of Macmillan's children's department. The educational focus of the imprint worked to circumscribe some of the artistic freedom Chambers had sought, since the majority of Topliner sales were to schools and the books were often used as class readers. Following the series of complaints about 'questionable' content and language in Topliner, Macmillan instituted a set of in-house guidelines intended to govern the content of Topliners. In-house editor Martin Pick stated:

> It is important for ME [Macmillan Education] that AC gradually develops a Macmillan view, rather than one which represents him only. Otherwise I am sure that there will be continuing tests of strength over what is considered acceptable.[63]

The reference to 'tests of strength' is indicative of the fact that Chambers was prepared to champion potentially controversial material in the face of opposition both within Macmillan and beyond. Archival evidence suggests, however, that in practice the limits placed on him by Macmillan were relatively few; an impression borne out by his own account. *Up the Road and Back* (1977), one of the most controversial titles on the list, was championed by Martin Pick, who stated: 'It is just the sort of book I think we should be publishing in Topliners; it shows a personality growing and changing through exposure to other people and their feelings'.[64] Despite the need to conform to commercial pressures, Macmillan were willing to support Aidan Chambers in pushing at the boundaries of acceptable content in publishing for young people.

---

[62]   Aidan Chambers, *The Reluctant Reader*, p. 141.

[63]   Martin Pick memo to Michael Wace, 11 April 1977, UoA, Box 110/111 02, Folder: Topliner: in-hand materials, f 3. Unfortunately, it was not possible to obtain a copy of the guidelines developed to represent the 'Macmillan view'.

[64]   Martin Pick to John Crompton, 17 February, 1976, UoA, Box 42, Folder: Macmillan Correspondence 1 October 1975–25 March 1976.

A key aspect of Aidan Chambers' commitment to creating a more inclusive literature in the Topliner list was the inclusion of books which addressed the social and ethnic diversity of Britain in the 1960s and 1970s. The work of Petronella Breinburg and Farrukh Dhondy illustrates the ways in which realistic books by and about characters of colour challenged the boundaries of content and language in literature for young people. Attempts to tackle the issue of racism and to reflect experiences of race risked potential for criticism both from those who felt that 'too much' realism was potentially damaging to young readers, and from those who feared that realistic portrayals of racism ran the risk of perpetuating racist attitudes. Joan Tate's *Clipper*, in which a young couple from a provincial town move to the West End of London, is characteristic of the conflict inherent in presenting a realistic picture of their experiences. The racial diversity of the tenants in their new home is new to Nibs and Clee, and their reactions to their neighbours are friendly but undoubtedly racist:

> It was Moses, standing there just as he had on Saturday night, holding out a 5p bit, a towel over his arm this time.
>
> 'O.K. if I have it [a bath] now?'
>
> His face was expressionless, shiny and brown, his eyes restless. He looked down at me. He had to, as he was about six foot two or three.
>
> [...] I looked at Nibs.
>
> 'Do you think he comes every night?'
>
> 'Must be trying to wash himself white,' said Nibs.[65]

The passage clearly contains racism, not only in Nibs's reaction, but also in the othering of Moses through the description of him as 'expressionless [...] restless'. Nevertheless, it is a realistic portrayal of the assumptions and reactions of a young 1960s couple with no experience of people of colour, and the book as a whole sees Nibs and Clee come to recognise their neighbours as people rather than as the other: it closes with their decision to stay in the house with their friends rather than move to a better – and whiter – neighbourhood. The passage quoted, however, comes from a revised edition of the book published in 1976: Jessica Yates notes that the difficulty inherent in portraying Nibs's and Clee's racist attitudes prompted Macmillan to cut some of the material which appeared in the 1969 edition of *Clipper*.[66] Although Aidan Chambers was prepared to challenge accepted standards of content in children's literature, the changing sensibility of the 1970s made the representation of racist attitudes more problematic.

---

[65]   Joan Tate, *Clipper*, rev. edn (London: Macmillan, 1976), p. 68.

[66]   Jessica Yates, 'Censorship in Children's Paperbacks', *Children's Literature in Education*, 11:4 (December 1980), 180–91, p. 186. Unfortunately it was not possible to obtain a copy of the 1969 edition of *Clipper* for the purpose of comparison.

Us Boys of Westcroft, the first title in Topliner to tackle race from the perspective of a writer of colour, was also the most controversial title to appear on the Topliner list. Aidan Chambers recalls:

> I was attacked in the House of Commons. The then–Conservative MP for South Derbyshire said he'd come across this book, which was purported to be published by a firm run by an ex–Prime Minister of Britain, one of the most distinguished publishing houses in the world and that he could not believe such a book would be published by that firm. That it contained language that was quite disgraceful. Now, of course, it wasn't about that at all […] It was because it was about black kids.[67]

Chambers' account of events is a little unreliable, but it is undoubtedly true that the book provoked more intense criticism than the levels of explicit content would seem to merit.[68] Archival material shows that there was a surge in the number of complaints about Topliner following the publicity about the book in 1977. One correspondent wrote:

> I read in the 'Yorkshire Post' of 10th November the comments of a Derbyshire M.P. on a Macmillan school publication: 'Us Boys of Westcroft'. […] I make no comment about the book itself, which I have before me, but it seems to me that Mr. Chambers has an elastic view of 'teenage adulthood'.[69]

Despite such criticisms, *Us Boys of Westcroft* remained in print. Aidan Chambers' account suggests that his defence of the book was supported by Macmillan as a whole: after the press coverage brought it to the attention of Harold Macmillan, who responded with a memo expressing his personal distaste for the book but saying he was sure that the editors knew what they were doing.[70] The support within the firm itself suggests that Aidan Chambers had succeeded in establishing some of the artistic freedom he had sought for teenage literature.

One of the most frequent reasons for complaint about Topliner was the inclusion of 'bad' language. The non-standard English used in *Us Boys of Westcroft* was a target for critics, despite the degree to which Aidan Chambers had standardised Petronella Breinburg's attempt to represent black vernacular. The attempt to provide more realistic books demanded the inclusion of both vernacular English and of offensive language, both issues which sat uneasily with the schools market which Topliner served. One head teacher wrote to complain about Christine Dickenson's *Last Straw* (1975):

---

[67]   Aidan Chambers, Interview with Lucy Pearson, 27 April 2009.

[68]   The precise details of the event are unclear: no record appears in Hansard, and so it seems likely that the comments which appeared in the Yorkshire Post were not delivered in the House of Commons. However, it is clear that an MP did publicly criticise the book.

[69]   D. Hartley to Macmillan Topliner, 13 November 1977, UoA, Box 110/111 02, Folder: House Editor.

[70]   Harold Macmillan, quoted by Aidan Chambers, Interview with Lucy Pearson, 27 April 2009.

One of our greatest problems is to teach girls to express themselves in acceptable English when they wish to be forceful. They – and we – know the unacceptable words, unacceptable by our standards and by the standards of their parents. I have a duty to parents and children to offer them the best.[71]

The reference to offering children 'the best' indicates that the material included in Topliner fell outside accepted parameters of quality in literature for young people. The complainant returned the book to the supplier: by pushing at the boundaries of acceptable content in Topliner, Macmillan risked losing sales. The same outcome resulted after a school librarian received complaints from students about 'rude' books: she cancelled her standing order for the series, stating:

Until recently I had found Topliners to be an excellent source of material for the reluctant reader in the senior school but I am afraid I no longer find it possible to trust your recommendation.[72]

House Editor Alyn Shipton's rueful note to Aidan Chambers that 'there is another of those letters from a book buying teacher, complaining about the low moral standard of Topliners', indicates that such criticisms were not unusual.[73]

Aidan Chambers argued in *The Reluctant Reader* that sex and relationships were at the forefront of teenage concerns, and this belief is reflected in the number of books centring around romance and relationships. While many of these titles remained in the same innocent territory explored by Beverly Cleary in *Fifteen*, Chambers' willingness to push at the boundaries of what was deemed acceptable is also evident in the inclusion of more explicit material. John Crompton's *Up the Road and Back* followed the adventures of an adolescent boy hitch-hiking from south-east England to Scotland. At the heart of the novel is his sexual coming-of-age: before he sets off on his journey he states, 'I had great ideas of having it with some willing girl or other and coming back all ready to do it with Patsy', but although by the end of the book he has had a number of sexual adventures, his emotional development is more complex than either he or the reader expects.[74] The book is in fact far less explicit than Barry Hines's *The Blinder*, which had provoked controversy when it appeared in Peacock, but whereas Kaye Webb took the decision to withdraw Hines's book from Peacock, Macmillan responded to the complaints by adding warnings of controversial content in the Topliner catalogue. A note on the catalogue for 1978 states: 'The story and idiom of **Up the Road and Back** are such we recommend all teachers to read the book before giving it

---

[71] J.M. Pennington, Headmistress of Wheatley High School for Girls, Doncaster, to Martin Pick, 9 January 1976, UoA, Box 42, Folder: Macmillan Correspondence 1 October 1975–25 March 1976.

[72] Mrs. R. Young, Librarian of Wodensborough High School, to Macmillan Education, 15 November 1977, UoA, Box 110/111 02, Folder: House editor.

[73] Alyn Shipton to Aidan Chambers, 17 January 1978, UoA, Box 110/111 02, Folder: House editor.

[74] John Crompton, *Up the Road and Back* (London: Macmillan, 1977), pp. 7–8.

to their pupils'.[75] This approach reflects a belief that offering 'the best' in reading for teenagers meant providing more information about the books available, rather than limiting all titles to a prescribed range of content.

Less controversial than *Up the Road and Back*, but perhaps more ideologically groundbreaking, was Max Lungren's *Summer Girl*, published in Topliner a year after the publication of Judy Blume's controversial title *Forever* (1975) in the United States. While Blume's book was widely regarded as groundbreaking, Roberta Seelinger Trites has argued that it operates within significant ideological constraints, reiterating a patriarchal discourse which characterises 'good' women as vulnerable, sexually inexperienced and chaste.[76] By contrast, *Summer Girl* depicts its protagonist Evy as the more experienced partner, in a tender scene which conveys the emotional component of sex whilst unabashedly acknowledging the role of physical pleasure:

> It wasn't particularly good for me, but I wasn't miserable. Janne wasn't like all the others. He didn't get up and walk round as if he had committed the greatest heroic deed in the world (and neither had he, of course). And neither did he turn over and begin snoring. […] So we made love again and I cried nearly all the time. And it wasn't because of my body, as it felt really good now, and I helped Janne, and he learnt in a flash; it wasn't that. It was something completely different.[77]

Evy's sexual activity transgresses the boundaries defined by Judy Blume as necessary to a 'healthy' sexual relationship. Aged 14, she is below the age of consent both in Britain and in Sweden, where the book is set, and has had a number of loveless sexual encounters. Although the book clearly presents her sexual history as unhappy, Evy is neither condemned nor depicted as unable to enjoy a meaningful relationship. On the contrary, her previous experience arguably enables her to experience more pleasure with Janne, since she is able to 'help' him understand how to make sex feel really good. Furthermore, Evy's matter-of-fact attitude to sex – not the 'greatest heroic deed in the world' – moves the book away from the emphasis on virginity which contributes to the inadvertent reinforcement of negative attitudes to sexuality in *Forever*. This depiction of teenage sexuality reflects the more liberal attitudes of its Swedish author, but its publication in Topliner also reflects Aidan Chambers' desire to reflect more liberal ways of thinking in British teenage literature. By including not only explicit material by British authors, but also books which reflected the mores of countries elsewhere in Europe, Chambers established broader parameters for teenage literature than had been present in books for children.

---

[75] 'Topliner: 10th Anniversary: 1978–79 Illustrated Catalogue', UoA, Box 110/111 02, Folder: Topliner: in-hand materials, p. 3.

[76] Roberta Seelinger Trites, *Disturbing the Universe: Power and Repression in Adolescent Literature* (Iowa City: University of Iowa Press, 2000), pp. 88–92.

[77] Max Lundgren, *Summer Girl*, trans. Joan Tate (London: Macmillan, 1976), pp. 107–8.

A defining characteristic of Aidan Chambers' approach to teenage literature was his belief that offering 'the best' in books for young people was incompatible with the aim of policing the content of adolescents' reading. Kaye Webb had adhered to a view of children's publishing which positioned the publisher and editor in loco parentis and had removed controversial titles such as *The Blinder* from the Peacock list in order to maintain Puffin's reputation as a trustworthy arbiter of content. This role was one which Aidan Chambers explicitly rejected for Topliner. He responded to the complaint about 'rude' books on the list:

> You seem to think we are 'recommending' Topliners. In one sense we are, of course. We are publishing books we feel valuable to young readers, and especially those young readers who are not keen fiction readers. (The hundreds of letters we receive every year from Topliner readers suggests we have succeeded modestly in this aim.) But we have always made it clear that we respect the teacher's decision about which of the titles we publish shall be bought, and expect that teachers, especially school librarians, will make the choice after considering the books. This is why we offer the standing order and inspection copy services. Only the teacher concerned can know precisely the requirements of a school.[78]

The emphasis on the role of teachers in assessing the suitability of the books was evident in the decision to flag controversial titles in the Topliner catalogue. While this attitude shifted responsibility from the publisher to the school rather than unequivocally asserting teenagers' ability to make their own judgements about literary material, it also undermined the notion of a universally agreed standard for 'the best' literature. Chambers' insistence that Topliner were not 'recommending' the books for all readers positions acceptable content as subjective rather than objective, depending on the school and the individual – and, by implication, on the relative liberality of the teacher or librarian. This was a conscious rejection of the editorial model practised by Kaye Webb, in which she assumed personal responsibility for a presumed standard of objective quality. Topliner positioned teenage literature outside the safe space of children's literature, emphasising the responsibility of the individual reader.

Talkback: Aidan Chambers and the Reading Community

The educational sales model of Topliner made it inevitable that the list should be constrained by the needs and perspectives of the teachers and librarians who were responsible for buying most of the books. In seeking to develop a list based on teenagers' own reading preferences, however, Aidan Chambers was positioning the critical responses of adolescents themselves as legitimate and valuable. One of the hallmarks of Kaye Webb's success as editor of Puffin was her ability to respond to children's tastes and her success at reaching out to real child readers

---

[78]   Aidan Chambers to Mrs. R. Young, Librarian of Wodensborough High School, Wednesbury, 22 November 1977, UoA, Box 110/111 02, Folder: House editor, recto.

through the Puffin Club and *Puffin Post*. Aidan Chambers sought to adopt similar strategies with adolescent readers in Topliner.

Kaye Webb had founded the Puffin Club in order to provide a venue through which children could contact her and the authors and illustrators published in Puffin. Aidan Chambers attempted to achieve some of the same dialogue. Topliners carried a note in the back stating:

> The editor of Topliners is always pleased to hear what readers think of the books and to receive ideas for new titles. If you want to write to him please address your letter to: The Editor, Topliners [...] All letters received will be answered.[79]

Many teenagers did so, both on their own behalf and at the instigation of their teachers (a practice Chambers regarded rather ruefully). Reading and responding to their letters was one of Aidan Chambers' central concerns as editor; he commented:

> Writing letters to editors and readers is never a waste of time. That's why we encourage Topliner readers to send their comments to us, and why we take what they say seriously, making it a rule to answer every letter that reaches us, despite the chore it can be on an off day and despite too the high cost of postage nowadays.[80]

The practice of responding personally to every letter received helped to create some of the sense of community which Kaye Webb had created through the Puffin Club. The prevalence of original titles in the Topliner list also meant that Aidan Chambers was able to utilise comments about the books themselves more directly than could Kaye Webb: many of the extant letters are annotated in his hand, noting particular elements which might be fed back into the process of selecting and commissioning Topliners. Such letters helped to develop Chambers' ideas about what teenage readers could and would read, expanding his sense of the possibilities for teenage literature. On one letter he noted 'like unconventional narrative styles', an observation which had a discernible impact on his own writing for teenagers, which is highly experimental in form.[81]

As Chapter 2 has shown, through the *Puffin Post* Kaye Webb had not only opened up a means of communication with child readers, but also endeavoured to develop children's creativity and engagement with literature. Aidan Chambers attempted to achieve the same end with adolescent readers, arguing that a magazine for Topliner directly modelled on the *Puffin Post* had 'all kinds of possibilities,

---

[79] Promotional note in Joan Tate, *Sam and Me* (London: Macmillan, 1969), p. 96.

[80] Aidan Chambers, 'From Blyton to Doetovsky [sic]', typescript draft of article, 1975, UoA, Box 155, Folder: Topliner Readers' Letters.

[81] Aidan Chambers, annotation on a letter from Juliet Galliford to the Editor of Topliner, 1979, UoA, Box 155 – Aidan's correspondence, Folder: Readers' letters.

Maria Nikolajeva identifies Aidan Chambers as one of a number of modern writers pushing the boundaries of children's literature. (Maria Nikolajeva, 'Exit Children's Literature?', *The Lion and the Unicorn*, 22:2 (1998), 221–36.)

stretching beyond mere publicity and amusement'.[82] *Topliner Talkback* was advertised in the back of Topliners:

> Hey, how's about hearing the latest news about TOPLINERS? Reading letters, stories and poems you've sent us? Reading authors writing about themselves? Joining in jokes, competitions and Trailers?
>
> That's what TALKBACK is all about. We want you to talk back to us, and to talk back to each other.[83]

The somewhat awkward nature of this promotional text demonstrates that Chambers did not share Kaye Webb's gift for appealing marketing, but *Talkback* was an attempt to create the kind of reading community she had achieved through the Puffin Club, encouraging readers to talk about books as well as consuming them. The magazine was distributed through schools and supplied directly by mail to readers who requested it; the egalitarian ethos of Topliner as a whole is reflected in the fact that there was no subscription cost.

Talkback had a specific educational focus as well as a promotional one. In his proposal for the idea, Chambers argued:

> We would need to be able to use the magazine methods in an attempt from time to time to engage the young reader's interest in a subject he might not normally look at once, never mind twice. And because teachers would be crucially important to both the sale and the use made of the magazines their attitudes have to be taken into account, and their needs too. It might, therefore, be important to produce a 'teachers' guide' to each issue, an inexpensive booklet which explores the educational intention behind each article and the possibilities the editors have in mind for its use by teachers: suggestions for follow-up work, etc.[84]

The concept of the magazine as a teaching aid was partly a consequence of Topliner's position as an imprint of Macmillan Education: the chances of the firm funding the venture were higher if it could be presented as catering to their core market. However, it also fitted well with Aidan Chambers' central belief in Topliner as a means of bridging the gap between popular reading material and the full world of literary endeavour. As in the books themselves, he sought to build upon the popularity of popular magazines to lead readers towards material they would otherwise have ignored. In the Puffin Club, Kaye Webb had attempted to recreate some of the benefit she had enjoyed growing up in a literate environment; Aidan Chambers' experiences both as a reader and as an educationalist made him even more alive to the importance of a community which could help young people

---

[82] Aidan Chambers, 'A proposal for a TOPLINER MAGAZINE', 9 March 1973, UoA, Box 42, Folder: Topliners, f. 1.

[83] Promotional note in Joan Tate, *Clipper*, p. 125.

[84] Aidan Chambers, 'A proposal for a TOPLINER MAGAZINE', 9 March 1973, UoA, Box 42, Folder: Topliners, f. 5.

develop an appreciation of reading. His emphasis on the importance of the reading environment was to increase later in his career; reflecting on his own development as a 'literary' reader in *Tell Me: Children, Reading and Talk* (1993) he wrote: 'a certain kind of booktalk gave us the information we needed, the energy, the impetus, the will to explore beyond our familiar boundaries'.[85] *Talkback* demonstrates an attempt to provide this energy and impetus from a publishing perspective. Although Aidan Chambers' editorial ethos differed significantly from that of Kaye Webb, therefore, he shared with her a belief in the social and educational role of publishers.

Theorising Reading: The Reader in the Book

Aidan Chambers' decision to challenge the established boundaries of style and content in the Topliner list was part of an overtly ideological approach to the creation of teenage literature. The political and theoretical basis on which his editorial policies were based reflects a markedly more academic outlook on children's literature than was evident in Kaye Webb's work at Puffin: whereas Webb presented her response to children's literature as intuitive and unscholarly, Aidan Chambers sought to position children's books within a literary critical context. Kaye Webb's intuitive approach placed less emphasis on the social and ideological qualities of the books she published; Chambers' belief that the dominant ideologies inherent in much of the 'best' children's literature worked to exclude many readers demanded a more consciously analytical approach. By applying the work of critical theorists from the world of adult literature, Aidan Chambers also claimed greater cultural legitimacy for children's and young adult literature. This strategy is evident in his seminal 1977 essay 'The Reader in the Book', in which he employed the theories of Wolfgang Iser and Wayne C. Booth to establish a reader-response theory of children's literature.[86] Although the essay does not deal explicitly with teenage literature, it was developed during the period in which he was working closely on Topliner and on his own novels for adolescents, and the ideas he explores in his critical work correspond with some important aspects of his editorial work.[87]

The social and ideological focus of the Topliner list was part of a broader cultural move towards attempting to engage with real children through children's literature.

---

[85]   Aidan Chambers, *Tell Me: Children, Reading and Talk*, p. 14.

[86]   Aidan Chambers, first published as 'The Reader in the Book: Notes From Work in Progress', *Signal Approaches to Children's Books*, 23 (May 1977), 64–87. Reprinted as 'The Reader in the Book' in Aidan Chambers, *Booktalk: Occasional Writing onLliterature and Children*, 34–58. Further citations relate to the latter.

[87]   As Peter Hunt has noted, Aidan Chambers has refined his theoretical framework since, and his own work as a writer of young adult literature demonstrates a much more nuanced attempt to engage with some of the issues originally explored in 'The Reader in the Book'. (Peter Hunt, *Children's Literature: The Development of Criticism*, ed. by Peter Hunt (London: Routledge, 1993), p. 90.)

Chambers' attempt to reach out to the readers of Topliner through letters and *Talkback* magazine, and his desire to build a list which reflected the tastes and preferences of real adolescents, reflected a growing critical engagement with young people's responses to literature. As discussed in Chapter 1, however, the practice of using real or imagined children as a basis for assessing children's books was criticised by figures such as Brian Alderson. Alderson argued:

> It may be objected that to assess children's books without reference to children is to direct some absolute critical standard relating neither to the author's purpose nor to the reader's enjoyment. To do much less, however, is to follow a road that leads to a morass of contradictions and subjective responses, the most serious result of which will be the confusion of what we are trying to do in encouraging children to read.[88]

Although Alderson's criticisms do not obviate the need or possibility of creating a literature which more accurately reflects the society it represents, they do pose a challenge to the approach which Aidan Chambers had adopted in Topliner. Chambers' belief that definitions of quality which failed to consider the responses of real readers worked to exclude those from outside the white, middle-class demographic to whom editors like Eleanor Graham had primarily catered necessitated a more child-centred approach. 'The Reader in the Book' represents an attempt to reconcile this child-centred approach with more formal literary critical methods:

> We need a critical method which will take account of the child-as-reader; which will include him rather than exclude him; which will help us to understand a book better and to discover the reader it seeks. We need a critical method which will tell us about the reader in the book.[89]

The concept of 'the reader in the book' offered a critical approach which could take account of the child – or adolescent – reader without resorting to a real individual or to a constructed 'ideal' child. It was significant to Chambers' work at Topliner in a number of respects. By reclaiming the role of the reader in a critical context, Chambers was establishing legitimacy for the kind of audience-focused publishing he was practising at Topliner. By seeking a critical approach which would 'include rather than exclude' the reader, he was also extending the concept of a literature of recognition to the critical arena and attempting to develop a theoretical basis for assessing the ways in which texts could include or exclude their readers. Furthermore, the assertion that books seek a particular reader or readers was significant in the context of his belief that books for adolescents could constitute a separate and distinctive literature.

---

[88] Brian Alderson, 'The Irrelevance of Children to the Children's Book Reviewer' in *Children's Literature: The Development of Criticism*, ed. by Peter Hunt, 53–5, p. 55. Originally published in *Children's Book News*, January/February 1969.

[89] Aidan Chambers, 'The Reader in the Book', p. 34.

The theory of the implied reader as Aidan Chambers develops it in 'The Reader in the Book' positions the creation of textual meaning as a collaboration between author and reader:

> In effect it suggests that in his book the author creates a relationship with a reader in order to discover the meaning of the text. [...] To achieve this, an author, sometimes consciously, sometimes not, creates, in Warren C. Booth's words: 'an image of himself and another of his reader; he makes his reader, as he makes his second self, and the most successful reading is one in which the created selves, author and reader, can find complete agreement.' [The Rhetoric of Fiction, p. 138][90]

Chambers sidesteps some of the problems Brian Alderson had identified with critical recourse to real or imagined child readers by positing that the book itself provides an imagined reader. This implied reader is created through the rhetorical strategies of the text rather than the critic's perceptions of the kind of child who might or should read the book. The real reader, he argues, is encouraged to align him or herself with this implied reader:

> In the same way (and let me stress again, deliberately or otherwise) the reader's second self – the reader-in-the-book – is given certain attributes, a certain persona, created by narratives and techniques which help form the narrative. And this persona is guided by the author towards the book's potential meanings.[91]

This concept of the reader-in-the-book offers a basis from which the critic can talk about the possible effect on real readers, who can be compared with the imagined reader created by the text. Aidan Chambers utilises the concept of reader-response to identify the characteristics of children's literature, arguing that the distinctive nature of books for children is created by the ways in which they imply a child reader through strategies such as the use of a limited range of cultural reference points. It should be noted that this argument ultimately sidesteps rather than solves the problem of using an imagined or real child in critical approaches to children's literature, since the characteristics which Chambers identifies as indicators of an implied child reader can only be measured against the critic's perception of children's tastes and experience.[92] Nevertheless, it does establish some theoretical basis by which to identify the defining characteristics of a literature written for a specific audience. This critical framework was significant in the context of

---

[90]   Aidan Chambers, 'The Reader in the Book', p. 36.

[91]   Aidan Chambers, 'The Reader in the Book', p. 36.

[92]   Subsequent critics have returned to this issue: Jacqueline Rose has argued that the impossibility of escaping reference to a real or imagined child obviates the possibility of children's literature altogether, while Peter Hollindale follows Chambers in seeking signs of 'childness' in children's books. (Jacqueline Rose, *The Case of Peter Pan: or, the Impossibility of Children's Fiction*, rvd. edn (London: Macmillan, 1992); Peter Hollindale, *Signs of Childness in Children's Books* (Stroud: The Thimble Press, 1997).)

Chambers' assertion that a literature specifically for adolescents was both possible and desirable: while he does not address teenage literature in 'The Reader in the Book', the essay opens up the possibility of an implied adolescent reader.

The influence of the critical framework Aidan Chambers establishes in 'The Reader in the Book' is evident in some of his work on teenage literature from the same period. In a column for the American periodical *The Horn Book Magazine*, he compared William Mayne's *A Game of Dark* (1971) and Paul Zindel's *I Never Loved Your Mind* (1970) – written for a similar age group – arguing that the stylistic and cultural signals encoded in Mayne's book implied a British reader of a certain social class, exemplifying 'just how confined to the confines of its social and literary heritage the best English writing [still] is'.[93] By contrast, Chambers argued:

> Because America is so much more a polyglot society than England and is so much less specific in social class, an American writer approaches his craft differently from the way his English fellow does. The American has to establish his relationship with his audience with each book. He makes fewer, if any, class-based assumptions; there are fewer culturally narrow references, there is no confident literary elite. [...] Lacking a closely identified audience to speak to, the American writer is forced (free?) to do something else. He has to establish himself, his characters and his narrative in such a way that the reader is drawn into what he has to say.[94]

While he does not explicitly reference the concept of the implied reader in this piece, the strategies he uses to identify the characteristics which made North American literature accessible to British readers, while preventing passage in the opposite direction, are based on the concept of a narrowly defined implied reader within Mayne's work with whom readers from other cultural backgrounds are unable to relate. The concept of the implied reader therefore provides a formalised way of assessing the ideological impact of texts and the ways in which they include or exclude real readers.

A congruence between the real and implied reader is an important aspect of reading as Aidan Chambers presents it in 'The Reader in the Book'. His description of writing for teenagers as speaking to 'the sixteen-year-old adolescent within' bore strong similarities to the critical discourse explored in Chapter 1, which presented children's literature as a means of 'entering the child's world'. In 'The Reader in the Book', Chambers extends this concept further, presenting the 'childness' – in Peter Hollindale's word – of the implied author as a means of guiding readers towards the desired mode of reading:

> The child, finding within the book an implied author whom he can befriend because he is of the tribe of childhood as well, is thus wooed into the book.

---

[93]   Aidan Chambers, 'Letter From England: American Writing and British Readers' in *Booktalk*, 77–83, p. 80.

[94]   Aidan Chambers, 'Letter From England: American Writing and British Readers', pp. 81–2.

He adopts the image of the implied child reader and is thus willing, may even desire, to give himself up to the author and the book and be led through whatever experience is offered.

Thus the book's point of view not only acts as a means of creating the author-reader relationship but works powerfully as a solvent, melting away a child's non-literary approach to reading and forming him into the kind of reader the book demands.[95]

The idea that the children's author should exist within the book as part of 'the tribe of childhood' is reminiscent of Paul Hazard, but whereas Hazard presented his 'republic of childhood' as an arena of freedom and imagination, Chambers presents the affinity between implied child-author and implied child-reader as a potential source of power over the child. It is important for real child readers to willingly adopt the image of the implied child reader because it is only by doing so that they can be 'formed into the kind of reader the book demands'. This has important implications for Aidan Chambers' editorial approach at Topliner. His desire to produce more inclusive books in which adolescent readers could recognise their own lived experience – and therefore align themselves more easily with the implied reader – was closely linked to his belief that the right books could help adolescent readers transition 'from Blyton to Dostoevsky'. If books themselves can work to erode a 'non-literary approach to reading', then the social and educational power of the publisher is clear.

John Stephens criticises the model Aidan Chambers offers in 'The Reader in the Book' for the degree to which it presents a 'successful' reading as one in which the reader conforms to the ideology of the author.[96] The power relations inherent in the way Chambers constructs his theory of the implied reader have particular relevance in the context of young adult literature, which, Roberta Seelinger Trites has argued, is fundamentally concerned with power. Trites identifies the urge to help 'potentially out-of-control adolescents […] exist within institutional structures' as a primary motivator of young adult fiction.[97] Aidan Chambers' attempt to create a literature for adolescents took place in the context of a period during which there was intense anxiety about teenagers and their potentially destabilising effects upon society and culture. The congruence between the theory of reading he expresses in 'The Reader in the Book' and his work at Topliner reflects a response to this anxiety: by forming adolescents into the kind of readers able to access the literary realm represented by Dostoevsky, Topliner was aimed at acculturating and socialising this potentially threatening demographic.

---

[95]   Aidan Chambers, 'The Reader in the Book', p. 42.

[96]   John Stephens, *Language and Ideology in Children's Fiction* (London: Longman, 1992), p. 55.

[97]   Roberta Seelinger Trites, *Disturbing the Universe: Power and Repression in Adolescent Literature*, p. 7.

Aidan Chambers did not explicitly relate his work at Topliner with the theoretical framework presented in 'The Reader in the Book', and the degree to which the ideas in his literary critical work are reflected in his editorial practice should not be overstated. Nevertheless, the essay does include some themes which are relevant to the literary endeavour Chambers pursued through Topliner. The power dynamics which John Stephens identifies as problematic aspects of 'The Reader in the Book' are undoubtedly reflected in Chambers' desire to develop the reading tastes of the reluctant reader – albeit in a benevolent form. Chambers' own literary work in the 'Dance Sequence', which repeatedly questions the barriers between fiction and fact, and between the author and the reader, reflects an attempt to use the collaboration between implied author and implied reader as a means of empowerment rather than ideological colonisation. Despite the more educationally and socially motivated nature of the Topliner list, the same desire to create a critical reader can be seen in the development of Chambers' editorial work.

Axes for Frozen Seas: Creating Readers

In 'The Reader in the Book', Aidan Chambers presents a model of reading in which a successful book can lead the reader away from a 'non-literary approach to reading' and towards a desirable reading of the text. Some of the key aspects of the Topliner list itself appear to favour the 'non-literary' aspects of reading: whereas Kaye Webb emphasised the literary qualities of books on the Peacock list, Aidan Chambers' construction of quality in the Topliner list involved an emphasis on the social and educational functions of literature. Chambers' original proposal for a list which could do for adolescent readers what Penguin had done for adults suggests, however, that Topliner was intended to be more than a social and educational project. His later writing reveals a commitment to an ideal of literature as an end in itself. Speaking in 1981, he stated:

> I am not very interested – and never have been – in bringing children up as diversionary readers. I have always assumed that the idea was to bring children into their literary heritage, and to enable them in the act of the deepest possible and most avidly desired literary reading.[98]

Quoting Kafka, Chambers argued that a book should not simply make the reader happy, but should be 'the axe which smashes the frozen sea inside us'.[99] The educational focus of the Topliner list and the prevalence of books which addressed specific social and ideological issues tended to place an emphasis on the utilitarian aspects of reading, but the idea that it should aid the transition 'from Blyton to Dostoevsky' signals that it was also intended to 'bring children into their literary heritage' and enable them to access the transformative experience of reading to which Kafka refers.

---

[98] Aidan Chambers, 'Axes For Frozen Seas', in *Booktalk*, 14–33, p. 17.

[99] Aidan Chambers, 'Axes For Frozen Seas', p. 17.

Aidan Chambers' resistance to the definition of quality represented by the books which were awarded the Carnegie medal and his advocacy of the use of non-standard English by authors such as Farrukh Dhondy indicate that by 'literary reading' he did not mean the consumption of books which conformed to a particular set of linguistic and literary conventions. On the contrary, his work on Topliner illustrates his belief that the experience of the reader was an integral aspect of literary quality. If a successful reading is, as he suggests in 'The Reader in the Book', dependent upon the real reader's identification with the implied reader, then successful writing depends on the ability of the book to effect this identification. In a lecture in 1996, Chambers addressed the personal and spiritual aspects of literary experience:

> Because book-writing, by which I mean literary writing, is the best means by which we express what is innermost, and because book-reading leaves the entire act of interpretation to the reader's inner self, we not only come intimately closer to the consciousness of another person than is possible in any other way but are also engaged with our own consciousness more intricately and accurately than by any other means. This is why we so often feel when we have read a great book, a book that matters to us, that we have grown, that we are more aware of some aspect of our self, of other people, of life itself, than we were before. It is why, in adolescence especially, but throughout life, certain books are an epiphany, a showing forth, that help us know who we are and what we are and what we can be.[100]

For Chambers, the purpose of reading is intimately bound up in the effect of the book on the reader, not only on aesthetic but on deeply personal grounds. His description of reading as an 'epiphany' bears a strong resemblance to the view of 'numinous' literature evident in the work of critics such as Eleanor Cameron. Chambers' work on Topliner demonstrates, however, that the tendency to accept implicit ideologies which often accompanied this view was absent in his case. On the contrary, his belief in the importance of books which would enable the reader to 'engage with [their] own consciousness' was an important component of his desire to overturn dominant ideologies by publishing books which engaged directly with adolescents' lived experience.

The idea of reading as a way to 'help us know who we are and what we are and what we can be', and the particular importance of this in the adolescent years, is reflected in the titles chosen for the Topliner list. Many of the titles on the list dealt with periods of crisis or change in the lives of their adolescent protagonists, or focused on internal experiences. Evy, the heroine of *Summer Girl*, speaks of thinking '"right inside"', while Katie, in *Answering Miss Roberts*, tells the reader 'behind my face, behind these words, I am as different again: untouched, undissected'.[101] Joan Tate's *Sam and Me*, which appeared in the second batch of

---

[100] Aidan Chambers, 'Anne Frank's Pen', in *Reading Talk*, 9–28, p. 24.

[101] Christopher Leach, *Answering Miss Roberts*, p. 6.

titles for the list, foregrounds the idea of the need to be 'engaged with our own consciousness'. Jo, the protagonist, enters into her marriage with passive devotion for her husband, blind to his need for her to have her own sense of self. The story is told in the first person, starting *in medias res* at the height of Jo's personal crisis, and Jo's lack of understanding about herself forces the reader to join in the task of interpreting her experiences. At the end of the book, when Jo reflects, 'I would have to look hard at myself and if I were to change, then the only person who could do the changing was me, myself. Not anyone else', the reader shares in the same process of self-realisation.[102] Elaine Moss praised the book for its imaginative and skilful handling of physical and emotional problems; while it undeniably has flaws, not least in the heavy-handed presentation of Jo's realisation that she needs to change, its immediacy offers a way into self-reflection for the less accomplished reader.[103] Titles like this represent an attempt to provide reluctant readers with the directly personal and transformational experiences which Aidan Chambers viewed as integral to 'literary' reading.

The idea of reading as 'an axe to the frozen sea inside ourselves' suggests that books should not only encourage inward reflection, but also profoundly alter their readers. Aidan Chambers had praised Penguin for offering books which 'took the reader where he couldn't take himself'; by championing diversity in the Topliner list he sought to offer books which not only reflected readers' own lives, but also expanded readers' horizons. A key element of this endeavour was the inclusion of books by non-British writers. North America, where young adult literature was already well-established, was an obvious source of material for Topliner, and the list included several notable American titles, including Paul Zindel's *The Pigman* (1968; published in Topliner 1971), Sondra Rosenberg's *Will There Never Be a Prince?* (1970; published in Topliner 1974) and Felice Holman's *Slake's Limbo* (1974; published in Topliner 1980). Chambers also argued strongly for the importance of works in translation:

> One of the things that makes books from other cultures so interesting is that their view of the world is a little different from our own – a different perspective, a different set of attitudes and assumptions, not least assumptions about what is all right for children to know and read about. They take us, as Michael Ignatieff puts it, 'out of our own skins [...] on a trip into someone else's life' – a life culturally different from ours. And this is the difference that matters. This is a primary value, a principal reason for choosing to translate a book.[104]

During the 1980s, Chambers pursued this principle further through the Turton and Chambers imprint, which was dedicated to works in translation. His belief in the importance of books which could take readers 'out of [their] own skins'

---

[102] Joan Tate, *Sam and Me*, p. 94.

[103] Elaine Moss, 'Reluctant at fifteen', *Times Saturday Review*, 1968, SS, Pat Garratt Scrapbook 1 – 'The Times - Alderson - B.W.A.'.

[104] Aidan Chambers, 'In Spite of Being a Translation', in *Reading Talk*, 113–37, p. 119.

was also reflected in the unusually large number of works in translation on the Topliner list. Despite the additional cost inherent in purchasing foreign rights and commissioning translations, he consistently advocated the inclusion of books from non-English speaking countries. One reason for this was the sense that these books were, in the words of translator Patricia Crampton, doing something which British literature was not: Sweden, the Netherlands and Germany all developed a teenage literature in advance of Britain. The close involvement of Joan Tate, who was a professional translator of Swedish, facilitated the inclusion of a number of books by Swedish authors, including Gunnel Beckman's *Nineteen is Too Young to Die* and *A Room of His Own* (1976) and Max Lundgren's *Summer Girl* (1976) and *For the Love of Liza* (1976). From the Netherlands came *David and Dorothea* (1979), by Ingebourg Bayer and Hans-Georg Noack, while from Germany came Lotte Betke's *Lights By the Canal* (1979); all these titles were translated by Anthea Bell. As the treatment of sex in *Summer Girl* illustrates, these books reflected some significantly different attitudes from those which prevailed in Britain, offering a different cultural perspective to their readers. The use of books by foreign writers offered the possibility of expanding readers' horizons while maintaining some of the familiarity which Chambers had identified as important to the reluctant reader: everyday adolescent concerns offered a way into stories about different countries and cultures.

The overtly ideological nature of the Topliner list entailed an experience of reading which was not only transformative on a personal level, but also on a political one. The conscious decision to seek out writers of colour for the list and the decision to preserve vernacular English in the work of Farrukh Dhondy demonstrate that Aidan Chambers and the Topliner list as a whole were engaged in an overtly ideological construction of literature. Topliner author John Crompton argued this was an important aspect of literature which tended to be diminished by the conventional division between utilitarian and literary reading:

> The young reader is to understand the forms and leaflets in order to be able to comply with their requirements: the readers capable of appreciating the great works will be more sensitive, humane people. No particular action is implied, then: the effects of reading are internal only.

> But I want my readers to be moved to action! I do not want them passively to absorb whatever minute spark of an idea or an insight they may gain from me – I want them to follow it up.[105]

Crompton's argument presents the 'axe that smashes the frozen sea' as effecting not only a personal transformation, but also a political one. This element was present both in the ideological focus of the Topliner list as a whole, and in the inclusion of individual titles on the list. Farrukh Dhondy's *The Siege of Babylon*

---

[105] John Crompton, 'The Politics of Not Reading: Writing for Power', *Children's Literature in Education*, 11:2 (1980), 76–81, p. 78.

engaged directly with racial politics: the story of black liberationists whose botched attempt at a robbery turns into a bloody hostage situation, it addresses the uneasy relationship between black Britons and British society. The book does not advocate violent action, but the closing sentences suggest the need to acknowledge rather than ignore racial conflict. The sympathetic central character is visited in prison by one of the hostages:

> She talks about tomorrow and he never reminds her that tomorrow drags along its yesterday: it goes forward like a wounded animal dragging a trap. She talks of the new jobs she has, she talks to him of the trades he could learn, she tries to tell him that to make peace with Babylon he will have to forget.
>
> But Hurly doesn't want to forget, he wants to remember.[106]

The implication that it is important for Hurly to remember his experience – and by extension, that it is important for the reader to remember and seek to understand it – offers the possibility that the book might 'move its readers to action'. An even more overt political ethos was present in Dulan Barber's *Beasts* (1980), which contained a strong anti-vivisection message. The possibility that *Beasts* might move its readers to violent action caused a degree of controversy within Macmillan, but only the most extreme example of vivisection was removed before publication.[107] The inclusion of such overtly ideological titles in Topliner reflected the move towards more socially and politically conscious literature during the 1970s; however, although this trend was criticised for tending to prioritise the political over the literary, Aidan Chambers' construction of literary reading suggests that the two were not necessarily in opposition. On the contrary, the literary power of *The Siege of Babylon* lies in the potential for the book to 'smash the frozen sea within' by forcing the reader to question both the events in the book and the wider implications for society.

Aidan Chambers' critical approaches to children's and young adult literature demonstrate his profound belief in the importance of reading, not only as a tool for education and acculturation but also for its transformative effects. Whereas Kaye Webb's advocacy of literature focused primarily on its effect on the individual and rejected an ideologically-focused approach, however, Aidan Chambers' work at Topliner was intimately connected with the social and political. He was sometimes willing to sacrifice some of the literary quality of the books he published in

---

[106] Farrukh Dhondy, *The Siege of Babylon*, p. 160.

[107] Marni Hodgkin, memo to Alyn Shipton, 19 April 1978, UoA, Box 110/111 02, Folder: 'Dulan Barber: Colin's Story'; Aidan Chambers to Alyn Shipton, 22 May 1979, UoA, Box 110/111 02, Folder: 'Dulan Barber: Colin's Story'; Aidan Chambers to Dulan Barber, 7 June 1979, UoA Box 110/111 02, Folder: 'Dulan Barber: Colin's Story'.

Vivisection was a particularly sensitive topic within Macmillan because Marni Hodgkin's husband, Sir Alan Lloyd Hodgkin, was a prominent physiologist who engaged in animal experimentation and had been the subject of attacks by anti-vivisectionists.

order to pursue his ideological goals; however, his belief that genuine literary reading involved the ability to become 'engaged with [one's] own consciousness' demanded a literature which made this possible. His attempt to produce books which directly engaged with adolescent experience stemmed from a belief that self-identification was an important first step towards accessing such literary reading; while his ideological approach was fundamentally different from that of Kaye Webb, therefore, he shared with her a belief in the importance of 'the deepest possible and most avidly desired literary reading'.

Flimsy Stories? Failures and Successes in Topliner

The unique nature of the Topliner list posed some significant challenges, both in terms of critical response and in relation to the kind of authors it was able to attract. As a new and disputed genre, teenage literature met with a measure of critical hostility: reactions like that of Nina Bawden, discussed in Chapter 1, demonstrate that the concept of a specialist literature for adolescents was often regarded as indicative of 'dumbing down'. The desire to cater specifically for reluctant readers led credence to such accusations in the case of Topliner; although the only limit placed on the books was a length of 30,000 words, archival evidence suggests that Chambers was frequently obliged to refute the notion that they were also subject to vocabulary limitations. Early Topliners attracted criticism even from those who were broadly in sympathy with this list. The reviewer and critic Griselda Greaves – a personal friend of Chambers who had encouraged him to set up Topliner – greeted the first titles without enthusiasm. Reviewing the selection available in Topliner and in Heinemann's series for reluctant readers, Pyramid, she gave muted praise to a handful of books but concluded:

> The remainder of both series are heavy with Message and Social Consciousness, and their flimsy stories collapse under the dead weight. [...] The standard of "Pyramid Books" and "Topliners" is so uneven, and so generally low, that we are no better off. Despite all the good intentions, we are forced back to the slow sifting through publishers' lists to find the occasional book that is right for the teenager, not because it is written to order, but because the author has a story to tell, and the power to tell it that way.[108]

The problem of books 'written to order' was an unavoidable one: whereas Kaye Webb had reaped the benefits of near-monopoly of a paperback market well supplied with children's books from the hardback lists, the novelty of the Topliner list meant Aidan Chambers did not enjoy the same range of choice. Although he was able to source some books from countries such as the United States and Sweden, where young adult literature was already established, there were

---

[108] Griselda Greaves, 'The in-between and reluctant' in *Guardian*, Friday, 12 July, 1968, p. 7.

relatively few British titles which satisfied the criteria of the list. The majority of Topliners were therefore commissioned specifically, and a number of authors were approached 'cold'. Although commissioned literature attracted critical disapprobation, Aidan Chambers' belief in the need for publishers to lead the way in creating new avenues for literature made it an integral part of Topliner. He wrote to one Topliner author:

> Topliners are by no means masterpieces! My hope in publishing the ones that aren't really that good is to create an atmosphere in which better stuff will get written and published, and the publishing channels for this kind of literature got open.[109]

In this sense the ideological prevailed over the purely literary in Topliner: whereas Kaye Webb was committed to 'the best in children's books', Aidan Chambers was prepared to accept books of lower quality in order to pave the way for a new type of writing. The difference between Petronella Breinburg and Farrukh Dhondy demonstrates that this strategy did bear some fruit: whereas *Us Boys of Westcroft* was justifiably criticised for being unconvincing, Farrukh Dhondy's writing shows the mark of a more accomplished writer and a more confident editorial hand.

Although reviews like the one by Griselda Greaves demonstrate that Topliners were not always successful, the responses of readers and reviewers as the list developed indicates that the list did fill a need which had been hitherto ignored. One reader wrote of how the Topliner list had transformed her attitude to books:

> At one time I had no interest for reading. I only read books I had to, and they took me ages.
>
> While, one day, I was in my local library, I came across a book titled 'Orange Wendy'. I picked it up and read the book cover. It immediately took my fancy so I took it out of the library and read it that night. I never knew I could read a book so fast. [...] I now regularly take out Topliners from my library.[110]

While the fact that she was in the library suggests that this reader was not wholly reluctant, this account illustrates the effectiveness of Topliners in reaching some readers. The characteristics she identifies are those which Aidan Chambers had specifically addressed: the cover and blurb offered immediate interest, while the length and style of the book enabled her to read it fast and with avid enjoyment. Archival correspondence from other readers shows that this response was not unusual: many adolescents emphasised their lack of interest in books prior to discovering Topliners.

---

[109] Aidan Chambers to Dave Simpson, 18 October 1969, UoA, Box 110/111 01, Folder: Dave Simpson correspondence.

[110] Linda Balance to Editor of Topliner, 10 August 1979, UoA, Box 155, Folder: Topliner Readers' Letters.

Aidan Chambers noted that the fiercest criticism of the Topliner list came from people who were not in direct contact with the school environment, and was ameliorated and sometimes contradicted by the comments of teachers and librarians working directly with reluctant readers.[111] Responses from this group emphasised the fact that Topliners were catering to a market overlooked by existing imprints. An article by teacher and educationalist John L. Foster outlining 'A reading policy for a comprehensive school (11–16)' cited Topliner as one of the few series catering to 'those children who are most in danger of giving up reading for ever'.[112] Another teacher wrote to Aidan Chambers:

> For some, the reading of 'Topliners' provides the first committed and involved reading experience in their secondary school life. [...] Until recently it would appear that Penguin and Puffins have contributed greatly in making good literature available at a reasonable price. But without wishing to deprecate or devalue the literary merit of the 'Puffin Authors', I feel that many adolescents find the language of 'Puffins' too sophisticated, and the characters + values too middle class and somewhat alien to their current trends. The authors in the Topliner series help to restore the balance.[113]

This evaluation demonstrates that the Topliner list was achieving precisely what Aidan Chambers had envisaged. The idea that Topliner authors helped to balance the kind of quality which was found in the Puffin list suggests that the books were seen not only as educational tools but as possessing literary quality in their own right.

The success of Topliner increased as the list became more established. Aidan Chambers' conviction that new writers would explore teenage literature once a publishing venue existed was proven to be correct: while the growth in the number of suitable writers in part reflected wider trends in British children's literature, the speed at which the list developed suggests that Topliner played a significant role in encouraging writers. As early as 1969, Chambers was able to reject a manuscript by Irma Chilton on the grounds that it struck him as '"worked-out" rather than compulsively felt'. Outlining the book's flaws, he wrote, 'I must be honest: I'm quite sure that a year ago we would have published this one. Now we have seen, and can manage to try to achieve it, that the books must grow in quality'.[114] The later books in the Topliner list reflect this improvement: Farrukh Dhondy was the

---

[111] Aidan Chambers, 'Guest Editorial: Who Knows?' in *LINES: Librarians in Essex Schools: A Bulletin from Essex (Branch) S.L.A*, 2:2 (June 1968), UoA, Box 110/111 01, Folder: Series publicity, 1–4.

[112] John L. Foster, 'A Reading Policy for a Comprehensive School (11–16)', *Children's Literature in Education*, 17 (Summer 1975), 51–65, p. 53

[113] John Lloyd to Aidan Chambers, 14 May 1974, UoA, Box 155, Folder: Topliner Readers' Letters, f.1 verso, f. 2 recto.

[114] Aidan Chambers to Irma Chilton, 19 October 1969, UoA, Box 110/111 02, Folder: Irma Chilton correspondence, recto.

most notable writer on the list, but he was not the only Topliner author to achieve lasting success. Michael Morpurgo's first novel, *Long Way Home* (1975), was a Topliner original and is still in print today; Morpurgo went on to win a number of awards and held the post of Children's Laureate between 2003 and 2005. *Andra* (1971), the first novel by science fiction writer Louise Lawrence – best known for *Children of the Dust* (1985) – appeared in Topliner in 1975. In some cases the Topliner list simply provided inspiration: Aidan Chambers wrote encouragingly to Mary Hooper, commenting on her proposal for a new Topliner and advising her that while a diary form might appear clichéd to adult eyes, it could be successful in a list for adolescents. Hooper was never to appear on the Topliner list, but she later found success with *Megan* (1999), the story of a teenage pregnancy written in diary form. Aidan Chambers stated that the list never achieved the kind of literary quality to which he aspired: 'There was very competent stuff. I mean, Chris Leach's books were very competent writing [...] But my benchmark was *The Owl Service*, that's what I was looking for'.[115] In citing *The Owl Service*, however, Aidan Chambers perhaps reflects his growing sense of the broader possibilities for teenage literature rather than the potential scope of Topliner: Alan Garner's work is not typically suited to the needs of the reluctant reader. Relatively few of the books published in Topliner enjoyed the longevity of *The Owl Service*, but this reflects the topical nature of the books on the list as well as their quality: books which dealt directly with the experience of being a teenager in the 1970s were quick to date. Nevertheless, they did succeed in catering for the group at which they were primarily aimed, and the list helped to establish new avenues for teenage literature.

The successes of Topliner helped to convince the commercial publishing world that a list for teenagers was a viable proposition, but this resulted in a more difficult market for Topliner itself. Few authors were willing to accept the low returns and relative obscurity of an educational list when offered publication with a commercial list.[116] By the end of the 1970s, the opportunities for writers who wished to write 'with adolescents in mind' were far more diverse than at the end of the 1960s. Reluctant adolescent readers were catered for in other educational lists, including Nelson's Getaways and Knockouts by Longman, both of which included Topliner authors such as Gunnel Beckman. Commercial paperback lists such as Piccolo began to carry teenage literature, while more hardback lists entered the young adult market; for example, Gollancz published Judy Blume's *Forever* in the United Kingdom in 1976.[117] The degree to which Aidan Chambers had succeeded in helping to create a new genre of teenage literature is reflected in the fact that by 1980 the Topliner list was merely one among many.

---

[115] Aidan Chambers, Interview with Lucy Pearson, 27 April 2009.

[116] Aidan Chambers, Interview with Lucy Pearson, 27 April 2009.

[117] Steve Bowles, 'Be Our Guest...', *Books for Keeps*, 2 (May 1980), <http://www.booksforkeeps.co.uk/issue/2/childrens-books/articles/be-our-guest/be-our-guest> [accessed 18/01/10].

Topliner: A Legacy for Teenage Readers

Aidan Chambers' work at Topliner was part of a much wider-scale shift in perceptions of quality in children's literature which took place during the 1960s and 1970s. Although Topliner itself no longer exists, and the books published under the imprint have largely vanished into obscurity, it made a significant contribution to changing ideas about children's and young adult publishing in Britain. The trend towards more diversity in children's literature to which Topliner contributed has continued: books which feature the lives of working-class children in Britain are now commonplace, although the representation of Britain's diverse cultures and ethnicities remains a problematic area. Literature for young adults is now an accepted part of the literary landscape, and while the functions and characteristics of the genre remain contested, most British children's publishers now have a specialist teenage list. Aidan Chambers commented:

> It certainly showed the commercial publishers that there was a market they said there wasn't. That that market was adolescent readers, and they developed it. And indeed, Jacqueline Wilson is the example of that – highly skilled, highly competent, does it well, is prepared to talk about any topic.[118]

Jacqueline Wilson, one of Britain's most popular and successful writers for children and young adults, does reflect many of the characteristics of the Topliner list, notably in her direct, accessible style – she often utilises first-person narration – and her representation of children from working-class backgrounds. In Topliner, Aidan Chambers therefore anticipated some of the developments to come and helped to pave the way for their more widespread acceptance. While he was not solely responsible for these developments, which were part of a widespread trend during the period, the impact of specialist publishing imprints like Topliner in establishing new parameters for children's literature should not be underestimated. By offering a publishing venue for new types of books, publishers helped to effect change in British children's literature.

The ideological and literary characteristics of Aidan Chambers' ethos as editor of Topliner differed significantly from those of Kaye Webb at Puffin; however, as this chapter has shown, he shared with her a profound belief in the cultural and social importance of literature. In seeking to provide adolescent readers with cheap, high-quality books which would help them access the broader literary realm, Chambers saw himself as continuing the original Penguin ethos rather than subverting it. In challenging the constructions of quality which characterised Kaye Webb's work at Peacock, he was advocating a more inclusive rather than a more commercial literature. Although the two editors were profoundly different in their emphases and methods, in line with the characteristics of 'golden age' publishers in the 1960s and 1970s, they shared a commitment to publishing as a social rather than commercial endeavour.

---

[118] Aidan Chambers, Interview with Lucy Pearson, 27 April 2009.

Like Kaye Webb, Aidan Chambers was uncomfortable with some aspects of his legacy as editor. Although his work at Topliner had a specific ideological and social focus, by the 1980s he complained that the 'healthy egalitarian pluralism' he had sought had been replaced by a situation in which children's literature was subject to 'the judgement of groups of adults with other special interests (to do with, for instance, racism, politics, sexism, commercial bookselling and like preoccupations), who always claimed to be working on behalf of children's own opinions and "rights"'.[119] He also saw the commercial impact of the list as deleterious, commenting that 'it encouraged the populist view that whatever the kids like is good for them'.[120] Just as Kaye Webb's success at Puffin had demonstrated the commercial potential for children's paperbacks, inadvertently encouraging a more profit-driven model for children's publishing, Aidan Chambers' support for simpler, more immediately appealing books for teenagers helped to legitimise the creation of 'pulp' series for young people.

Despite Aidan Chambers' own reservations about the legacy of Topliner, the list demonstrably helped to expand the boundaries of children's literature in Britain. The precedents set by the list were not unique – Chambers' vision for teenage literature owed much to the American model – but in establishing a paperback imprint for this market he helped to legitimise teenage literature as a distinctive literature in itself, laying the foundations for more ambitious and innovative literature. By championing work by writers from non-traditional backgrounds, such as Farrukh Dhondy, he also helped to expand the diversity of literature for young people in Britain. Both in style and content, then, Topliners set a model which is still discernible in teenage literature today.

---

[119] Aidan Chambers, 'Axes for Frozen Seas', pp. 14–15.
[120] Aidan Chambers, Interview with Lucy Pearson, 27 April 2009.

Conclusion:
The Making of Modern
Children's Literature

The rapid growth and development which took place during the 1960s and 1970s radically changed the character of British children's literature. The period's reputation as a 'second golden age' is justified in the light of the breadth and depth of activity in almost every area. Commercially, creatively and critically, these two decades fundamentally shaped modern children's literature. Children's publishers and editors were at the heart of these developments: the work of Kaye Webb and Aidan Chambers illustrates the degree to which editors were involved in creating commercial, creative and ideological change. Crucially, although Webb and Chambers were in many respects unique, they were not exceptional figures. On the contrary, the second golden age was characterised by the existence of many figures who were similarly innovative, politically engaged and socially conscious.

The characterisation of this period as a 'golden age' and the consequent tendency to regard it as a benchmark for children's literature imply a consistency and consensus which was not reflected in the world of children's literature at the time. On the contrary, as the diverse approaches of the editors, critics and authors explored in Chapter 1 demonstrate, the period was characterised by a lack of consensus. The different discourses of the period served to problematize the concept of 'the best' in children's literature; while Kaye Webb sought to uphold the motto 'Puffins for the best in children's books' and to get Puffin books into the hands of more readers, Aidan Chambers was critiquing the Puffin standard for its potential to exclude many readers. Far from representing a unified model of 'the best' in children's literature, the unique character of the second golden age derives from the existence of vigorous debate over the nature and purpose of books for children, and the innovation and change which this produced.

A Quality Standard: The Second Golden Age

Despite the diversity of the second golden age, some important continuities are evident across the 1960s and 1970s which give the period its essential character. The editors, critics, authors and educationalists who were active during this period espoused a variety of different visions of children's literature, but they were united in a profound belief in the cultural and social importance of literature, and a corresponding desire to give children access to the full range of possibilities it offered. Kaye Webb and Aidan Chambers epitomise two contrasting approaches to this mission: while Kaye Webb followed critics such as Margery Fisher and Eleanor Cameron in emphasising the numinous and aesthetic effects of literature, relying on increased access to books as a way of offering more children access to these effects, Aidan Chambers adopted a similar approach to figures such as Leila Berg and Robert Leeson in his focus on the ideological and social aspects of children's books, and the need for more accessible as well as more available literature. The two were united, however, in their passionate belief in the transformative effects of literature and their conviction that what children read was of fundamental importance. This belief underpinned sometimes conflicting attempts to achieve the 'best' in children's literature.

Much of the conflict between different models of quality in children's literature during the 1960s and 1970s emerged from the ideological differences between the two groups which John Rowe Townsend characterised as the 'child people' and the 'book people'. Aidan Chambers' attempt to produce a popular literature for adolescents in the Topliner list emerged from the socially and educationally motivated perspective associated with the 'child people': the desire to cater for a particular demographic of readers, and to pursue particular ideological agendas on issues such as class, race and gender, outweighed concerns about the specifically literary quality of the books published on the Topliner list. By contrast, Kaye Webb's avowed adherence to a largely undefined notion of the 'best' in children's books focused more on the literary qualities of the books than on their educational or ideological components. As Peter Hollindale has argued, however, in practice the division between the 'child people' and the 'book people' was less extreme than it was perceived to be, and there are some key similarities between both editors' ideas about quality. It is notable that while Kaye Webb and Aidan Chambers pursued distinct and different literary, educational and ideological goals, both emphasised the importance of children's own tastes and perceptions. Kaye Webb's determination to ensure that children had the opportunity to choose their own books bears close similarities to Aidan Chambers' desire to provide adolescent readers with books which appealed directly to their interests and concerns.

The dramatic expansion of children's publishing during the 1960s and 1970s gave children's books commercial as well as cultural importance, and the growing focus on children's preferences in part positioned child readers as consumers. The work of Kaye Webb at Puffin and of Aidan Chambers at Macmillan Topliner is, however, indicative of the fact that a strong public service ethos prevailed over motives of profit in many sectors of the juvenile publishing industry. Kaye Webb's adherence to Allen Lane's 'swings and roundabouts' philosophy at Puffin exemplified an attempt to balance commercial exigencies with the desire to publish quality books with a less immediate appeal. Aidan Chambers' work at Topliner reflects a willingness to pursue new ideologies about the purpose and nature of children's literature, even when this presented both commercial and literary challenges. While both editors attempted to provide books which were appealing to young readers, this was not motivated by a desire to shape children into consumers, but by a belief that if children were provided with enjoyable reading material, they would be enabled to access the more challenging and transformative aspects of reading. Despite the difference in their methods and ideologies, the work of both editors manifests a strong social ethos. Kaye Webb's desire to reach a wide range of children through the Puffin Club and Aidan Chambers' attempt to cater for the 'reluctant' adolescent reader reflect the growing consciousness of the ways in which children's literature had tended to exclude some groups of children. This ethos is also powerfully evident in the work of figures such as Leila Berg, Rosemary Stones, Elaine Moss and Robert Leeson, who sought to cater for children from working-class and ethnic-minority backgrounds, and worked to expose some of the implicit ideologies in children's books. Children's literature was positioned as a means of access to the full range of cultural opportunity; attempts to develop children's abilities as readers and to provide greater access to books were part of a broader cultural attempt to create a more egalitarian society. This egalitarianism was a fundamental component of the second golden age.

The Legacy of the Second Golden Age

The developments of the 1960s and 1970s are significant not only because of their impact at the time, but also because of their lasting legacy. Although the beginning of the 1980s can be regarded as the end of the golden age, children's literature had been fundamentally altered by the developments of the previous two decades, and many of the trends which emerged during the 1960s and 1970s continued uninterrupted. The discourses shaped by the authors and critics of the period, and by publishers and editors like Kaye Webb and Aidan Chambers, defined many of the characteristics of modern children's literature.

The lasting legacy of the 1960s and 1970s is evident in the business context of modern children's literature. The trend towards paperback editions which began in this period has now become the norm in children's publishing. Whereas in 1961, when Kaye Webb began work at Puffin, paperback publishing accounted for a tiny percentage of the children's market, today paperbacks account for the majority of children's books sold. Similarly, Aidan Chambers' decision to build the Topliner list almost exclusively from paperback originals was regarded as a radical departure from prevailing standards, whereas today's British children's writers frequently make their debut in paperback: Bloomsbury famously produced only 500 hardback copies of the first book by little-known author J.K.Rowling, *Harry Potter and the Philosopher's Stone*, although by the time *Harry Potter and the Deathly Hallows* was published, they were able to rely on guaranteed sales for their initial print-run of 12 million copies of the hardback edition.[1] In this context, hardback editions frequently function as a symbol of prestige rather than a genuine opportunity for increased profit margins: with retailers competing to offer the greatest discounts on high-volume titles like *Harry Potter*, the increased profit margin on hardback editions is quickly swallowed up.[2] The dominance of the paperback format in the British market is indicative not only of a move towards

---

[1]   Abebooks, 'The Holy Grail of Harry Potter Books', *abebooks.co.uk*, <http://www.abebooks.co.uk/docs/harry-potter/hp-holy-grail.shtml> [accessed 01/12/09].

[2]   Nadia Crandall explores the reasons behind retailers' adherence to high discounts in 'The UK Children's Book Business 1995–2004: A Strategic Analysis', *New Review of Children's Literature and Librarianship*, 12:1 (April 2006), 1–18, pp. 12–13.

more private ownership of books – one of the key elements of Aidan Chambers' and Kaye Webb's championship of paperbacks and most enduring legacies – but also of a shift in the perception of paperbacks. Aidan Chambers' assertion that paperbacks are 'democratic, unthreateningly attractive, affordable' has been borne out in the increasing popularity of the format, which no longer carries the inferior connotations which prevailed at the beginning of the 1960s; public preference for paperbacks is manifested in the growing trend for their use in libraries, traditionally the core market for the more robust hardback.[3]

The affordable nature of the paperback format encouraged Kaye Webb to move Puffin away from a conservative model of publishing focused on the creation of a small personal library, and towards an image of paperback publishing which was more closely related to the regular publication and disposability of magazines. Her vision of Puffin as a brand which could lend a sense of familiarity to unfamiliar authors or titles and encourage children to buy books on a regular basis was based on a desire to encourage children to access a range of reading material. Similarly, Aidan Chambers' use of branding in the Topliner series was an attempt to use the marketing strategies of the magazine world to tempt readers to access more solid material. However, the period immediately following their editorships saw the emergence of many series books – including the successful Fighting Fantasy games books published by Puffin – which show a clear debt to the strong branding Webb achieved in Puffin, but little of the diversity. During the 1980s and 1990s, children's publishing was dominated by heavily branded series such as Scholastic's Point Horror titles, in which the identity of individual authors was secondary to identification with the series and the short gaps between new titles in the series encouraged readers to treat the books as collectibles. Multiple-authored series like Point Horror are less prominent in the contemporary children's market, but series identification is an important element in the popularity of the most prominent contemporary authors: fans of J.K. Rowling, Eoin Colfer, Anthony Horowitz, Robert Muchamore and Louise Rennison can all 'count on' regular additions to their favourite series. Authors who produce stand-alone novels are also heavily branded: Jacqueline Wilson is 'serialised' by the consistency of her cover art, all produced by cartoonist Nick Sharratt, and although she writes both for younger readers and for adolescents, little distinction between the two readerships is evident in the way she is marketed. Many of the most heavily branded series originated in the North American publishing industry, but the success of figures like Kaye Webb helped to pave the way for the adoption of similar practices in the British market.

The trend towards heavily branded series has been a focus for criticism among those who have identified a decline in the quality of what is published for children. Jack Zipes asserts that 'Children's books are formulaic and banal, distinguishable from one another only by their brand labels'.[4] The move away

---

    [3]   Aidan Chambers, 'Pick Up a Penguin' in *Reading Talk* (Stroud: Thimble Press, 2001), 99–112, p. 112.

    [4]   Jack Zipes, 'The Cultural Homogenization of American Children', in *Sticks and Stones: The Troublesome Success of Children's Literature From Slovenly Peter to Harry Potter* (London: Routledge, 2002), 1–23, p. 7.

from multi-authored series like Point Horror and towards series by individual authors may be characterised as an attempt to avoid the formulaic, insofar as the formula is based on the particular strengths of an author rather than a corporately agreed template. However, Daniel Hade argues that the promotion of individual authors or characters of the contemporary children's publishing industry stems from an increasingly profit-centred mentality:

> The corporate owners of children's book publishing really aren't in the business of publishing children's books anymore [...] these corporations are hoping that children are attracted not to books so much as to *any* product that carries the brand's name.[5]

Thus fans of the Harry Potter series can not only enjoy the books themselves, but can also purchase sticker books, games, clothing, DVDs, stationery and almost every other form of merchandise conceivable, so that the opportunities for consumption continue even now that Rowling has completed the series. The focus on profit which Hade identifies as the underlying cause of the shift from books to brands exposes some of the tensions inherent in golden age. The desire to put books in the hands of more children held the seeds of a more populist and commercial approach to children's books. Kaye Webb's success at marketing and selling books helped to shift British children's literature from a largely overlooked area of the publishing industry to a lucrative and financially important sector. By proving that children's books *could* make money, she laid the foundations for the idea that they *should* do so. Simultaneously, by disrupting a quality ideal which was firmly based on literary merits, and focusing attention on the kinds of literature popular with young people themselves, Aidan Chambers inadvertently helped to make space for more populist children's publishing. In this respect the legacy of the golden age has arguably been anything but golden. However, while Kaye Webb and Aidan Chambers both deplored the commercialisation of children's publishing during the 1980s and 1990s and saw it as antithetical to their own aims, the growing financial importance of children's books has had beneficial as well as negative effects. Writers and illustrators typically enjoy better pay and higher visibility, and children's literature occupies a more prominent position in publishing as a whole.

The child-centred ethos which is evident in the work of both Kaye Webb and Aidan Chambers is central to the creation of modern children's literature: its lasting effects are evident commercially, critically and artistically. While both editors emphasised the importance of creating books which appealed directly to young readers as a means of encouraging reading, this has had considerable commercial implications. In British children's publishing, the idea of books designed to appeal directly to the child reader has continued to play an important role in the ways that books are selected, marketed and sold. Despite the relatively high cost of books, book clubs aimed directly at children and adolescents have continued

---

[5]   Daniel Hade, 'Storyselling: Are Publishers Changing the Way Children Read?', *The Horn Book Magazine* (September/October 2002), 509–15, p. 510.

to thrive. Puffin school book clubs continue to operate, although the American company Scholastic now dominates the UK market with a monthly school book club and a school book fair service. The bright, attractive covers pioneered by Kaye Webb have also become a standard feature of contemporary children's books: a visit to the children's section of a bookshop will reveal books with wrap-around jacket images, embossed cover art, television and film tie-in covers and striking imagery. The adult presentation of many titles aimed at teenage readers also show similarities to Aidan Chambers' initiative at Topliner: in particular, the descendants of the close-up portrait photographs which characterised early Topliners are evident among books aimed at young women. While these trends are largely a result of the more market-conscious nature of modern children's publishing rather than an attempt to reproduce the work of editors like Webb and Chambers, they reflect the ways in which developments in the 1960s and 1970s prepared the way for key aspects of modern children's literature. More recently, the re-launch in 2009 of the Puffin Club and the *Puffin Post* – discontinued by Puffin during the 1980s when subscriptions dropped – suggests a more conscious attempt to revive the achievements of Kaye Webb and to encourage children to engage with literature. However, the fact that the Club was re-launched not by Puffin, but by the direct sales company The Book People, and that the £45 subscription included the purchase of eight books a year indicates that the endeavour was more closely linked to sales than Webb's original Puffin Club.[6] Perhaps because it was more focused on branding than innovation, the relaunch was unsuccessful: the new Puffin Post was discontinued at the end of 2012.[7]

Aidan Chambers' work at Topliner was explicitly aimed towards the creation of modern children's literature through the development of a specialist teenage literature. The lasting impact of Topliner and other proponents of teenage literature during the 1960s and 1970s is evident in the position of young adult books in modern children's literature. Whereas in 1968, the concept of books written especially for adolescent readers was a source of contention, teenage literature is now an established part of the publishing world. Since the 1980s, a growing number of British authors have begun writing for adolescents: Robert Swindells, Melvin Burgess, Kevin Brooks and Anne Cassidy have all emerged as notable young adult authors. Chambers' assertion that he was 'creating a literature' is borne out by the fact that young adult books have gained a foothold not only commercially, but also in a broader cultural sense. More than half the books nominated for the Carnegie Medal between 2002 and 2012 were aimed at readers aged 12 or older, and a substantial proportion of these was aimed at readers of 14

---

[6]   Caroline Horn, 'Puffin Post to Fly With The Book People', *The Bookseller* (19 September 2009), <http://www.thebookseller.com/news/67362-puffin-post-to-fly-with-the-book-people.html.rss> [accessed 20/01/10].

[7]   Alison Flood, 'Puffin Post to Become Extinct', *Guardian* (17 December 2012), <http://www.guardian.co.uk/books/2012/dec/17/puffin-post-penguin-become-extinct> [accessed 28/04/13].

or above.[8] In 2003, the charity Booktrust launched an award especially for young adult literature: the Booktrust Teenage Prize aims to 'recognise and celebrate contemporary fiction written for teenagers'.[9] Such cultural recognition indicates that young adult literature has progressed beyond the specifically educational and social parameters which characterised the original Topliner list, assuming a significant position as a literature in its own right.

The ideological movements which were a dominant feature of the 1970s have had a mixed impact upon modern children's fiction. The move towards the depiction of more diverse childhoods which was advocated by activists such as Robert Leeson and Leila Berg, and which helped to shape the Topliner list, is reflected in contemporary children's and young adult literature. Children's literature is no longer an exclusively middle-class domain: working-class childhoods are represented not only in realistic novels such as Jacqueline Wilson's *Diamond Girls* (2004), but also in adventure stories such as Robert Muchamore's CHERUB books. Female protagonists are also more widely represented in children's books: notable examples of fully realised and active female protagonists in recent books for children and young adults include Philip Pullman's Sally Lockhart and Lyra Silvertongue, Neil Gaiman's Coraline and Philip Reeve's Hester. However, the ideological demands for more ethnically diverse children's literature which took place in the 1960s and 1970s are only partially reflected in modern British writing for children. While gender and class are more broadly represented in British children's literature, ethnic and cultural diversity remain relatively under-represented. Benjamin Zephaniah and Bali Rai stand out for their books on the experience of non-white young people in urban Britain, while Malorie Blackman has explored issues of race in her popular science fiction series beginning with *Noughts and Crosses*, but there are still relatively few writers of colour relative to the population of modern Britain. Nevertheless, while the ideological movements of the 1970s have not been fully realised in modern children's literature, they worked to create a very different literature than had prevailed up until the 1950s. Writers like Jacqueline Wilson now enjoy such widespread popularity that they no longer appear unusual, but both the style and content of books like hers emerge directly from the developments of the 1960s and 1970s.

Looking Forward and Looking Back: The Second Golden Age and Now

The impact of the second golden age on the making of modern children's literature was significant. The focus on childhood and literature which was present in almost every aspect of British life produced significant and lasting artistic, ideological and commercial changes in children's literature. Although divisions existed

---

[8]   Based on Carnegie shortlist. Suggested age ranges are provided by the Carnegie judges.

[9]   Booktrust, 'The Booktrust Teenage Prize 2010', *Booktrust Children's Books* (2010), <http://www.booktrustchildrensbooks.org.uk/show/feature/Booktrust-Teenage-Prize-2010> [accessed 20/01/10].

between commentators who wished to focus on the purely literary and aesthetic aspects of children's books and those who saw children's literature as a means of engaging with social and ideological issues, figures on both sides of the debate were governed by egalitarian motives. The different discourses of the period were driven by a desire to give children from all social backgrounds access to the cultural and spiritual opportunities which literature provides. It laid the foundation for a more diverse and egalitarian children's literature, expanding the boundaries of an area which had previously been focused on the needs of the white, middle-class, literate child. However, it also helped to produce the populism and commerciality which critics have argued effaces altruistic ideals of quality in modern publishing.

Nicholas Fisk's assertion that Kaye Webb 'set the scene' illuminates many of its key characteristics: her editorship of Puffin exemplifies both the innovation, diversity and social focus of the era, and the shift towards an increasingly prominent and lucrative children's market. Even more fundamental to the spirit of the age, however, was the Puffin Club and its role in making books 'exciting, alive and vigorous'. The Puffin Club itself was of central importance in fostering a sense of excitement around children's literature, but also epitomises the more general sense of children's literature as culturally significant. The widespread cultural concern with children and the sense that children were navigating and creating the new, post-war world gave children's publishing in this period a sense of excitement and a social focus which helped to foster innovation.

Despite the often-divided discourse surrounding children's literature in the 1960s and 1970s, the similarities between Kaye Webb's ethos at Puffin and Aidan Chambers' ethos at Topliner reveal some important continuities. Both editors were ultimately guided by a sense of publishing as a public service, and of children's books as transformative on both an individual and a personal level. Although Topliner challenged the status quo in a number of ways – most notably by asserting the existence and value of a specialist *teenage* literature – Aidan Chambers' assertion that a lack of access to good books was analogous to 'poor food and poor air' was consonant with Kaye Webb's ideal of a 'butter and eggs' children's literature. This philosophy was notably present in children's literature as a whole during this period. While both Webb and Chambers are notable individuals, their importance lies partly in the degree to which they exemplify some of the key trends of the 1960s and 1970s.

Kaye Webb was characteristic of the type of editor who dominated children's publishing in the 1950s and 1960s: she was one of a group of charismatic female editors – among them Mabel George at the Oxford University Press, Grace Hogarth at Constable, Marni Hodgkin at Macmillan, and Judy Taylor and Margaret Clark at the Bodley Head – who were both adventurous and passionately committed to 'the best in children's books.'[10] Indeed, much of Webb's success

---

[10]   See Kimberley Reynolds and Nicholas Tucker (eds), *Children's Book Publishing in Britain Since 1945* (Aldershot: Scolar Press, 1998) and Sue Bradley (ed.), *The British Book Trade: An Oral History* (London: The British Library, 2008) for further interviews and accounts by publishing figures of this period.

as a paperback publisher rested on the existence of these similarly innovative editors on the hardback lists, on which she relied for new titles. Robert Westall's challenging realist novels, for example, were first published by Macmillan, where he worked closely with Marni Hodgkin; Maurice Sendak's *Where the Wild Things Are* appeared as a Puffin picture book after being championed by Judy Taylor at the Bodley Head; and William Mayne, one of Webb's own favourites, was published by Mabel George at the OUP. All these editors worked closely together, aided by the formal network established in the Children's Book Circle, and it was their genuine passion for children's books and willingness to experiment which fostered the outstanding authors and illustrators of the period.

Aidan Chambers is similarly representative of a new generation of editors, writers and educationalists who had been inspired by the values of the previous generation but were frustrated by the limitations of what was available. The importance of Penguin Books as a model for Aidan Chambers own editorial vision illustrates not only the link between his work and Webb's, but more fundamentally reflects the degree to which he and others like him had been shaped by the intellectual and public service ethos of the 1940s and the post-war years. The efforts of figures like Aidan Chambers, Leila Berg (also part of the Macmillan family as editor of *Nippers*) and librarians such as Elaine Moss and Rosemary Stones helped to expand ideas of what children's literature could and should be.

The second golden age was characterised by the existence of innovative and socially-focused people who were deeply concerned with children's literature and its effects. However, perhaps the most fundamental element of the period was the existence of high levels of funding for education and libraries. Both the wide-ranging and innovative work of the major publishing imprints like Puffin, and the experimentation of niche imprints like Topliner owed their existence to a commercial environment which supported children's books as a whole. The developments of the period emerged from a fundamental belief that the creation of meaningful and appealing books and the provision of the skills needed to read them were goals worth investing in. Investment in schools and libraries offered children's publishers a greater commercial safety net, encouraging the publication of 'risky' titles, while the availability of social funding provided a basis for political and charitable initiatives around children's literature. Recession in the late 1970s and the 1980s, combined with cuts in public spending by the Conservative government during the same period, was one of the most significant factors in replacing the second golden age with the more commercially focused environment criticised by Jack Zipes and others. In the context of today's children's market, which is faced with a changing technological and cultural environment in the context of global recession, the impact of social investment should not be underestimated. The challenges facing children's literature at the beginning of the twenty-first century will require new and creative solutions, but understanding the factors and legacies of the second golden age can help us foster and protect quality – in all senses of the word, as we continue the process of 'making modern children's literature'.

Appendix:
Interview with Aidan Chambers

This is a partial transcript of an interview with Aidan Chambers, conducted by Lucy Pearson at his home in Woodchester, Stroud on the 27th of April 2009. Text in square brackets indicates where material is missing or inaudible.

LP: Aidan, could you tell me a bit to begin with about how you came to set up Topliner?

AC: I was teaching – my second job – in a secondary modern school, in Stroud. I was the librarian as well as a teacher of English. I was told my job was to get the pupils to read more. And the first thing I was told to do was to build a library. The local authority gave us extra money to do that. After about three years there were 6,000 volumes, 75% of which was fiction. But there were swathes of them I just couldn't get anyone to read. So I began to look at what it was they were reading, which was popular magazines, special interest books, that kind of thing, but very rarely any fiction. Except for some titles. There were one or two that they really loved. The breakthrough was *Fifteen* by Beverly Cleary, which Puffin published in an edition very cleverly edited by Kaye Webb, to make it less American. Even the boys adored this rather silly, comic story of a girl and her boyfriend. I started making a lot of notes and writing to Joan Tate, who was a writer, a translator out of Swedish, and a journalist. She had written for Heinemann Education some special educational books – very short stories – based on the ordinary life of young people – teenagers – because she believed that's what they needed.

I got in touch because her books were so successful, but were not commercial books – they weren't trade books – and we started talking about what was needed. She said to me 'You know exactly what is needed. Why don't you write that down and I'll take it to Heinemann Education' (who were her publishers). We wrote to each other every day for six years – it was almost like a love affair! The first thing I did when I got to school each morning was write to her, and there was always a letter in the post from her. So this conversation went on. She was a fierce lady – she called herself the Dragon of Shrewsbury (she lived in Shrewsbury). She took me to Heinemann Educational Books after I'd written my first play for the kids at school – *Johnny Salter* – saying to them, 'You should see this man, you should meet him.' I was at the time a monk, of course, so I was a bit odd. And Heinemann were superb, they were a wonderful firm. Tony Beale, who was then the managing director, was a superb guy and a specialist in D.H. Lawrence, so we had a lot to talk about. He read the play and offered to publish it. And he said, 'We hear you're thinking about what should be done for teenagers'. So I wrote a long document, which not only analysed the situation, but described the kind of books that did work. It had a section on illustrations and covers, and what the covers should be like – that they should be in paperback. At that time nobody believed in that. They said that you can't originate in paperback, you'd have to do it in hardback. I submitted my report to them and Tony said, 'We would love to do this, but we're not a commercial trade paperback imprint'. And I said, 'That's a condition – that has to be part of it. I don't mind having educational editions but we have to have commercial ones as well, otherwise to the kids this is not grown-up publishing, it's school stuff.' And they tried and tried. They tried to convince William Heinemann – who they were part of – to take this up, but William Heinemann's only paperback outlet was Pan, they part-owned Pan, with Macmillan and one other publisher – I can't remember who it was. And Heinemann said no, we can't go to Pan because there's no way they can publish this, they don't even have a children's list. And so I said, 'Okay, that's it, I'm not going to do it'. And Joan said 'Do not do it – forget it. If we can't do it the way we want it then we don't want to do it'.

Just before that, Michael Wace had gone to Macmillan, from Hart Davis, I think, and was put in charge of the schools publishing. He sent me a letter, having read an article I had published in *The Times Educational Supplement* [...] called the Newsom Young. He wrote to me saying, 'I'm interested in what you say, can we talk?' I wrote back saying, 'No, I'm sorry, I can't, I'm having talks with Heinemann'. And he wrote back saying, 'Well, if it doesn't work out with Heinemann come to us'. I'd forgotten that, but when I was clearing out the file, intending to put it away, because the whole thing had come to nothing, I came across Michael's letter. So I wrote to him, saying, 'It didn't work out with Heinemann, do you want to try it?' He took me to lunch with the Macmillan children's editor Marni Hodgkin. I don't think she wasn't too keen on the idea, she was a very up market, from a highly literary family. I think at least three of her relatives were Nobel prize-winners, and her husband was Master at Trinity. She was unhappy about this idea that we might be doing what she regarded as totally popular, rather low-level [unliterary work]. But Michael was very keen, and so they took it on, which is how it arrived at Macmillan. I think it took a year to get everything through. Heinemann had said to me, 'We don't think any writers will actually write books for you. It's all very well making a paperback edition of an already existing book, which is not what you're proposing. You want to originate in paperback. We don't think it will work, particularly at educational rates,' which was a 7 1/2 per cent royalty, not the usual 10 percent. But I'd already talked to one or two writers, so I knew they would.

All the librarians in the country told me it wouldn't work, the booksellers said they'd never sell, other people – other publishers – said there was no market for this. So everybody was against us. Tony Beale could see there was a market, he was a very astute, intelligent publisher, and Michael Wace knew there was, but they didn't know how to get to it. So Heinemann had said to me, in the period that I was working with them, 'If you can get six books, we'll do it', and I went round and [...] Joan had already written a book, which was in her drawer. I can remember talking to her and she said, 'What kind of book do you want?' And I told her. And she opened the drawer and picked out this typescript and said, 'Is it that?'

That was *Sam and Me*, the most successful book we did in Topliners. So we had that, we had one I'd written. There was writer called Reginald Maddocks, who was head of a secondary modern school in the Wirral, really back-end street kids, who was writing books, one of which had been published in hardback. I went to a writer called Christopher Leach, published a novel I admired called *The Long Play*, an adult novel set in a school, who had stopped writing because he thought nobody was interested in what he was doing, a lovely man. He said 'Yes, I'll do something', and he produced *Answering Miss Roberts*. So I got six. But then Heinemann said, 'No, we can't do it.' So these were the books that I took to Macmillan, except for mine, which Heinemann had insisted on keeping. They started a list called Pyramids, in hardback, which was never really successful, it wasn't really what I was looking for, but it was based on what I had said, so they tried to do it themselves as a hardback. None of those books I don't think ever went into paperback. That's how it started and I became General Editor of Topliners [...]

LP: What was the initial standing on which you were involved with them? There's – very early on – a letter that you wrote to the *Times* correcting them, saying 'You've described me as the editor, I'm not the editor', but you clearly were the editor later on – did you start out in a different capacity?

AC: Okay, this was Joan. Joan had very high moral and ethical standards about editors being paid as part of a royalty on an author's book. She said it was outrageous, this was nothing to do with the editor, why should the editor take part of the royalties? And Macmillan were saying, the only way in which I could be paid was on a royalty, in the same way that Heinemann paid the Serralliers for the New Windmill series, which was hugely successful. They got a penny a book, which made them very well-off. And Macmillan were saying we can't take you on as staff, otherwise you become a fulltime and in any case you have a job as a teacher. We don't quite see how to do it – we can pay you a fee for each book but that's the same thing in the end, it's got to be based on [sales]. Joan said, 'If you take a royalty, you're behaving disgracefully, and I will not stand for it'. So, there was this. And also the community, the monks, were saying, 'We can't have you doing this, it's not what we do'. So I was in a very difficult position. Finally, that was got rid of, and I was called the General Editor. I worked on a freelance basis, and at first I was paid a low fee per year. And that went on for, oh – I can't remember when I wrote to them saying, 'Sorry, not doing this any more, want more money', because it was so much work. They were paying all my expenses, and every Friday I went up to London, got to the office about 11, did an hour's work, then we went to a really good restaurant, usually with an author, we were there until three o'clock, came back to the office and I got the five o'clock train back home. [...] Classic old fashioned, gentlemanly publishing. Michael was superb. When I left the monastery, I had no money, I had nothing. I got the train up to him, and I had a jacket on over my habit, because I thought well, I was no longer a monk, and I said, 'I've got some news for you'. And I said 'I need money'. 'How much do you want?' And I remember saying '£150', which was an awful lot of money then. And he went upstairs, and an hour later came back with a 150 quid. I couldn't have survived without that. He was just superb. And he gave me my head, he believed in what I was doing. I wrote all the publicity, dictated the covers, I wrote the cover blurbs, all that, as much of the whole thing was mine as it could be. But I was not a member of the staff. So I had no power inside the firm, and without Michael, who was the boss of that department, it wouldn't have happened. Where I failed was because they got Pan to do a trade edition, and it didn't work. They wanted 20,000 copies sale per year, and we couldn't achieve that quickly. We learned that you have to have about 50 titles in paperback before the dam breaks. And they couldn't live with it that long. Whereas we did. And after three years the sales were excellent [...]

LP: That's interesting when you say that about the tipping point, because one of the things that's come across really strongly in Kaye's work – and she seems to have got the idea from Grace – is that a children's book is a slow burner, that you put something in a list and it takes at least five years to take off.

AC: Yes, that was generally true.

LP: But how did that work for Topliners? Because –

AC: Ah, we couldn't wait that long. Pan wouldn't have stood for it. It was not our sort of publishing. And the education publishers had no experience of paperback publishing. Indeed none of the children's publishers did. Puffin were working off very low sales. Now, Macmillan couldn't do that with this list. They had to have considerable sales. The point was, it was the right thing at the right time. So within two years it was selling hugely well. *Sam and Me* was selling 20,000 copies a year. It was what – you've forgotten what happened – [...] in the sixties, in education, we really felt we'd made the breakthrough. We thought we'd cracked it, we're were going to educate a literate community, we were going to make secondary moderns literate and exciting and all the rest – you know, people like me believed in those schools, because we knew what those kids were like, and they didn't have to sit public exams. The chairperson of the governors of Archway School was an old suffragette, a big socialist, and she believed that secondary moderns should be craft schools, they should teach crafts, they should teach music, they should teach drama, they should teach literature. That was the way that you create an intelligent, literate community. At the time, in the 1960s, we really felt we'd cracked it. What went wrong was that the very things we took to be advantages, like the more informal methods we used, the use of coursework instead of exam work, the more informal relationships inside school between the teachers and the kids, in the seventies that went wrong. It went too far the other way. And so you got [...] bad order. My generation had been taught you can only teach when you have order. You've got to establish order first. Not discipline but order. Unless you've got order it doesn't work. And it was the order that got lost. I remember going into schools in the late seventies, and thinking, 'What the hell has gone wrong?' They were dreadful. I mean, they were a mess. Kids were behaving in the most extraordinary manner that I would never have put up with. So, although in the seventies a lot of good things were happening, the whole culture had shifted.

And then you got Thatcher, of course, who stopped it, and wrecked it, and every administration since then has followed suit and it's got worse and worse and worse. But at the time, Topliners were the right thing at the right time. And that was why it worked. Very quickly the commercial publishers got onto it and Gollancz Lions started with it. You see Penguin, Puffin, Kaye never really had any sympathy with teenagers. She really couldn't stand them. She interviewed me for the job of editing Peacocks, which was meant to be Puffin's teenage list. I remember she took me to dinner at her house. There were two other people there. Both very middle-class business men. And the name Leon Garfield came up. Kaye said of course you would take Leon Garfield; I said 'No'. She just adored Leon, adored his books, and that was the end of it. The job didn't happen.

[Kaye Webb] also knew I had views about the kind of language you could use, the kinds of subjects you could tackle, the kind of books you could do which she didn't agree with. She believed strongly that you have to have the parents on your side.

LP: What would you have done differently if you'd run Peacock?

AC: I held the view that the key book was Alan Garner's *The Owl Service*. When *The Owl Service* came out, I remember vividly, in 1967, we still hadn't got Topliners going. However, I thought that book was a great youth book. I still do. I don't think we've got beyond it. Both Philippa Pearce and Edward Blishen wrote reviews saying, 'This is not a children's book, this is an adult book, how can you publish this on a children's list? This is a very fine piece of literary work.' The implication being that, if it was a fine literary work, it couldn't be for children. Now, I was incensed by that, and wrote condemning it. To me it was the benchmark. So I was saying we need this kind of book that includes children who are not found in literature. That's what makes them reluctant. It is not a question of difficulty of language. So for me I was creating a literature, not creating an educational prop that was meant to help children who had some sort of difficulty. We used to be accused of writing to a certain vocabulary level, which we never did – we never told the authors that there was any limit at all, except length. The kids had dictated they wanted short books. To them that was about 30,000–35,000 words, which was how we started. We'd just say 128 pages, but we didn't dictate language, nor did we actually dictate content. We never actually received anything that pushed us to the point where we had to say, 'No, you can't do that', although I was attacked in the House of Commons over *Us Boys of Westcroft* by Petronella Breinburg. This was the first novel – it's a novella – written by a black person living in England about black kids living in England. I worked on it for three years. I over edited it. Of course, Petronella was using Surinese [?] English, and I thought, 'We just can't do this' – quite wrongly – I took too much of it out. And I was attacked in the House of Commons. The then-Conservative MP for South Derbyshire said he'd come across this book, which was purported to be published by a firm run by an ex-Prime Minister of Britain, one of the most distinguished publishing houses in the world and that he could not believe such a book would be published by that firm. That it contained language that was quite disgraceful. Now, of course, it wasn't about that at all [...] It was because it was about black kids. And there was a terrible furore. Harold Macmillan (then retired) sent a memo to the office saying. 'I'd like to see this book.' And I was sent a copy of the memo he sent back, saying he read the book and though he didn't like it he was sure the editors knew what they are doing [...]. That was in 1977 or 1978. He saved my bacon!

LP: Did you see yourself as creating a literature?

AC: Yes, absolutely. No question. That was always the problem. I did in the run-up to the list. I talked to Gollancz, for example, I talked to Hodder, Joan and I tried various commercial publishers, to get the list taken, before Heinemann took an interest. Because that's what we wanted. But we believed it had to be in paperback. And there was the problem, because paperback publishing was not then as it is now, and people were not originated in paperback. So Topliners was unusual, it was one of the first to do this. Oh, there were original paperbacks, there were [...] paperbacks within educational publishing, but they were educational books. They looked it: they had comprehension questions in them, that kind of thing. I was against it [...] They were terrible-looking. They were one of the reasons the kids weren't reading. So, the basis of it was the literature of recognition. I'd gone back to myself. I became a reader when I found myself, my own culture, my own kind, my own way of living in fiction, and I made that equation – until you find yourself written, you don't exist, and you're not so keen to read the literature written for another kind of person. So I was creating a literature, and I always wanted it to be a trade thing, and it never became that. But the other trade publishers did cotton on, but none of them wanted me.

LP: Did you make a point of seeking out writers of colour?

AC: Yes, we did. Petronella Breinburg was one of the first. Farrukh Dhondy was another, for instance. [...] We didn't have a lot of success. It was difficult because finding the black writers who were able to write the kind of book we were looking for were hard to come by. Petronella Breinburg we got through Judy Taylor of The Bodley Head, because she'd done some picture books – *My Brother Sean*, one of the first black books. Judy had published it. And Judy said to me, 'Petronella could write a very good Topliner'. [...] It took I think over three years, again because of this prejudiced belief about black English not being proper English. And we didn't have a lot of contact with black teachers working in schools who were writers, or black writers, but we kept on looking. We were trying.

LP: What would have been on that list?

AC: We wanted to find books that were about areas of life that were not being covered. For instance, one of the books that was read by my kids, that was a kind of model for Topliners, was a book by Josephine Kamm, *Young Mother*. It was about a teenage girl who gets pregnant. Now, there was terrible controversy about it. But I was teaching 15-year-old girls who would have children two or three years down the line. They loved it. Josephine was a wonderful woman. Her son was Anthony Kamm, a wonderful publisher, the only publisher that was entirely devoted to children, Brockhampton Press, which later became part of Hodder.

[…] So we were asking, 'What is the ordinary life of the ordinary teenager, and who writes that? How do we get that written without prescribing it? Because there was a great prejudice, quite rightly, against commissioning fiction. The literary publishers said, 'You can't commission fiction […] you're just going to get journalism'. Now, of course, Jacqueline Wilson has cracked it. Remember, *Jackie* magazine is named after her. That's where she started. […] She's the epitome of a Topliner writer. All her books are the kind of books we'd have published. And it shows you the shift that's taken place, because she's been hugely supported by the trade, published by publishers who'd never have looked at Topliners, they'd have turned their noses up. Now I think it's gone too far, we've gone the other way. You know, now I look for the literary book, which is my natural mode. I was starting out as a teacher […] literature should cover all the areas […] and we were talking to authors. We weren't saying, 'We'd like you to write such–and–such', we were saying, 'What kinds of things interest you about being a teenager?'

LP: Do you feel it got easier to find good books as Topliners went on?

AC: No, that was one of the problems. Because by the time got easier, the commercial publishers were in on the act, quite rightly […] Topliners had made the point, it had shown the market, but it wasn't the right way to do it, once it was established. […] I used to argue that publishing was about opportunity. Once you showed the opportunity, people would write. Once they saw, 'Oh, you can publish this, I want to do that,' they would write it. Until it's there, people don't think of it. I would say you have to start with the publisher.

LP: Was there any book in Topliners that achieved what you wanted at a literary level?

AC: No. […] When I say there was nothing of literary quality, that's to set the bar very high. There was very competent stuff. I mean, Chris Leach's books were very competent writing […] But my benchmark was *The Owl Service*, that's what I was looking for.

LP: [Asks his opinion of Kaye Webb]

AC: She wanted to sell books. And she was very good at it. […] She wasn't an intellectual – fine. She was a publisher, and she was very, very good at it. Now, that was not true of Eleanor Graham. Nor was it true of Margaret Clark, who should have had that job.

[…] Now, I'm not sure what Kaye would have been aiming at, other than this delight in having a vibrant market where kids were reading a lot […] She wanted to sell the books she wanted to sell, and in that sense her standards were high. But they were very middle-brow standards. They were created by the middle-brow reading that the English love. They're not really very comfortable with people like Virginia Woolf. They like straightforward stories.

LP: What would you see as Topliners' legacy?

AC: In one sense, it has been deleterious. I think it encouraged the populist view that whatever the kids like is good for them and that's what they should be given. It think it had a part in that, which was not intentional at all. What I think it did that is not now thought of, because it never thought of as in the mainstream of children's publishing, because it was done by an educational publisher – it certainly showed the commercial publishers that there was a market they said there wasn't. That that market was adolescent readers, and they developed it. And indeed, Jacqueline Wilson is the example of that: highly competent, does it well, is prepared to talk about any topic [...] My beef is that we're into the problem of what you mean about literary standards, but what I would think of as literary literature for the young hasn't happened. And I think there are reasons for that which are much deeper than simply publishing, and the causes are cultural, they're to do with the culture. [...] But it certainly opened up that market, it sensitised publishers to a lot of what was going on. It showed a lot of writers and teachers that you could say the sort of things everyone knew teenagers think. I think it did those things. I'm not sure it did much more. At the peak of its time it was doing extremely well commercially, quite as good as the paperback lists.

I spoke to a teacher who said, 'I have kids who will only read what they call the books with the black spines' – that was Topliners. And I thought then, 'Hang on, that's not what I'm about. I'm not about creating a reader who only reads Topliners'. Now, whether the idea of needing a bridge literature has merit – clearly for some people it does. I think that on the whole all it created was readers of that kind of books. I don't think it did much more than that. So, my view of what should happen to people who are not literate is not to approach it in that way. I would not do that now. The only reason I would do it is to create a literature which doesn't exist. That has certainly happened. To that extent it worked. It did not work to produce the kind of literary writing I wanted, or lead children beyond that kind of book because it had helped them.

Bibliography

Archive Material

Please note: The majority of the archive material used in the preparation of this book was uncatalogued or only partially catalogued at the time of access. The fullest possible location descriptors have therefore been provided in order to assist future scholars.

Titles given in quotation marks are the title given on the material. Where no quotation marks are used, the title is a description of the material accessed. Where the item is a draft or copy of published material, publication details are also given if known.

Alderson, Brian to Kaye Webb, 1988, Kaye Webb Collection, Seven Stories, the National Centre for Children's Books, KW/11/01/16

'AMW', memo to Executive Board, 'Art dept.', 26 May 1965, Penguin Archive, University of Bristol, DM/1843/16

Anonymous, Review of Peacock Books, *Spectator*, 7 June 1963, press cutting, Penguin Archive, University of Bristol, DM1107/PK05

Anonymous review, 'Dichotomy of Adolescence', *Times Educational Supplement*, 25 August 1967, photocopy, Penguin Archive, Bristol University, DM/1107/PK66

Balance, Linda to Editor of Topliner, 10th August 1979, Chambers Collection, University of Aberystwyth, Box 155, Folder: Topliner Readers' Letters

Banks, Lynne Reid, c. 1979, 'Puffin scrapbook', Penguin Archive, University of Bristol, DM1952/File 742

Beck, Linda Howe, 'Puffin Books "Made with Butter and Eggs"', unidentified newspaper clipping in 'Press Cuttings for Puffins' scrapbook, n.d., Kaye Webb Collection, Seven Stories, the National Centre for Children's Books, KW/16/06

Breinburg, Petronella to Aidan Chambers, 21 February 1979, Chambers Collection, University of Aberystwyth, Box 110/111 02, Folder: Petronella Breinburg

Brockhampton Press, 'Knight Books', promotional leaflet, 1967, University of Aberystwyth, Chambers archive, Box 110/111 02, Folder: Series Publicity

Carrington, Noel, 'The Puffin Picture Books', typescript draft, 29 March 1971, Penguin Archive, University of Bristol, DM.1294/17.ii

Chambers, Aidan to Alyn Shipton, 22 May 1979, Chambers Collection, University of Aberystwyth, Box 110/111 02, Folder: 'Dulan Barber: Colin's Story'

Chambers, Aidan, memo to Alyn Shipton, 2 January 1978, Chambers Collection, University of Aberystwyth, Box 110/111 02, Folder: House editor

Chambers, Aidan, to Alyn Shipton, 19 December 1977, Chambers Collection, University of Aberystwyth, Box 110/111 02, Folder: House editor

Chambers, Aidan to Anthea Joseph, 6 May 1966, Chambers Collection, University of Aberystwyth, Box 110/111 01, Folder: Michael Joseph Ltd. Correspondence

Chambers, Aidan to Barbara Bell, 10 May 1966, Chambers Collection, University of Aberystwyth, Box 156, Folder: Barbara Bell correspondence

Chambers, Aidan to Celia Harcourt, 19 January 1976, Chambers Collection, University of Aberystwyth, Box 42, Folder: Macmillan Correspondence 1 October 1975–25 March 1976

Chambers, Aidan to Dave Simpson, 18 October 1969, Chambers Collection, University of Aberystwyth, Box 110/111 01, Folder: Dave Simpson correspondence

Chambers, Aidan to Dulan Barber, 7 June 1979, Chambers Collection, University of Aberystwyth, Box 110/111 02, Folder: 'Dulan Barber: Colin's Story'

Chambers, Aidan to Irma Chilton, 19 October 1969, Chambers Collection, University of Aberystwyth, Box 110/111 02, Folder: Irma Chilton correspondence

Chambers, Aidan to Irma Chilton, 13 September 1969, Chambers Collection, University of Aberystwyth, Box 110/111 02, Folder: Irma Chilton correspondence

Chambers, Aidan to Irma Chilton, 5 August 1967, Chambers Collection, University of Aberystwyth, Box 110/111 02, Folder: Irma Chilton correspondence

Chambers, Aidan to Josephine Kamm, 11 December 1966, Chambers Collection, University of Aberystwyth, Box 110/111 01, Folder: Josephine Kamm

Chambers, Aidan to Josephine Kamm, 4 June 1966, Chambers Collection, University of Aberystwyth, Box 110/111 01, Folder: Josephine Kamm

Clark, Charles to Kaye Webb, c. 1972, Kaye Webb Collection, Seven Stories, the National Centre for Children's Books, KW/07/01/05/02/01

Chambers, Aidan, to Mrs. R. Young, Librarian of Wodensborough High School, Wednesbury, 22 November 1977, Chambers Collection, University of Aberystwyth, Box 110/111 02, Folder: House editor

Chambers, Aidan to Stuart Jackman, 13 February 1967, Chambers Collection, University of Aberystwyth, Box 110/111 01, Folder: Stuart Jackman

Chambers, Aidan, 'Aidan - Revised blurb suggested for Topliners pamphlet', typescript draft, c. 1968, Chambers Collection, University of Aberystwyth, Box 110/111 01, Folder: Series publicity

Chambers, Aidan, 'From Blyton to Doetovsky [sic]', typescript draft of article, 1975, Chambers Collection, University of Aberystwyth, Box 155, Folder: Topliner Readers' Letters

Chambers, Aidan, 'Guest Editorial: Who Knows?' in *LINES: Librarians in Essex Schools: A Bulletin from Essex (Branch) S.L.A*, 2:2 (June 1968), Chambers Collection, University of Aberystwyth, Box 110/111 01, Folder: Series publicity

Chambers, Aidan, 'THE NEWSOM YOUNG REED BOOKS: a new and growing market', typescript proposal for a teenage publishing imprint, August 1966, Chambers Collection, University of Aberystwyth, Box 110/111 01, Folder: Series Publicity

Chambers, Aidan, 'Peacock Books', typescript editorial proposal. Enclosure with letter, Chambers, Aidan to Kaye Webb, 5 January, 1968, Chambers Collection, University of Aberystwyth, Box 155, Folder: Penguin - Puffin

Chambers, Aidan, 'A proposal for a TOPLINER MAGAZINE', 9 March 1973, Chambers Collection, University of Aberystwyth Box 42, Folder: Topliners

Chambers, Aidan, 'Suggestions for a Reading Library for early teenage (13–16 years) of average and below average ability in Secondary Modern and Comprehensive Schools', November 1965, Chambers Collection, University of Aberystwyth, Box 110/111 01, Folder: Series publicity

'CHILDREN'S BOOK CIRCLE ELEANOR FARJEON AWARD: Winner of the 1969 Award: Kaye Webb', press release, 1970, Kaye Webb Collection, Seven Stories, the National Centre for Children's Books, KW/11/01/06

Editorial file: A.P. Herbert, *The Water Gypsies*, 1973–1975, Penguin Archive, University of Bristol, DM/1952, Box 361, ISBN 047.069 7

Editorial file: Alan Garner, *The Owl Service*, Penguin Archive, University of Bristol, DM/1107/PK66

Fisk, Nicholas to Kaye Webb, 12 November 1979, Kaye Webb Collection, Seven Stories, the National Centre for Children's Books, KW/07/06/11

Fox, Geoff, 'Where the Kids Are', *Times Educational Supplement*, 6 February 1976, Chambers Collection, University of Aberystwyth, Box 42 – Woodchester Post Office, Folder: Macmillan Correspondence 1 October 1975–25 March 1976

Galliford, Juliet to the Editor of Topliner, 1979, Chambers Collection, University of Aberystwyth, Box 155 – Aidan's correspondence, Folder: Readers' letters

Garner, Lesley, 'The Queen of Puffinland' in Nova (August 1972), clipping in 'Press Cuttings for Puffins' scrapbook, Kaye Webb Collection, Seven Stories, the National Centre for Children's Books, KW/16/06

Godwin, Anthony to Kaye Webb, 3 February 1961, Kaye Webb Collection, Seven Stories, the National Centre for Children's Books, KW/07/01/01/04

Graham, Eleanor, to Kaye Webb, c.1961, Kaye Webb Collection, Seven Stories, the National Centre for Children's Books, KW/07/01/05/05/01

Gregory, Dave, 'A Bibliography of Penguin Books: Part 1: Peacock Series', typescript copy, Kaye Webb Collection, Seven Stories, the National Centre for Children's Books, KW/01/04/047/011

Griffin, John to Kaye Webb, 12 September 1977, Penguin Archive, University of Bristol, DM 1952/047.0964

'The Guardian Award: "Both Real and Magical"', *Guardian*, Friday March 29, 1968, p. 14, photocopied press clipping, Penguin Archive, University of Bristol, DM/1107/PK66'Now Peacocks join the Penguin and Puffin family', *Smiths Trade News*, c. 1962, clipping in 'Press Cuttings for Puffins' scrapbook, Kaye Webb Collection, Seven Stories, the National Centre for Children's Books, KW/16/06

Hartley, D., to Macmillan Topliner, 13 November 1977, Chambers Collection, University of Aberystwyth, Box 110/111 02, Folder: House Editor

Higgins, Judith, 'Publishing Children's Paperbacks: A Talk With Puffin's Kaye Webb' in *Publishers Weekly*, February 24, 1975, Clipping in 'Puffin' scrapbook, Kaye Webb Collection, Seven Stories, the National Centre for Children's Books, KW/16/03

Hodgkin, Marni, memo to Alyn Shipton, 19 April 1978, Chambers Collection, University of Aberystwyth, Box 110/111 02, Folder: 'Dulan Barber: Colin's Story'

Kennedy, Richard to Kaye Webb, n.d., Kaye Webb Collection, Seven Stories, the National Centre for Children's Books, KW/01/02/43/17

Lane, Allen to Kaye Webb, 3 March 1958, Kaye Webb Collection, Seven Stories, the National Centre for Children's Books, KW/07/01/01/01

Lane, Peter A. to Kaye Webb, 24 March 1978, Penguin Archive, University of Bristol, DM 1952/047.0964

'List of 100 Best-selling Puffins', typescript, n.d., Kaye Webb Collection, Seven Stories, the National Centre for Children's Books, KW/07/04/08/24 'New from Penguins', black and white photograph, c. 1960s, Kaye Webb Collection, Seven Stories, the National Centre for Children's Books, KW/07/08/01

Lloyd, John to Aidan Chambers, 14 May 1974, Chambers Collection, University of Aberystwyth, Box 155, Folder: Topliner Readers' Letters

MacRae, Julia to Kaye Webb, February 1970, Kaye Webb Collection, Seven Stories, the National Centre for Children's Books, KW/11/01/16

Marley, Kathleen to Kaye Webb, 17 September 1964, Penguin Archive, University of Bristol, DM1107 / PS175

McKay, Jenny, 'M.P. slams sexy books for kids', *Sunday Sun*, 13 November 1977, press cutting, Penguin Archive, University of Bristol, DM 1952/047.0964

Moloney, Eileen to Kaye Webb, c. 1979, Kaye Webb Collection, Seven Stories, the National Centre for Children's Books, KW/01/04/073/01

Moss, Elaine, 'Reluctant at fifteen', *Times Saturday Review*, 1968, Kaye Webb Collection, Seven Stories, the National Centre for Children's Books, Pat Garratt Scrapbook 1 - 'The Times - Alderson - B.W.A.'

Nuttall, Gwen, 'Puffin's winning gambler', *Sunday Times Business*, 6 April 1975, Penguin Archive, University of Bristol, 'Puffin' green publicity folder

Orr, Mr and Mrs J.C. to Kaye Webb, 5 April 1975, Penguin Archive, University of Bristol, DM/1952/047.069 7

Paroissien, H.F. to Eunice Frost, 23 June 1965, Penguin Archive, University of Bristol, Frost Papers 19, DM/1843/16

'Penguin Books Limited: Net Sales and Trading Profit for the Year Ending 31 December 1968', Penguin Archive, University of Bristol, DM/1843/16

Pennington, J.M., Headmistress of Wheatley High School for Girls, Doncaster, to Martin Pick, 9 January 1976, Chambers Collection, University of Aberystwyth, Box 42, Folder: Macmillan Correspondence 1 October 1975–25 March 1976

Pick, Martin to John Crompton, 17th February, 1976, Chambers Collection, University of Aberystwyth, Box 42, Folder: Macmillan Correspondence 1 October 1975–25 March 1976

Pick, Martin, memo to Michael Wace, 11th April 1977, Chambers Collection, University of Aberystwyth, Box 110/111 02, Folder: Topliner: in-hand materials

Savage, Ian, memo to Kaye Webb, 25 November 1975, Penguin Archive, University of Bristol, Folder: Puffin Annual No 2, Memos & Correspondence with non-contributors, DM/1952 box 529

Shipton, Alyn to Aidan Chambers, 17 January 1978, Chambers Collection, University of Aberystwyth, Box 110/111 02, Folder: House editor

Thirsk, John (illustrator), 'The Blinder', jacket proof, Penguin Archive, University of Bristol, DM 1952, Box 362, 047.0964

'Topliner sales', sales ledger, 1971–1977, Chambers Collection, University of Aberystwyth, Box 110/111 02, Folder: Topliner: In-Hand Materials

'Topliner: 10th Anniversary: 1978–79 Illustrated Catalogue', Chambers Collection, University of Aberystwyth, Box 110/111 02, Folder: Topliner: in-hand materials

'Total Sales – to end of March 1966', typescript, c. 1966, Penguin Archive, University of Bristol, Folder: 'Misc Puffin History (incl Kaye Webb)', DM1294/17.ii

Townsend, John Rowe, 'Operation Junior Egghead', *Guardian*, 3 April 1989. Clipping in 'Press Cuttings for Puffins', scrapbook, Kaye Webb Collection, Seven Stories, the National Centre for Children's Books, KW/16/06

Webb, Kaye to Aidan Chambers, 10 January 1968, Chambers Collection, University of Aberystwyth, Box 155, Folder: Penguin – Puffin

Webb, Kaye, to C. Dolley, 1970, Kaye Webb Collection, Seven Stories, the National Centre for Children's Books, KW/07/01/01/12

Webb, Kaye to C. Walter Hodges, 20 August 1964, Penguin Archive, University of Bristol, DM/1107/PS146

Webb, Kaye to Dave Gregory, 1988, Kaye Webb Collection, Seven Stories, the National Centre for Children's Books, KW/01/04/047

Webb, Kaye, memo to John Rolfe, 31 March 1978, Penguin Archive, University of Bristol, DM 1952/047.0964

Webb, Kaye to John Rowe Townsend, 22 March 1966, Penguin Archive, University of Bristol, DM/1107/PS299

Webb, Kaye to Julia MacRae, 1978, Kaye Webb Collection, Seven Stories, the National Centre for Children's Books, KW/07/01/05/07

Webb, Kaye to Michael Powell, 1981, Kaye Webb Collection, Seven Stories, the National Centre for Children's Books, KW/01/03/101/02

Webb, Kaye to Noel Streatfeild, 26 July 1961, Penguin Archive, University of Bristol, DM1107 / PS 157

Webb, Kaye, to Robert Westall, 10 January 1975, Robert Westall Collection, Seven Stories, the National Centre for Children's Books, RW/14/01/20

Webb, Kaye, to Tony Godwin, 1961, Kaye Webb Collection, Seven Stories, the National Centre for Children's Books, KW/07/01/01/03

Webb, Kaye to Yehudi Menuhin, series of correspondence, 1975–1995, Kaye Webb Collection, Seven Stories, the National Centre for Children's Books, KW/01/03/086

Webb, Kaye, 'Australian Broadcasting Commission: Guest of Honour: Kaye Webb', broadcast transcript, 11 July 1971, Kaye Webb Collection, Seven Stories, the National Centre for Children's Books, KW/07/01/04/03/12

Webb, Kaye, 'A Beggar's Knock', draft of Kaye Webb's autobiography transcribed in Charles Kennedy's hand, c. 1988, Kaye Webb Collection, Seven Stories, the National Centre for Children's Books, KW/01/02/43/19

Webb, Kaye, 'Brief Record of K.W.'s Employment with Penguins', typescript notes, n.d., Kaye Webb Collection, Seven Stories, the National Centre for Children's Books, KW/07/01/03/01

Webb, Kaye, 'The Children's Market Grows Up', typescript draft of article for *The Bookseller*, c. 1980s, Kaye Webb Collection, Seven Stories, the National Centre for Children's Books, KW/07/04/08/19

Webb, Kaye, 'Draft talk on Odway', n.d., Kaye Webb Collection, Seven Stories, the National Centre for Children's Books, KW/07/04/03/01

Webb, Kaye, 'Eleanor Farjeon Award', typescript draft for acceptance speech, 1970, Kaye Webb Collection, Seven Stories, the National Centre for Children's Books, KW/11/01/01

Webb, Kaye, 'Getting to Children', typescript notes, n.d., SS, KW/07/04/08/12d

Webb, Kaye, 'History of Puffin Books', typescript, 1972, Kaye Webb Collection, Seven Stories, the National Centre for Children's Books, KW/07/04/08/02

Webb, Kaye, 'NOT IN FRONT OF THE CHILDREN (Pas devant les Enfants)', typescript draft, probably for a radio broadcast, Kaye Webb Collection, Seven Stories, the National Centre for Children's Books, KW/07/04/08/20

Webb, Kaye, 'Notes For Speech', typescript draft, n.d., Seven Stories, the National Centre for Children's Books, KW/07/04/08/12

Webb, Kaye, Notes for a speech on children's reading, n.d., Kaye Webb Collection, Seven Stories, the National Centre for Children's Books, KW/07/04/08/13

Webb, Kaye, 'On Being a Children's Book Editor', typescript draft of an article for *School Bookshop News*, c. 1975, Kaye Webb Collection, Seven Stories, the National Centre for Children's Books, KW/11/03/35

Webb, Kaye, 'On Being a Children's Editor', typescript draft, Kaye Webb Collection, Seven Stories, the National Centre for Children's Books, KW/15/32

Webb, Kaye, 'Paperback Buyer', typescript draft of article for *Paperback Buyer*, c. 1978, Kaye Webb Collection, Seven Stories, the National Centre for Children's Books, KW/07/01/05/09/03

Webb, Kaye, 'Puffin Books - Marketing Plan 1967', 1967, Penguin Archive, University of Bristol, DM/1879/23/5

Webb, Kaye, 'Puffin notes in diary form', March 15 1962, Kaye Webb Collection, Seven Stories, the National Centre for Children's Books, KW/07/01/03/04

Webb, Kaye, 'A Red Letter Day for Children (or the Rewarding Road to the 1000th Puffin)', typescript draft of article, c. 1977, Kaye Webb Collection, Seven Stories, the National Centre for Children's Books, KW/07/01/05/09/03

Webb, Kaye, 'SIDELIGHTS: Kaye Webb Revised text, September 1991', typescript draft of article, September 1991, KW/15/32

Webb, Kaye, Speech notes, typescript draft, c. 1986, Seven Stories, the National Centre for Children's Books, KW/07/04/08/17

Webb, Kaye, typescript draft of speech, c. 1980, Kaye Webb Collection, Seven Stories, the National Centre for Children's Books, KW/07/04/08/31

Williams, Gladys, 'Queen of the Puffins: Kaye Webb' in *Books and Bookmen*, magazine clipping, [n.d, c. 1969], Kaye Webb Collection, Seven Stories, the National Centre for Children's Books, KW/16/03

Willox, Michael to Puffin Staff, n.d, Kaye Webb Collection, Seven Stories, the National Centre for Children's Books, KW/07/04/01/04/09

Wood, Dorothy to Diana Mackey, Michael Joseph Ltd, 17 February 1976, Penguin Archive, University of Bristol, DM 1952/047.0964

'Young Elizabethans', *Birmingham Weekly Post*, 22 April 1955, press cutting in 'Press Cuttings Album', Kaye Webb Collection, Seven Stories, the National Centre for Children's Books, KW/16/03

Young, Mrs. R., Librarian of Wodensborough High School, to Macmillan Education, 15 November 1977, Chambers Collection, University of Aberystwyth, Box 110/111 02, Folder: House editor

Primary Sources

Adams, Philippa, *Hitch on the Way* (London: Macmillan, 1976)

Adams, Philippa, *Nine Months* (London: Macmillan, 1977)

Adams, Richard, *Watership Down* (London: Rex Collings, 1972)

Aiken, Joan, *Night Fall* (London: Macmillan, 1969)

Aiken, Joan, *The Whispering Mountain* (Harmondsworth: Puffin, 1970) [1969]

Alcott, L.M., *Little Women* (Harmondsworth: Puffin, 1994) [1868]

Ashley, Bernard, *All My Men* (Oxford: Oxford University Press, 1977)

Ashley, Bernard, *A Kind of Wild Justice* (Oxford: Oxford University Press, 1978)

Ashley, Bernard, *The Trouble with Donovan Croft* (Harmondsworth: Puffin, 1977) [1974]

Bagnold, Enid, *National Velvet* (Harmondsworth: Penguin, 1962) [1935]

Bannerman, Helen, *Little Black Sambo* (New York: HarperCollins, 1990) [1899]

Barber, Dulan, *Beasts* (London: Macmillan, 1980)

Bawden, Nina, *Carrie's War* (Harmondsworth: Puffin, 1974) [1973]

Bawden, Nina, *Squib* (Harmondsworth: Puffin, 1983) [1971]

Bayer, Ingebourg and Hans-Georg Noack, *David and Dorothea* (1979)

Beckman, Gunnel, *Admission to the Feast*, trans. Joan Tate (London: Macmillan, 1971)

Beckman, Gunnel, *Mia*, trans. Joan Tate (London: Longman, 1975) [1974]

Beckman, Gunnel, *Nineteen is Too Young to Die*, trans Joan Tate (London: Macmillan, 1971)

Berg, Leila, *Fish and Chips for Supper* (London: Macmillan, 1968)

Berg, Leila, *Grandad's Clock* (London: Macmillan, 1976), <http://www.aspects.net/~leilaberg/Grandad.htm> [accessed 02/09/09]

Betke, Lotte, *Lights by the Canal*, trans. Anthea Bell (London: Macmillan, 1979)

Blackman, Malorie, *Noughts and Crosses* (London: Corgi, 2001)

Blume, Judy, *Are You There, God? It's Me, Margaret* (New York: Dell, 1983) [1970]

Blume, Judy, *Blubber* (New York: Yearling, 1986) [1974]

Blume, Judy, *Forever* (London: Macmillan, 2001) [1975]

Blume, Judy, *Then Again, Maybe I Won't* (New York: Dell, 1983) [1971)]

Bond, Michael, *A Bear Called Paddington* (London: Armada Lions, 1972) [1958]

Boston, Lucy M., *The Children of Green Knowe* (Harmondsworth: Puffin, 1975) [1954]

Boston, Lucy M., *The Chimneys of Green Knowe* (Hemingford Grey: Oldknow Books, 2003) [1958]

Boston, Lucy M., *An Enemy at Green Knowe* (Hemingford Grey: Oldknow Books, 2003) [1964]

Boston, Lucy M., *The River at Green Knowe* (Hemingford Grey: Oldknow Books, 2003) [1959]

Boston, Lucy M., *The Stones of Green Knowe* (Hemingford Grey: Oldknow Books, 2003) [1976]

Boston, Lucy M., *A Stranger at Green Knowe* (Hemingford Grey: Oldknow Books, 2003) [1961]

Breinburg, Petronella and Errol Lloyd (illustrator), *My Brother Sean* (London: Bodley Head, 1973)

Breinburg, Petronella, *Us Boys of Westcroft* (London: Macmillan, 1975)

Brennan, Sarah Rees, *The Demon's Lexicon* (London: Simon and Schuster Children's, 2009)

Brooks, Kevin, *Black Rabbit Summer* (London: Penguin, 2008)

Buchan, John, *Greenmantle* (Harmondsworth: Peacock, 1964) [1961]

Buchan, John, *The House of the Four Winds* (Harmondsworth: Peacock, 1966) [1935]

Buchan, John, *The Three Hostages* (Harmondsworth: Peacock, 1963) [1924]

Burton, Hester, *A Time of Trial* (Oxford: Oxford University Press, 1979) [1963]

Calder-Marshall, Arthur, *The Fair to Middling* (Harmondsworth: Puffin, 1973) [1959]

Chambers, Aidan, *Breaktime* (London: Red Fox, 2000) [1978]

Chambers, Aidan, *Cycle Smash* (London: Heinemann, 1967)

Chambers, Aidan, *Dance on My Grave* (London: Red Fox, 2000) [1982]

Chambers, Aidan, *Johnny Salter* (London: Heinemann, 1966)

Chambers, Aidan, *Now I Know* (London: Red Fox, 2000) [1987]

Chambers, Aidan, *Postcards From No Man's Land* (London: Red Fox, 2001) [1999]

Chambers, Aidan, *This Is All: The Pillow Book of Cordelia Kenn* (London: The Bodley Head, 2005)

Chambers, Aidan, *The Toll Bridge* (London: Red Fox, 2000) [1992]

Clarke, Pauline, *The Twelve and the Genii* (Harmondsworth: Puffin, 1977) [1962]

Cleary, Beverly, *Fifteen* (London: Puffin, 1995) [1956]

Colfer, Eoin, *Artemis Fowl* (London: Viking, 2001)

Colfer, Eoin, *Artemis Fowl: The Arctic Incident* (London: Viking, 2002)

Colfer, Eoin, *Artemis Fowl: The Eternity Code* (London: Viking, 2003)

Colfer, Eoin, *Artemis Fowl: The Lost Colony* (London: Viking, 2006)

Colfer, Eoin, *Artemis Fowl: The Opal Deception* (London: Viking, 2005)

Colfer, Eoin, *Artemis Fowl: The Time Paradox* (London: Viking, 2008)

Collodi, Carlo, *The Adventures of Pinocchio / Le Avventura di Pinocchio*, trans Nicholas J. Perella (Berkeley: University of California Press, 2005) [1883]

Coolidge, Susan, *What Katy Did* (Harmondsworth: Puffin, 1995) [1872]

Cooper, Susan, *The Dark is Rising* (Harmondsworth: Puffin, 1976) [1973]

Cooper, Susan, *Greenwitch* (Harmondsworth: Puffin, 1977) [1974]

Cooper, Susan, *The Grey King* (Harmondsworth: Puffin, 1977) [1975]

Cooper, Susan, *Over Sea, Under Stone* (Harmondsworth: Puffin, 1968) [1965]

Cooper, Susan, *Silver on the Tree* (Harmondsworth: Puffin, 1979) [1977]

Cormier, Robert, *I Am the Cheese* (London: Collins, 1995) [1977]

Crompton, John, *Up the Road and Back* (London: Macmillan, 1977)

Dahl, Roald, *Charlie and the Chocolate Factory* (Harmondsworth: Puffin, 1995) [1964]

Dhondy, Farrukh, *East End At Your Feet* (London: Macmillan, 1976)

Dhondy, Farrukh, *The Siege of Babylon* (London: Macmillan, 1978)

Dickenson, Christine, *Last Straw* (London: Macmillan, 1975)

Dickinson, Peter, *The Blue Hawk* (Harmondsworth: Puffin, 1977) [1975]

Dickinson, Peter, *The Devil's Children* (Harmondsworth: Puffin, 1970) [1970]

Dickinson, Peter, *Heartsease* (Harmondsworth: Puffin, 1982) [1969]

Dickinson, Peter, *The Weathermonger* (Harmondsworth: Puffin, 1970) [1968]

Doubtfire, Dianne, *Girl in a Gondola* (London: Macmillan, 1980)

Dowd, Siobhan, *Bog Child* (Oxford: David Fickling, 2008)

Downham, Jenny, *Before I Die* (Oxford: David Fickling, 2007)

Forester, C.S., *Hornblower Goes to Sea* (Harmondsworth: Peacock, 1963) [1948]

Friedan, Betty, *The Feminine Mystique* (London: Penguin, 2010) [1963]

Fuller, Roy, *With My Little Eye* (Harmondsworth: Penguin, 1963) [1948]

Gaiman, Neil, *Coraline* (London: Bloomsbury, 2002)

Gardam, Jane, *Bilgewater* (Harmondsworth: Peacock, 1979) [1976]

Garner, Alan, *Elidor* (London: Armada Lions, 1974) [1965]

Garner, Alan, *The Owl Service* (Harmondsworth: Penguin, 1969) [1967]

Garner, Alan, *Red Shift* (London: Lions, 1975) [1973]

Garner, Alan, *The Weirdstone of Brisingamen* (Harmondsworth: Puffin, 1963) [1960]

Glanville, Brian, *A Bad Lot* (Harmondsworth: Penguin, 1977)

Gray, Keith, *Ostrich Boys* (London: Definitions, 2008)

Guy, Rosa, *The Friends* (Harmondsworth: Puffin, 1994) [1973]

Haddon, Mark, *The Curious Incident of the Dog in the Night-time* (Oxford: David Fickling, 2003)

Harnett, Cynthia, *The Load of Unicorn* (London: Methuen, 1959)

Harnett, Cynthia, *The Wool-pack* (Harmondsworth: Puffin, 1974) [1951]

Harris, Rosemary, *The Moon in the Cloud* (London: Faber, 1989) [1968]

Hearn, Lian, *Heaven's Net is Wide* (London: Macmillan, 2007)

Herbert, A.P., *The Water Gypsies* (London: Methuen, 1930)

Heyer, Georgette, *Devil's Cub* (Harmondsworth: Peacock, 1963) [1932]

Hildick, Wallace, *Jim Starling* (London: Chatto and Windus, 1958)

Hine, Barry, *The Blinder* (Harmondsworth: Penguin, 1969) [1966]

Holman, Felice, *Slake's Limbo* (London: Macmillan, 1980) [1974]

Hooper, Mary, *Megan* (London: Bloomsbury, 1999)

Horowitz, Anthony, *Ark Angel* (London: Walker, 2005)

Horowitz, Anthony, *Crocodile Tears* (London: Walker, 2009)

Horowitz, Anthony, *Eagle Strike* (London: Walker, 2003)

Horowitz, Anthony, *Point Blanc* (London: Walker, 2001)

Horowitz, Anthony, *Scorpia* (London: Walker, 2004)

Horowitz, Anthony, *Skeleton Key* (London: Walker, 2002)

Horowitz, Anthony, *Stormbreaker* (London: Walker, 2000)

Jones, Diana Wynne, *Charmed Life* (London: HarperCollins, 2001) [1977]

Jones, Diana Wynne, *The Ogre Downstairs* (London: HarperCollins, 2002) [1974]

Kamm, Josephine, *Young Mother* (London: Heinemann Educational Books, 1968) [1965]

Kästner, Erich, *Emil and the Detectives*, trans. Rod Smith (Harlow: Pearson Education, 2000) [1929]

Kemp, Gene, *The Turbulent Term of Tyke Tiler* (London: Faber and Faber, 2002) [1977]

King, Clive, *Stig of the Dump* (Harmondsworth: Puffin, 1987) [1963]

L'Engle, Madeline, *A Wrinkle in Time* (Harmondsworth: Puffin, 1967) [1962]

Lanagan, Margo, *Tender Morsels* (Oxford: David Fickling, 2009) [2008]

Larrabeiti, Michael de, *The Borribles* (New York: Tor, 2005) [1976]

Lawrence, D.H., *Sons and Lovers* (Oxford: Oxford University Press, 2009) [1913]

Lawrence, Louise, *Andra* (London: Macmillan, 1975) [1971]

Lawrence, Louise *Children of the Dust* (Cambridge: Cambridge University Press, 1996) [1985]

Le Guin, Ursula, *The Farthest Shore* (Harmondsworth: Puffin, 1974) [1971]

Le Guin, Ursula, *Tehanu* (London: Penguin, 1992) [1990]

Le Guin, Ursula, *The Tombs of Atuan* (Harmondsworth: Puffin, 1972) [1971]

Le Guin, Ursula, *A Wizard of Earthsea* (Harmondsworth: Puffin, 1971) [1968]

Leach, Christopher, *Answering Miss Roberts* (London: Macmillan, 1968)

Leeson, Robert, *The Third-Class Genie* (London: Collins, 2000) [1975]

Lewis, C.S., *The Horse and His Boy* (London: Fontana Lions, 1986) [1954]

Lewis, C.S., *The Last Battle* (London: Fontana Lions, 1986) [1956]

Lewis, C.S., *The Lion, the Witch and the Wardrobe* (London: Fontana Lions, 1986) [1950]

Lewis, C.S., *The Magician's Nephew* (London: Fontana Lions, 1986) [1955]

Lewis, C.S., *Prince Caspian* (London: Fontana Lions, 1986) [1951]

Lewis, C.S., *The Silver Chair* (London: Fontana Lions, 1986) [1953]

Lewis, C.S., *The Voyage of the Dawntreader* (London: Fontana Lions, 1986) [1955]

Lingard, Joan *The Twelfth Day of July* (London: Puffin, 2003) [1970]

Lipsyte, Robert, *The Contender* (London: Macmillan, 1969) [1967]

Lively, Penelope, *The Ghost of Thomas Kempe* (London: Heinemann, 1975) [1973]

Lively, Penelope, *A Stitch in Time* (London: Mammoth, 2000) [1976]

Loeff, An Rutgers van der, *Avalanche*, trans Dora Round (Harmondsworth: Puffin, 1967) [1954]

Loeff, An Rutgers van der, *Children on the Oregon Trail*, trans Dora Round (Harmondsworth: Puffin, 1963) [1949]

Lofting, Hugh, *The Voyages of Doctor Dolittle* (Harmondsworth: Puffin, 1967) [1922]

Lowry, Lois, *A Summer to Die* (Harmondsworth: Kestrel, 1979) [1977]

Lundgren, Max, *For the Love of Liza*, trans. Joan Tate (London: Macmillan, 1976)

Lundgren, Max, *Summer Girl*, trans. Joan Tate (London: Macmillan, 1976)

Maddock, Reginald, *The Pit* (London: Macmillan, 1972) [1966]

Mark, Jan *Thunder and Lightnings* (Harmondsworth: Kestrel, 1976)

Martin, Vicky, *September Song* (London: Macmillan, 1969)

Mayne, William, *Earthfasts* (London: Puffin, 1969) [1966]

Mayne, William, *A Game of Dark* (Harmondsworth: Puffin, 1974) [1971]

Meyer, Stephenie, *Breaking Dawn* (London: Atom, 2008)

Meyer, Stephenie, *Eclipse* (London: Atom, 2008) [2007]

Meyer, Stephenie, *New Moon* (London: Atom, 2007) [2006]

Meyer, Stephenie, *Twilight* (London: Atom, 2007) [2005]

Morpurgo, Michael, *Long Way Home* (London: Macmillan, 1975)

Muchamore, Robert, *Brigands, M.C.* (London: Hodder, 2009)

Muchamore, Robert, *Class A* (London: Hodder, 2004)

Muchamore, Robert, *Divine Madness* (London: Hodder, 2006)

Muchamore, Robert, *The Fall* (London: Hodder, 2006)

Muchamore, Robert, *The General* (London: Hodder, 2008)

Muchamore, Robert, *The Killing* (London: Hodder, 2005)

Muchamore, Robert, *Mad Dogs* (London: Hodder, 2007)

Muchamore, Robert, *Man vs Beast* (London: Hodder, 2006)

Muchamore, Robert, *Maximum Security* (London: Hodder, 2005)

Muchamore, Robert, *The Recruit* (London: Hodder, 2004)

Muchamore, Robert, *The Sleepwalker* (London: Hodder, 2008)

Paterson, Katherine, *A Bridge to Terabithia* (London: Puffin, 2006) [1977]

Pearce, Philippa, *A Dog So Small* (Harmondsworth: Puffin, 1964) [1962]

Pearce, Philippa, *Tom's Midnight Garden* (Harmondsworth: Puffin, 1976) [1958]

Peyton, K.M., *The Edge of the Cloud* (Harmondsworth: Puffin, 1979) [1969]

Peyton, K.M., *Flambards* (Harmondsworth: Puffin, 1976) [1967]

Peyton, K.M., *Flambards in Summer* (Harmondsworth: Puffin, 1977) [1969]

Porter, Sheena, *Nordy Bank* (London: Oxford University Press, 1971) [1964]

Pullman, Philip, *The Amber Spyglass* (London: Scholastic, 2000)

Pullman, Philip, *Northern Lights* (London: Scholastic, 1995)

Pullman, Philip, *The Ruby in the Smoke* (London: Scholastic, 2006) [1985]

Pullman, Philip, *The Shadow in the North* (London: Scholastic, 2007) [1986]

Pullman, Philip, *The Subtle Knife* (London: Scholastic, 1997)

Pullman, Philip, *The Tiger in the Well* (London: Scholastic, 2007) [1991]

Pullman, Philip, *The Tin Princess* (London: Scholastic, 2007) [1994]

Ransome, Arthur, *Pigeon Post* (Harmondsworth: Puffin,1969) [1936]

Ransome, Arthur, *Swallows and Amazons* (Harmondsworth: Puffin, 1974) [1930]

Reeve, Philip, *A Darkling Plain* (London: Scholastic, 2006)

Reeve, Philip, *Infernal Devices* (London: Scholastic, 2005)

Reeve, Philip, *Mortal Engines* (London: Scholastic, 2001)

Reeve, Philip, *Predator's Gold* (London: Scholastic, 2003)

Rennison, Louise, *...And That's When It Fell Off in My Hand* (London: Piccadilly, 2004)

Rennison, Louise, *Angus, Thongs and Full-Frontal Snogging* (London: Piccadilly, 1999)

Rennison, Louise, *Are These My Basoomas I See Before Me?* (London: HarperCollins Children's, 2009)

Rennison, Louise, *Dancing in my Nuddy-Pants* (London: Piccadilly, 2003)

Rennison, Louise, *It's OK, I'm Wearing Really Big Knickers* (London: Scholastic, 2001)

Rennison, Louise, *Knocked Out by my Nunga-Nungas* (London: Scholastic, 2002)

Rennison, Louise, *Luuurve is a Many Trousered Thing* (London: HarperCollins Children's, 2007)

Rennison, Louise, *...Startled by His Furry Shorts* (London: HarperCollins Children's, 2006)

Rennison, Louise, *Stop in the Name of Pants!* (London: HarperCollins Children's, 2008)

Rennison, Louise, *...Then He Ate My Boy Entrancers* (London: HarperCollins Children's, 2005)

Rodman, Maia, *Tuned Out* (London: Macmillan, 1976) [1968]

Rosenberg, Sondra, *Will There Never Be a Prince?* (London: Macmillan, 1974) [1970]

Rowling, J.K., *Harry Potter and the Chamber of Secrets* (London: Bloomsbury, 1998)

Rowling, J.K., *Harry Potter and the Deathly Hallows* (London: Bloomsbury, 2007)

Rowling, J.K., *Harry Potter and the Goblet of Fire* (London: Bloomsbury, 2000)

Rowling, J.K., *Harry Potter and the Half-Blood Prince* (London: Bloomsbury, 2005)

Rowling, J.K., *Harry Potter and the Order of the Phoenix* (London: Bloomsbury, 2003)

Rowling, J.K., *Harry Potter and the Philosopher's Stone* (London: Bloomsbury, 1997)

Rowling, J.K., *Harry Potter and the Prisoner of Azkaban* (London: Bloomsbury, 1999)

Sagan, Françoise, *Bonjour Tristesse*, trans. Irene Ash (London: Penguin, 2007) [1954]

Salinger, J.D., *The Catcher in the Rye* (Boston: Little Brown, 2001) [1951]

Schlee, Ann, *The Vandal* (London: Magnet, 1983) [1979]

Serailler, Ian, *The Silver Sword* (Harmondsworth: Puffin, 1979) [1956]

Smith, Dodie, *I Capture the Castle* (London: Virago, 1995) [1948]

Southall, Ian, *Josh* (London: Angus and Robertson, 1971)

Sparks, Beatrice, *Go Ask Alice* (New York: Simon and Schuster, 1988) [1971]

Spock, Dr. Benjamin, *The Pocket Book of Baby and Child-Care* (New York: Pocket Books, 1951) [1946]

Stewart, Maureen, *Orange Wendy* (London: Macmillan, 1974)

Storr, Catherine, *Marianne Dreams* (Harmondsworth: Puffin, 1964) [1951]

Streatfeild, Noel, *Ballet Shoes* (Harmondsworth: Puffin, 1983) [1936]

Sutcliff, Rosemary, *Knight's Fee* (London: Oxford University Press, 1960)

Sutcliff, Rosemary, *The Lantern Bearers* (Oxford: Oxford University Press, 2007) [1959]

Sutcliff, Rosemary, *Warrior Scarlet* (London: Oxford University Press, 1958)

Sutcliff, Rosemary, *Witch's Brat* (London: Oxford University Press, 1970)

Tate, Joan, *Clipper*, rev. edn (London: Macmillan, 1976)

Tate, Joan, *Sam and Me* (London: Macmillan, 1969)

Tate, Joan, *Whizz Kid* (London: Macmillan,1969)

Thompson, Kate, *Creature of the Night* (London: Bodley Head, 2008)

Todd, Barbara Euphan, *Worzel Gummidge* (Oxford: Oxford University Press, 2001) [1936]

Tolkien, J.R.R., *The Hobbit* (London: HarperCollins, 2001) [1937]

Townsend, John Rowe, *Goodnight, Prof, Love* (Harmondsworth: Puffin, 1989) [1973]

Townsend, John Rowe, *Gumble's Yard* (Harmondsworth: Puffin, 1967) [1961]

Trease, Geoffrey, *Bows Against the Barons* (Nottingham: Five Leaves, 2009) [1934]

Walsh, Jill Paton, *The Emperor's Winding Sheet* (Harmondsworth: Puffin, 1976) [1974]

Walsh, Jill Paton, *Unleaving* (London: Bodley Head, 1985) [1976]

Webb, Charles, *The Graduate* (London: Penguin, 2009) [1963]

Webb, Kaye, ed., *I Like This Story: A Taste of Fifty Favourites* (Harmondsworth: Puffin, 1986)

Westall, Robert, *The Machine Gunners* (London: Macmillan, 2001) [1975]

Wilson, Jacqueline, *Diamond Girls* (London: Doubleday, 2004)

Wilson, Jacqueline, *Girls in Love* (London: Doubleday, 1997)

Wilson, Jacqueline, *Girls in Tears* (London: Doubleday, 2002)

Wilson, Jacqueline, *Girls out Late* (London: Doubleday, 1999)

Winberg, Anna Greta, *When Someone Splits*, trans. Patricia Crampton (London: Macmillan, 1978)

Wodehouse, P.G., *Very Good, Jeeves!* (Harmondsworth: Peacock, 1965) [1930]

Zindel, Paul, *I Never Loved Your Mind* (London: Bodley Head, 1971) [1970]

Zindel, Paul, *My Darling, My Hamburger* (London: Red Fox, 1992) [1969]

Zindel, Paul, *The Pigman* (London: Red Fox, 1993) [1968]

Secondary Sources

Abebooks, 'The Holy Grail of Harry Potter Books', *abebooks.co.uk*, <http://www.abebooks.co.uk/docs/harry-potter/hp-holy-grail.shtml> [accessed 01/12/09]

Aiken, Joan, 'A Free Gift' in *The Thorny Paradise: Writers on Writing For Children*, ed. by Edward Blishen (Harmondsworth: Kestrel, 1975), 36–52

Alderson, Brian, 'The Irrelevance of Children to the Children's Book Reviewer' in *Children's Literature: The Development of Criticism*, ed. by Peter Hunt (London: Routledge, 1990), 53–5

Alderson, Brian, 'Puff puff Puffin along: Brian Alderson on the publication of the thousandth Puffin', *Times Educational Supplement* (No. 3272), 10 March 1978, p. 1

Anonymous, 'Through Literature to Life?', *Signal*, 11 (May 1973), 102–7

Ariès, Philippe, *Centuries of Childhood: A Social History of Family Life*, trans. Robert Baldick (London: Jonathan Cape, 1973)

Armstrong, Eileen, ed., *Riveting Reads: Boys into Books 11–14* (Swindon: School Library Association, 2007)

Avery, Gillian, *Nineteenth Century Children: Heroes and Heroines in English Children's Stories 1980–1900* (London: Hodder & Stoughton, 1965)

Barker, Keith, 'Prize-fighting' in *Children's Book Publishing in Britain Since 1945*, ed. by Kimberley Reynolds and Nicholas Tucker (Aldershot: Scolar Press, 1998), 42–59

Barker, Martin, 'Getting a Conviction: Or, How the British Horror Comics Campaign Only Just Succeeded' in *Pulp Demons: International Dimensions of the Postwar Anti-Comics Campaign*, ed. John A. Lent (London: Associated University Presses, 1999), 69–92

Barker, Martin, *A Haunt of Fear: The Strange History of the British Horror Comics Campaign* (Jackson, MS; London: University Press of Mississippi, 1992)

Bawden, Nina, 'A Dead Pig and My Father' in *Writers, Critics and Children: Articles from Children's Literature in Education*, ed. by Geoff Fox et al. (London: Heinemann Educational Books, 1976), 3–14

Bawden, Nina, 'The Imprisoned Child' in *The Thorny Paradise: Writers on Writing for Children*, ed. by Edward Blishen (Harmondsworth: Kestrel, 1975), 62–4

BBC News, 'Record print run for final Potter', *BBC News*, 15 March 2007, <http://news.bbc.co.uk/1/hi/entertainment/6452987.stm> [accessed 29/4/07]

Berg, Leila, *Reading and Loving* (London: Routledge, 1977)

Bettelheim, Bruno, *The Uses of Enchantment: The Meaning and Importance of Fairy Tales* (Harmondsworth: Penguin, 1991)

Blishen, Edward, ed., *The Thorny Paradise* (Harmondsworth: Kestrel, 1975)

Booktrust, 'The Booktrust Teenage Prize 2010', *Booktrust Children's Books* (2010), <http://www.booktrustchildrensbooks.org.uk/show/feature/Booktrust-Teenage-Prize-2010> [accessed 20/01/10]

Bowles, Steve, 'Be Our Guest...', *Books for Keeps*, 2 (May 1980), <http://www.booksforkeeps.co.uk/issue/2/childrens-books/articles/be-our-guest/be-our-guest> [accessed 18/01/10]

Bradley, Sue, ed., *The British Book Trade: An Oral History* (London: The British Library, 2008)

Bridgmann, Joan, 'Richard Adams at Eighty', *Contemporary Review*, 277:1615 (2000), 108–12

Britton, James, 'The role of fantasy' in *The Cool Web: The Pattern of Children's Reading*, ed. by Margaret Meek et al. (London: Bodley Head, 1977), 40–47

Bullock, Alan, 'A Language for Life' (London: HMSO, 1975), *Education in England*, <http://www.educationengland.org.uk/documents/bullock/> [accessed 02/08/12]

Butler, Charles, *Four British Fantasists: Place and Culture in the Children's Fantasies of Penelope Lively, Alan Garner, Susan Cooper, and Diana Wynne Jones* (Oxford: Children's Literature Association and Scarecrow Press, 2006)

Butts, Dennis, *Children's Literature and Social Change: Some Case Studies from Barbara Hofland to Philip Pullman* (Cambridge: Lutterworth Press, 2010)

Byatt, A.S., 'Harry Potter and the Childish Adult', *The New York Times*, 7 July 2003, <http://www.nytimes.com/2003/07/07/opinion/harry-potter-and-the-childish-adult.html?scp=10&sq=A.S.Byatt&st=nyt&pagewanted=1> [accessed 03/01/10]

Cadogan, Mary and Patricia Craig, *You're a Brick, Angela!: A New Look at Girls' Fiction From 1839 to 1975* (London: Gollancz, 1976)

Cameron, Eleanor, *The Green and Burning Tree: On the Writing and Enjoyment of Children's Books* (Boston, Toronto: Little, Brown, 1969)

Cate, Dick, 'Forms of storying: the inner and outer worlds: uses of narrative' in *The Cool Web: The Pattern of Children's Reading*, ed. by Margaret Meek et al. (London: Bodley Head, 1977), 24–31

Chambers, Aidan, 'Alive and Flourishing: A Personal View of Teenage Literature' in *Booktalk: Occasional Writing on Literature and Children* (Stroud: Thimble Press, 1995), 84–91

Chambers, Aidan, 'All of a Tremble to See His Danger', in *Reading Talk* (Stroud: Thimble Press, 2001), 29–50

Chambers, Aidan, 'Anne Frank's Pen', in *Reading Talk* (Stroud: Thimble Press, 2001), 9–28

Chambers, Aidan, 'Axes For Frozen Seas', in *Booktalk: Occasional Writing on Literature and Children* (Stroud: Thimble Press, 1995), 14–33

Chambers, Aidan, *Booktalk: Occasional Writing on Literature and Children* (Stroud: Thimble Press, 1995)

Chambers, Aidan, 'The Dance Sequence', *Aidan Chambers*, <http://www.aidanchambers.co.uk/sequence.htm> [accessed 06/01/10]

Chambers, Aidan, 'In Spite of Being a Translation', in *Reading Talk* (Stroud: Thimble Press, 2001), 113–37

Chambers, Aidan, Interview with Lucy Pearson, 27 April 2009

Chambers, Aidan, 'Letter From England: American Writing and British Readers' in *Booktalk: Occasional Writing on Literature and Children* (Stroud: Thimble Press, 1995), 77–83

Chambers, Aidan, 'Pick Up a Penguin' in *Reading Talk* (Stroud: Thimble Press, 1995), 99–112

Chambers, Aidan, 'The Reader in the Book' in *Booktalk: Occasional Writing on Literature and Children* (Stroud: Thimble Press, 1995), 34–58

Chambers, Aidan, 'The Reader in the Book: Notes From Work in Progress', *Signal Approaches to Children's Books*, 23 (May 1977), 64–87

Chambers, Aidan, *The Reading Environment* (Stroud: Thimble Press, 1991)

Chambers, Aidan, *Reading for Enjoyment: For 11 Year Olds & Up* (London: Children's Booknews Ltd, 1975)

Chambers, Aidan, *Reading Talk* (Stroud: Thimble Press, 1995)

Chambers, Aidan, *The Reluctant Reader* (London: The Pergamon Press, 1969)

Chambers, Aidan, *Tell Me: Children, Reading and Talk* (Stroud: Thimble Press, 1993)

Chambers, Nancy, 'A Note From the Editor', *Signal Approaches to Children's Books*, <http://www.claas-kazzer.de/signal/about.html> [accessed 10/12/07]

Chambers, Nancy, ed., *Reading the Novels of Aidan Chambers: Seven Essays* (Stroud: Thimble Press, 2009)

Chesney, Ann, 'The young idea', *Guardian*, 9 December 1964, p. 8

Children's Book Circle, 'Eleanor Farjeon Award', *Children's Book Circle*, <http://www.childrensbookcircle.org.uk/farjeon.asp> [accessed 03/07/09]

Children's Rights Workshop, *Sexism in Children's Books: Facts, Figures and Guidelines* (London: Writers and Readers Pub. Cooperative, 1976)

Childs, David, *Britain Since 1945: A Political History*, 5th edition (London & New York: Routledge, 2001)

Chukovsky, K., 'There is no such thing as a shark' in *The Cool Web: The Pattern of Children's Reading*, ed. by Margaret Meek et al. (London: Bodley Head, 1977), 48–50

CILIP, 'The CILIP Carnegie Medal Nominations for 2010', *The CILIP Carnegie and Kate Greenaway Children's Book Awards* (2010), <http://www.carnegiegreenaway.org.uk/pressdesk/press.php?release=pres_nom_car_2010.html> [accessed 03/01/10]

Copson, Belinda, 'Geoffrey Trease (1909–1998)', *British Children's Historical Novels*, <http://www.collectingbooksandmagazines.com/history.html> (1999) [accessed 28/08/2009]

Costa Book Awards, 'Past Winners', *Costa Book Awards*, <http://www.costabookawards.com/awards/previous_winners_archive.aspx> [accessed 25/05/09]

Crampton, Patricia, 'Will It Travel Well?' *Signal,* 17 (May 1975), 75–80

Crandall, Nadia, 'The UK Children's Book Business 1995–2004: A Strategic Analysis', *New Review of Children's Literature and Librarianship*, 12:1 (April 2006), 1–18

Crompton, John, 'The Politics of Not Reading: Writing for Power', *Children's Literature in Education*, 11:2 (1980), 76–81

Croome, Lesley, 'A million a month', *T.L.S Children's Books*, 15 June 1973, pp. 1–2

Crouch, Marcus, *Treasure Seekers and Borrowers: Children's Books in Britain, 1900–1960* (London: The Library Association, 1962)

Cunningham, Hugh, *The Invention of Childhood* (London: BBC Books, 2006)

Darton, F.J. Harvey, *Children's Books in England* (Cambridge: Cambridge University Press, 1982)

Davis, Kenneth C., *Two-Bit Culture: The Paperbacking of America* (Boston: Houghton Mifflin, 1984)

Demers, Patricia, *From Instruction to Delight: An Anthology of Children's Literature to 1850*, 2nd edn (Oxford: Oxford University Press, 2004)

Dickinson, Peter, 'A Defence of Rubbish' in *Writers, Critics and Children: Articles from Children's Literature in Education*, ed. by Geoff Fox et al. (London: Heinemann Educational Books, 1976), 73–6

Dixon, Bob, *Catching Them Young 1: Sex, Race and Class in Children's Fiction* (London: Pluto Press, 1977)

Egoff, Sheila, G.T. Stubbs and L.F. Ashley, eds, *Only Connect: Readings on Children's Literature* (Toronto, New York: Oxford University Press, 1969)

Engelhardt, Tom, 'Reading May Be Harmful To Your Kids: In the Nadirland of Today's Children's Books', *Harper's Magazine*, June 1991, pp. 55–62

Eyre, Frank, *20th Century Children's Books* (London: Longman, Green and Co, 1952)

Eyre, Frank, *British Children's Books in the Twentieth Century* (London: Longman, 1971)

Federation for Children's Book Groups, The, 'General Information', *The Federation for Children's Book Groups*, <http://www.fcbg.org.uk/general-information/> [accessed 01/07/09]

Fisher, Margery, *Intent upon Reading: A Critical Appraisal of Modern Children's Fiction* (Leicester: Brockhampton Press, 1961)

Flood, Alison, 'Puffin Post to Become Extinct', *Guardian* (17 December 2012), <http://www.guardian.co.uk/books/2012/dec/17/puffin-post-penguin-become-extinct> [accessed 28/04/13]

Forbes, 'The Celebrity 100: J.K. Rowling', *Forbes.com*, 16 November 2008, <http://www.forbes.com/lists/2008/53/celebrities08_JK-Rowling_CRTT.html> [accessed 29/10/09]

Foster, John L., 'A reading policy for a comprehensive school (11–16)', *Children's Literature in Education*, 17 (Summer 1975), 51–65

Fox, Geoff, et al., eds, *Writers, Critics, and Children: Articles from Children's Literature in Education* (London: Heinemann Educational Books, 1976)

Franklin, Bob, *British Television Policy: A Reader* (London: Routledge, 2001)

Gatiss, Mark, *On the Outside it Looked Like an Old Fashioned Police Box*, BBC Radio 4 broadcast, 23 June 2009

Glistrup, Eva, *The Hans Christian Andersen Awards 1956–2002* (Copenhagen: Gyldendal, 2002)

Graham, Judith, 'Picture Books', in *Children's Book Publishing in Britain Since 1945*, ed. by Kimberley Reynolds and Nicholas Tucker Tucker (Aldershot: Scolar Press, 1998), 60–85

Graves, Peter, 'Swedish Children's Books in Britain', *Signal* 18 (September 1975), 137–41

Greaves, Griselda, 'The in-between and reluctant' *Guardian*, Friday, July 12, 1968, p. 7

Green, Roger Lancelyn, *Tellers of Tales: Children's Authors and Their Books of the Last 100 Years* (London: Ward, 1946)

Green, Roger Lancelyn, *Tellers of Tales: Children's Books and Their Authors from 1800 to 1964*, rev. edn (London: Ward, 1965)

Greenway, Betty, *Aidan Chambers: Master Literary Choreographer* (Lanham, MD: Scarecrow Press, 2006)

Grenby, Matthew, *Children's Literature* (Edinburgh: Edinburgh University Press, 2008)

Gritten, Sally, *The Story of Puffin Books* (Harmondsworth: Penguin, 1991)

Grove, Valerie, *So Much To Tell* (Harmondsworth: Viking, 2010)

Hade, Daniel, 'Storyselling: Are Publishers Changing the Way Children Read?', *The Horn Book Magazine*, September/October 2002, pp. 509–15

Halliford, Deborah, 'Children's Books in Translation', *Carousel*, 31 (Autumn 2005), <http://www.carouselguide.co.uk/pdf/31p40.pdf> [accessed 12/12/09]

Halliford, Deborah, *Outside In: Children's Books in Translation* (London: Millet, 2005)

Harding, D.W., 'Psychological processes in the reading of fiction' *The Cool Web: The Pattern of Children's Reading* (London: Bodley Head, 1977), ed. by Margaret Meek et al., 58–72

Hare, Steve, *Penguin Portrait: Allen Lane and the Penguin editors, 1935–1970* (London: Penguin, 1995)

Haviland, Virginia, 'A New Internationalism' in *Children and Literature: Views and Reviews*, ed. by Virginia Haviland (London: Bodley Head, 1974), 328–34

Haviland, Virginia, 'A Second Golden Age? In a Time of Flood', in *Children and Literature: Views and Reviews*, ed. by Virginia Haviland (London: Bodley Head, 1974), 88–97

Hazard, Paul, *Books, Children and Men*, trans. Marguerite Mitchell (Boston: The Horn Book, 1965)

Hendrick, Harry, 'Children and Childhood', *ReFresh: Recent Findings of Research in Economic and Social History*, 15 (Autumn 1992), 1–4

Hildick, Wallace, *Children and Fiction* (London: Evans, 1970)

Hill, Janet, *Reading for Enjoyment: For 8 to 11 Year Olds* (London: Children's Booknews Ltd, 1975)

Hobbs, Sandy and David Cornwell, '"The Lore and Language of Schoolchildren": A Study of Scholars' Reactions', *Folklore*, 102:2 (1992), 175–82

Hoffman, Mary, 'Children's paperbacks in a state of change', *The Bookseller*, No. 4132, 2 March 1985, pp. 855–9

Holbrook, David, 'The Problem of C.S. Lewis' in *Writers, Critics and Children: Articles from Children's Literature in Education*, ed. by Geoff Fox et al. (London: Heinemann Educational Books, 1976), 116–24

Hollindale, Peter, *Choosing Books for Children* (London: Elek, 1974)

Hollindale, Peter, *Ideology and the Children's Book* (Stroud: Signal, 1988)

Hollindale, Peter, *Signs of Childness in Children's Books* (Stroud: The Thimble Press, 1997)

Hollindale, Peter and Zena Sutherland, 'Internationalism, Fantasy and Realism: 1945–1970' in *Children's Literature: An Illustrated History*, ed. by Peter Hunt (Oxford: Oxford University Press, 1995), 252–88

Horn Book, The, 'About Us', *The Horn Book*, <http://www.hbook.com/aboutus/> (2009) [accessed 27/07/09]

Horn, Caroline, 'Puffin Post to Fly With The Book People', *The Bookseller* (19 September 2009), <http://www.thebookseller.com/news/67362-puffin-post-to-fly-with-the-book-people.html.rss> [accessed 20/01/10]

Hunt, Peter, 'Childist Criticism: The Subculture of the Child, the Book and Critic', *Signal*, January 1984, 42–59

Hunt, Peter, *Children's Literature* (Oxford: Blackwell, 2001)

Hunt, Peter, *An Introduction to Children's Literature* (Oxford: Oxford University Press, 1994)

Hunt, Peter, 'Questions of Method and Methods of Questioning: Childist Criticism in Action', *Signal*, September 1984, 180–200

Hunt, Peter, ed., *Children's Literature: The Development of Criticism* (London: Routledge, 1993)

Inglis, Fred, *The Promise of Happiness: Value and Meaning in Children's Fiction* (Cambridge: Cambridge University Press, 1981)

Jago, Wendy, '"A Wizard of Earthsea" and the Charge of Escapism', *Children's Literature in Education*, 3:2 (1972), 21–9

Jenkins, Henry, 'The Sensuous Child: Dr. Benjamin Spock and the Sexual Revolution' in *The Children's Culture Reader*, ed. by Henry Jenkins (New York: New York University Press, 1998), 209–30

Jenkins, Janet, *Reading for Enjoyment: 9 to 11 Year Olds* (London: Children's Booknews Ltd, 1970)

Jenkins, Sue, 'Growing Up in Earthsea', *Children's Literature in Education*, 16:1 (March 1985), 21–31

Kennerley, Peter, ed., *Teenage Reading* (London: Ward Lock Educational, 1979)

Knapp, Nancy Flanagan, 'In Defense of Harry Potter: An Apologia', *School Libraries Worldwide*, 9:1 (2003), 78–91

Lambert, J.W. and Michael Ratcliffe, *The Bodley Head: 1887–1987* (London: The Bodley Head, 1987)

Larbalestier, Justine, 'Ain't That a Shame (Updated)', *Justine Larbalestier: Writing, Reading, Eating, Drinking, Sport*, 23 July 2009, <http://justinelarbalestier.com/blog/2009/07/23/aint-that-a-shame/> [accessed 12/01/10]

Le Guin, Ursula K., *Earthsea Revisioned* (Cambridge: Green Bay Publications, 1993)

Lesnik-Oberstein, Karín, 'Childhood and Textuality: Culture, History, Literature' in *Children in Culture: Approaches to Childhood*, ed. by Karín Lesnik-Oberstein (Basingstoke: Macmillan Press, 1998), 1–27

Lesnik-Oberstein, Karín, *Children's Literature: Criticism and the Fictional Child* (Oxford: Clarendon Press, 1994)

Lewis, C.S., 'On Three Ways of Writing For Children' in *Only Connect: Readings on Children's Literature*, ed. by Sheila Egoff, G.T. Stubbs and L.F. Ashley (Toronto, New York: Oxford University Press, 1969), 207–22

Lewis, Naomi, *The Best Children Books of 1963* (London: Hamish Hamilton, 1964)

Lochhead, Marion, 'Clio Junior: Historical Novels for Children' in *Only Connect: Readings on Children's Literature*, ed. by Sheila Egoff, G.T. Stubbs and L.F. Ashley (Toronto, New York: Oxford University Press, 1969), 233–43

Lourie, Helen, 'Where is Fancy Bred?', *Only Connect: Readings on Children's Literature*, ed. by Sheila Egoff, G.T. Stubbs and L.F. Ashley (Toronto, New York: Oxford University Press, 1969), 106–10

Manners, Elizabeth, *The Vulnerable Generation* (London: Cassell, 1972)

McDonald, Jill (illustrator), Cover artwork, *Puffin Post*, 5:1 (1971)

McDonald, Jill (illustrator), 'Odway', *Puffin Post*, 4:1 (1970), p. 3

McDowell, Myles, 'Fiction for Children and Adults: Some Essential Differences' in *Writers, Critics and Children: Articles from Children's Literature in Education*, ed. by Geoff Fox et al. (London: Heinemann Educational Books, 1976), 140–56

Meek, Margaret et al., eds, *The Cool Web: The Pattern of Children's Reading* (London: Bodley Head, 1977)

Morpurgo, J.E., *Allen Lane, King Penguin: A Biography* (London: Hutchison, 1979)

Moss, Elaine, 'The Adult-eration of Children's Books' in *Part of the Pattern: A Personal Journey Through the World of Children's Books, 1960–1985* (London: The Bodley Head, 1986), 113–8

Moss, Elaine, 'A Mirror in The Market Place', in *Part of the Pattern: A Personal Journey Through the World of Children's Books, 1960–1985* (London: The Bodley Head, 1986) 119–23

Moss, Elaine, *Part of the Pattern: A Personal Journey Through the World of Children's Books, 1960–1985* (London: The Bodley Head, 1986)

Moss, Elaine, 'Reluctant at Fifteen', in *Part of the Pattern: A Personal Journey Through the World of Children's Books, 1960–1985* (London: The Bodley Head, 1986) 31–3

Moss, Elaine, 'Review of Young Mother' in *Part of the Pattern: A Personal Journey Through the World of Children's Books, 1960–1985* (London: The Bodley Head, 1986), 23

Moss, Elaine, 'The Seventies in Children's Books', in *Part of the Pattern: A Personal Journey Through the World of Children's Books, 1960–1985* (London: The Bodley Head, 1986), 136–60

Moss, Elaine, ed., *Children's Books of the Year 1974* (London: Hamish Hamilton, 1975)

Moss, Elaine, ed., *Children's Books of the Year 1976* (London: Hamish Hamilton, 1977), 5–10

Ness, Patrick, *The Knife of Never Letting Go* (London: Walker Books, 2008)

Nettell, Stephanie, 'Obituary: Philippa Pearce', *Guardian*, 2 January 2007, <http://www.guardian.co.uk/news/2007/jan/02/guardianobituaries. booksforchildrenandteenagers> [accessed 23/07/09]

Newsom, John, 'Half Our Future' (London: HMSO, 1963), *Education in England*, <http://www.educationengland.org.uk/documents/newsom/> [accessed 02/08/12]

Nikolajeva, Maria, 'Exit Children's Literature?', *The Lion and the Unicorn*, 22:2 (1998), 221–36

Nodelman, Perry, 'The Case of the Disappearing Jew', *Children's Literature in Education*, 10:1 (1979), 44–8

Opie, Iona and Peter, *Children's Games in Street and Playground* (Oxford: Clarendon Press, 1969)

Opie, Iona and Peter, *The Lore and Language of Schoolchildren* (London: Oxford University Press, 1967)

Pearce, Philippa, 'Competition Winners', *Guardian*, 16 July 1975, p. 16

Pearce, Philippa, 'Interview with Kimberley Reynolds and Nicholas Tucker, 1995', in *Oral Archives: A Collection of Informal Conversations with Individuals Involved in Creating or Producing Children's Literature since 1945*, compiled by Kimberley Reynolds and Nicholas Tucker (London: Roehampton University, 1998), 289–305

Pearson, Lucy and Kimberley Reynolds, 'Realism' in *The Routledge Companion to Children's Literature* (London: Routledge, 2010), 63–74

Penguin Books, *Complete Catalogue of the Publications of Penguin Books* (Harmondsworth: Penguin, 1970)

Penguin Books, *Fifty Penguin Years* (Harmondsworth: Penguin, 1985)

Pinsent, Pat, 'Historical Studies', in *Teaching Children's Fiction*, ed. by Charles Butler (Basingstoke: Palgrave Macmillan, 2006), 6–28

Plowden, Bridget and The Central Advisory Council for Education (England), *The Plowden Report: Children and their Primary Schools* (London: HMSO, 1967), Volume 1, Chapter 2, <http://www.educationengland.org.uk/documents/ plowden/> [accessed 14/08/09]

Postman, Neil, *The Disappearance of Childhood* (New York: Vintage, 1994)

Puffin Books, 'The History of Puffin', *Puffin Books*, <http://www.puffin.co.uk/ static/aboutpuffin/historyofpuffin/> [accessed 20/01/10]

Puffin Books, 'The Story of Puffin', *Puffin Books*, <http://www.puffin.co.uk/nf/ shared/SharedDisplayTable/0,15126_1,00.html> [accessed 29/4/07]

Rabinovitch, Dina, 'The greatest stories ever told', *Guardian*, 31 March 2005, <http://books.guardian.co.uk/news/articles/0,6109,1448965,00.html> [accessed 29/04/07]

Ray, Sheila, *The Blyton Phenomenon: The Controversy Surrounding the World's Most Successful Children's Writer* (London: Andre Deutsch, 1982)

Ray, Sheila, 'The Development of the Teenage Novel' in *Reluctant to Read?*, ed. by John Foster (London: Ward Lock Educational, 1977), 46–67

Rees, David, 'Skin Colour in British Children's Books, *Children's Literature in Education*, 11:2 (June 1980), 91–7

Reynolds, Kimberley, 'Publishing Practices and the Practicalities of Publishing' in *Children's Book Publishing in Britain Since 1945*, ed. by Kimberley Reynolds and Nicholas Tucker (Aldershot: Scolar Press, 1998), 20–41

Reynolds, Kimberley, and Nicholas Tucker, 'Interview with Judy Taylor (The Bodley Head), 21 February 1995', in *Oral Archives: A Collection of Informal Conversations with Individuals Involved in Creating or Producing Children's Literature since 1945*, compiled by Kimberley Reynolds and Nicholas Tucker (London: Roehampton University, 1998), 332–47

Reynolds, Kimberley, and Nicholas Tucker, 'Interview with Kaye Webb, 7 February 1995', in *Oral Archives: A Collection of Informal Conversations with Individuals Involved in Creating or Producing Children's Literature since 1945*, compiled by Kimberley Reynolds and Nicholas Tucker (London: Roehampton University, 1998), 366–88

Reynolds, Kimberley, and Nicholas Tucker, 'Interview with Paul Binding (Oxford University Press), 10 March 1997' in *Oral Archives: A Collection of Informal Conversations with Individuals Involved in Creating or Producing Children's Literature since 1945*, compiled by Kimberley Reynolds and Nicholas Tucker (London: Roehampton University, 1998), 57–68

Reynolds, Kimberley and Nicholas Tucker, eds, *Children's Book Publishing in Britain Since 1945* (Aldershot: Scolar Press, 1998)

Roberts, Nesta, 'The playground their world' *Guardian*, 16 March 1960, p. 7

Rose, Jacqueline, *The Case of Peter Pan: Or, The Impossibility of Children's Fiction*, rev. edn (London: Macmillan, 1992)

Rowman, A.J., 'Irresponsible teenagers', *Manchester Guardian*, 9 April 1958, p. 6

Rudd, David, *Enid Blyton and the Mystery of Children's Literature* (Basingstoke: Palgrave, 2000)

Sandberg, Rosemary, 'The Relevance of Books for Older Children' in *Teenage Reading*, ed. by Peter Kennerley (London: Ward Lock Educational, 1979), 29–34

Shippey, Tom, 'Tolkien as a Post-War Writer' in *Proceedings of the J.R.R. Tolkien Centenary Conference*, ed. by Patricia Reynolds and Glen H. GoodKnight (Altadena: Mythopoeic Press, 1995), 84–93

Sinfield, Alan, *Literature, Politics and Culture in Postwar Britain* (London, New York: Continuum, 2004)

Smith, Lillian H., 'News From Narnia' in *Only Connect: Readings on Children's Literature*, ed. by Sheila Egoff, G.T. Stubbs and L.F. Ashley (Toronto, New York: Oxford University Press, 1969), 170–75

Spencer, Ian R.G., *British Immigration Policy Since 1939: The Making of Multi-racial Britain* (London & New York: Routledge, 1997)

Springhall, John, *Coming of Age: Adolescence in Britain, 1860–1960* (Dublin: Gill and Macmillan)

Stephens, John, *Language and Ideology in Children's Fiction* (London and New York: Longman, 1992)

Stones, Rosemary, '13 Other Years: The Other Award 1975–1987', *Books For Keeps*, 53 (November 1988), <http://www.booksforkeeps.co.uk/issue/53/childrens-books/articles/other-articles/awards> [accessed 12/01/10]

Stones, Rosemary, 'Multi-cultural Publishing: What it Took to Get Us Where We Are' in *Diversity in Publishing*, <http://www.diversityinpublishing.com/Recommended-Reads/MEDIA-ARTICLES/Multi-cultural-Publishing-What-it-took-to-get-to-where-we-are> [accessed 11/02/08]

Stuart, Malcolm, 'Plight of the school leavers', *Guardian*, 28 September 1971, p. 8

Sutton, Roger, 'Potter's Field', *The Horn Book Magazine*, 76 (May/June 2000), p. 1

Thwaite, M.F., *From Primer to Pleasure: An Introduction to the History of Children's Books in England, from the Invention of Printing to 1900* (London: The Library Association, 1963)

Townsend, John Rowe, 'Standards of Criticism in Children's Literature' in *Children's Literature: the Development of Criticism*, ed. by Peter Hunt (London: Routledge, 1990), 57–70

Townsend, John Rowe, *Written for Children: An Outline of English Children's Literature* (London: Garnet Miller, 1965)

Townsend, John Rowe, *Written for Children: An Outline of English-language Children's Literature*, 2nd rev. edn (Harmondsworth: Kestrel, 1983)

Townsend, John Rowe, and Jill Paton Walsh, 'Interview with Kimberley Reynolds and Nicholas Tucker, 2 May 1995', in *Oral Archives: A Collection of Informal Conversations with Individuals Involved in Creating or Producing Children's Literature since 1945*, compiled by Kimberley Reynolds and Nicholas Tucker (London: Roehampton University, 1998), 262–88

Trease, Geoffrey, 'The Revolution in Children's Literature' in *The Thorny Paradise: Writers on Writing For Children*, ed. by Edward Blishen (Harmondsworth: Kestrel, 1975), 13–24

Trease, Geoffrey, *Tales Out of School*, 2nd edn (London: Heinemann Educational Books, 1964)

Triggs, Pat, 'Authorgraph No. 4', *Books For Keeps*, 4 (September 1980), <http://www.booksforkeeps.co.uk/issue/4/childrens-books/articles/authorgraph/authorgraph-no4-farrukh-dhondy> [accessed 12/01/10]

Triggs, Pat, 'The Other Award 1981', *Books For Keeps*, 11 (November 1981). <http://www.booksforkeeps.co.uk/issue/11/childrens-books/articles/awards/awards> [accessed 01/09/09]

Trites, Roberta Seelinger, *Disturbing the Universe: Power and Repression in Adolescent Literature* (Iowa City: University of Iowa Press, 2000)

Trites, Roberta Seelinger, 'Historiography and Children's Literature', paper presented at *The Best of Three: The 36th annual Children's Literature Association Conference*, Charlotte, NC, USA, 12 June 2009

Tucker, Joan and Alan Tucker, *Reading for Enjoyment: For 6 to 8 Year Olds* (London: Children's Booknews Ltd, 1975)

Tucker, Nicholas, 'Depressive Stories for Children', *Children's Literature in Education*, 37:3 (September 2006), 199–210

Tucker, Nicholas, 'How Children Respond to Fiction' in *Writers, Critics and Children: Articles from Children's Literature in Education*, ed. by Geoff Fox et al. (London: Heinemann Educational Books, 1976), 177–89

Tucker, Nicholas, 'Setting the Scene' in *Children's Book Publishing in Britain Since 1945*, ed. by Kimberley Reynolds and Nicholas Tucker (Aldershot: Scolar Press, 1998), 1–19

Tucker, Nicholas, ed., *Suitable for Children? Controversies in Children's Literature* (Sussex: Sussex University Press, 1978)

Walsh, Jill Paton 'Seeing Green' in *The Thorny Paradise*, ed. by Edward Blishen (Harmondsworth: Kestrel, 1975), 58–61

University of Bristol, 'Penguin Archive Project', University of Bristol, <http://www.bristol.ac.uk/penguinarchiveproject/> [accessed 20/12/09]

Warnock, Mary, 'Escape into Childhood', *New Society*, 13 May 1971, p. 823

Webb, Kaye, ed., *Puffin Post*, 1:1 (Spring 1967)

Westall, Robert, 'The Vacuum and the Myth' in *Teenage Reading*, ed. by Peter Kennerley (London: Ward Lock Educational, 1979), 35–42

Williams, Alec, 'Afterwords: An Interview With Aidan Chambers', *The School Librarian*, 54:4 (2006), 168

Williams, Gladys, *Children and Their Books* (London: Duckworth, 1970)

Wood, Anne, '"Books For Your Children" – the first ten years', *Children's Literature in Education*, 6:1 (1975), 31–8

Yates, Jessica, 'Censorship in children's paperbacks', *Children's Literature in Education*, 11:4 (December 1980), 180–91

Zipes, Jack, 'The Cultural Homogenization of American Children', in *Sticks and Stones: The Troublesome Success of Children's Literature From Slovenly Peter to Harry Potter* (London: Routledge, 2002), 1–23

Zipes, Jack, 'The Phenomenon of Harry Potter, or Why All the Talk?', in *Sticks and Stones: The Troublesome Success of Children's Literature From Slovenly Peter to Harry Potter* (London: Routledge, 2002), 170–89

Zipes, Jack, *Sticks and Stones: The Troublesome Success of Children's Literature From Slovenly Peter to Harry Potter* (London: Routledge, 2002)

Index

Abelard Schulman 23
adolescent literature, *see* teenage literature
Aiken, Joan 112
    on 'Filboid Studge' and issue novels 57
    Night Fall 129, 140
    The Whispering Mountain 57
Alderson, Brian 10, 24, 113
    'The Irrelevance of Children to the
        Children's Book Reviewer'69–70,
        153–4
Andre Deutsch, *see also* Philippa Pearce 16
Ariès, Philippe 24–5
Armada, *see* Collins, Armada
Ashley, Bernard
    All My Men 56
    A Kind of Wild Justice 56
    The Trouble with Donovan Croft 50, 56
Avery, Gillian
    on allegory 37–8
    on gender in children's books 46
    on 'mealy mouthed' children's books
        54
    on moral tales 41
    Nineteenth Century Children 27

Banks, Lynne Reid 64, 105
Bannerman, Helen
    Little Black Sambo 43, 48
Bawden, Nina 55, 57, 66, 136, 162
    Carrie's War 55, 66
    Squib 55
Beckman, Gunnel
    Admission to the Feast [*Nineteen is too*
        Young to Die] 136, 166
    Mia 66
Berg, Leila
    Nippers 13, 22, 53–4, 119, 177
    on representations of working-class
        children in children's literature 54–4
Binding, Paul, *see also* Oxford University
    Press 22

Blume, Judy 55–6, 60
    Are You There, God? It's Me, Margaret 55
    Blubber 55
    Forever 55, 62, 148, 165
    Then Again, Maybe I Won't 55
Blyton, Enid 21, 127–8, 139, 156–7
    criticisms of 67–8
    Kaye Webb's response to 91–2
Bodley Head, *see also* Clark, Margaret;
    Taylor, Judy 1, 75, 176, 177, 184
    Books for New Adults 60, 119, 134
Bologna Children's Books Fair 19
book ownership 4, 82, 124
Books for Your Children, see also Wood,
    Anne 23
Bookstart 116
Booktrust 175
    Booktrust Teenage Prize 175
Boston, Lucy M.
    The Children of Green Knowe 95–6
    A Stranger at Green Knowe 92
Bowlby, John 9, 25
Breinburg, Petronella 135–6, 163, 184
    My Brother Sean 140, 184
    Us Boys of Westcroft 140–41, 143, 183
    controversy over 146
    jacket design 135
Brockhampton Press, *see also* Anthony
    Kamm 3, 75, 184
    Knights 21
    Black Knights 21, 119, 134
Bullock Report (1962) 26, 46–7, 117

Cameron, Eleanor 32–3, 36, 93–4, 98–9
Carnegie Medal
    criticisms of 129, 158
    establishment of 1, 20, 24
    influence on Kaye Webb 92
    realism in 66–7
    representations of class in winners of 45,
        52, 54–5

representations of race in winners of 44
winners of
　The Edge of the Cloud 61, 65
　The Emperor's Winding-Sheet 66
　Josh 19, 66–7
　The Lantern Bearers 19
　The Machine Gunners 101
　The Moon in the Cloud 44
　Nordy Bank 42
　The Owl Service 38
　Postcards from No-Man's Land 121
　A Stranger at Green Knowe 44, 53
　A Time of Trial 61
　Tom's Midnight Garden 16, 33
　The Turbulent Term of Tyke Tiler 49
　The Twelve and the Genii 33
　Watership Down 87
　The Wool-pack 42
Carrington, Noel, *see also* Puffin 75, 78
Chambers, Aidan, *see also* Macmillan
　　　Education, Topliner
　bridging literature, belief in 127–8
　diversity, emphasis on 49, 140–45
　early career 121
　editorial ethos 119–20
　Eleanor Farjeon Award, receipt of 7
　Eleanor Graham, criticism of 129
　experiences as a young reader 123
　experiences as teacher-librarian 16,
　　　121–2, 125–6
　interdisciplinarity 121
　literature of recognition, advocacy of
　　　52, 135, 139
　literary critical approach 152–7
　literary reading, advocacy of 157–62
　literary works
　　Breaktime 64–5
　　Cycle Smash 122
　　Dance Sequence 157
　　Johnny Salter 122, 179
　　Postcards from No-Man's Land 121
　Macmillan Education, working
　　　relationship with 144–5
　opinions of 'controversial' material in
　　　books for teenagers 143–4
　Peacock Books
　　opinion of 108
　　proposal for 125–6
　popular literature, advocacy of 130–31

postwar generation, part of 133
public service role of publishers, belief
　　in 123–4, 152
quality literature, attitude towards 129
reading community, creation of 149–51
reader-response theory
'The Reader in the Book' 23, 152–7
realism, emphasis on 59–60
reluctant reader, interest in 128–32
The Reluctant Reader 59, 135, 153–7
Signal Review of Children's Books,
　　establishment of 27
significance of 2–3, 13
teenage literature, creation of 126–7, 132
teenage publishing
　advocacy of specialist 122–7, 144
transformative effects of literature,
　　belief in 157–62
Turton and Chambers, establishment
　　of 121
working-class background of 134, 139
Chambers, Nancy, *see also Signal Review
　　of Children's Books* 27
child-centred approach
　in childcare and education 31–2
　in children's literature 9, 33–4, 115,
　　　124, 130–32, 149–52, 173–4,
　in children's literature criticism 10–11,
　　　152–7
　criticism of 69–70
　in sociology and anthropology 25, 31
childhood
　anxiety about shortening of 9–10
　changing attitudes to 9–10, 50–51
　connection to fantasy and imagination
　　　30–35, 93, 99
　constructions of 29
　extension of 57–8
　post-war attitudes to 51–2
Children's Book Circle, *see also* Eleanor
　　　Farjeon Award 6–7, 177
Children's Book News, see also Chambers,
　　　Nancy 23–4
Children's Literature in Education (CLE) 26
children's publishing
　after 1979 7–8
　amateur status of 75–6, 79–80, 84–5
　commercial mentality of (1970s on)
　　　7–8, 173–4

cultural influence of 2, 6–7, 11, 74, 122–3
early 20th century 3, 73
economic decline, effects on 22, 115
expansion of 3–5, 20–22, 82–3, 85–6,
    117, 170–71
diversification of 5–6, 20–23, 119–20, 126
female-dominated nature of 75–7
golden age of 1, 3–7
hardback 22
ideology and 10–11
impact of libraries on 21–2
impact of World Wars on 3
international 19
in USA, *see also* USA 20–21
paperback 20–21, 81–2, 85–6, 124–5,
    170–76
public service ethos of 8–9, 74–5,
    115–17, 170–72
quality ethos of 8–9
scholarship on 2, 12–13
status of 80–81, 85–6
Children's Rights Workshop 49, 142
Children and Young Persons (Harmful
    Publications) Act (1955) 68
Chukovsky, Kornei 90, 97, 35
Clark, Charles, *see also* Penguin 116
Clark, Margaret, *see also* Bodley Head,
    Puffin 75, 77, 80, 90, 176, 185
Clarke, Pauline
The Twelve and the Genii 33–4, 40, 45, 95
class
    bias, criticisms of 48
    changing dynamics of 4, 47, 62
    literary representations of
        middle-class 8, 45, 113–14, 155, 164
        working-class 37–8, 51–6, 63–4,
            131, 138–40, 166, 175
Club 75, *see* Macmillan Education, Club 75
Collins
    Armada 21
    Armada Lions 22
    Fontana Lions 23. 60
Collins, William 85
comics
    attitudes towards 68
    Horror Comics Act *see* Children
        and Young Persons (Harmful
        Publications) Act (1955)
Constable, *see also* Grace Hogarth 3, 6, 176

Cooper, Susan 5
The Dark is Rising 19, 30, 36, 40, 95
Greenwitch 31
Over Sea, Under Stone 45
Silver on the Tree 41
Cormier, Robert 60–61
I Am the Cheese 66
Crompton, John 160
Up the Road and Back 138, 144, 147–8
Crouch, Marcus 24

Dahl, Roald 91–2
Charlie and the Chocolate Factory
    44, 48
unpublished chapter of 91–2
Darton, Harvey 24
depressive literature 65–7
Dhondy, Farrukh 145, 158, 163–4, 167, 184
East End At Your Feet 141–3
The Siege of Babylon 143, 160–61
Dickinson, Peter
The Blue Hawk 57
'A Defence of Rubbish' 68–70
The Weathermonger 40
didacticism in children's books 41–57
Dixon, Robert (Bob) 40, 47, 139

education
    extension of compulsory 17, 57
    investment in 177
    new trends in 182–3, 51–2, 126–7
    reforms of 4, 9
    professionalisation of (teacher training) 25
    secondary 57–9, 133
Education Act (1944) 4, 51, 133
education reports and legislation, *see*
    Education Act (1944); Bullock
    Report; Newsom Report; Plowden
    Report
educational publishing, *see also* Macmillan
    Education 182, 119–20
Eleanor Farjeon Award, *see also* Children's
    Book Circle
    Aidan Chambers, receipt of 7
    establishment of 6–7
    Kaye Webb, receipt of 7, 112–13
Exeter Conference (1969) 26, 68–9
Eyre, Frank *see also* Oxford University
    Press 1–2

fantasy
   connection to childhood 30–35, 94
   moral and educational value of 35–8, 41
   psychological functions of 37–40, 97
   realism in 39–40
   regressive aspects of 39–40
Federation of Children's Book Groups, *see
   also* Wood, Anne 6, 23
feminism, *see also* gender 47–8
Fontana Lions, *see* Collins, Fontana Lions

Gardam, Jane 64
   Bilgewater 106
Garner, Alan 5, 22, 30, 36, 90
   Elidor 51
   The Owl Service 37–8, 63–4, 70, 83,
      97, 104–5, 108, 112, 165, 183
   Red Shift 6, 63–5
   The Weirdstone of Brisingamen 51
gender, *see also* feminism 45–50
George, Mabel, *see also* Oxford University
   Press 5, 176–7
Getaways, *see* Nelson, Getaways
Godwin, Anthony (Tony), *see also* Penguin
   76, 78, 80
golden age of children's literature
   second
      egalitarian ethos of 170–71
      key characteristics of 7–10, 70–71,
         169–71
      legacy of 171–7
      social funding and investment in 2–4,
         10, 177
   third, claims for 7
Gollancz 165, 184
Grasshopper 23
Green, Roger Lancelyn 24, 27
Guardian Award 6, 24
   winners of
      The Blue Hawk 57
      Charmed Life 57
      The Owl Service 38
      Thunder and Lightnings 99
      The Vandal 66
      Watership Down 87

Hans Christian Andersen Award 18–19, 21
Hazard, Paul 18, 30–39, 68, 90, 93–8, 113,
   121, 156

Heinemann 122, 124, 179
   Pyramid Books 59, 162, 181
Hildick, Wallace 51–2
   Jim Starling 51
Hill, Janet 48, 67, 112, 140
historical fiction 42–3, 61, 95–6
Hodgkin, Marni, *see also* Macmillan 1, 20,
   75, 144, 161n, 176–7, 180
Hogarth, Grace *see also* Constable 3, 6, 20,
   75, 176
Hollindale, Peter 10–11, 24, 62
Honey magazine 128
Horn Book Magazine 20

ideology, *see also* class, gender, race 43–50
immigration 10, 47
implied reader, *see also* Aidan Chambers,
   reader response 154–7
International Board on Books for Young
   People (IBBY) 17–18
international children's literature 18–21
International Research Society for
   Children's Literature (IRSCL) 17

Jackie Magazine 128, 134, 138, 185
Jones, Diana Wynne 5, 40
   Charmed Life 57
   The Ogre Downstairs 56

Kamm, Josephine 122n
   Young Mother 41–2, 184
Kemp, Gene
   The Taming of Tyke Tiler 49, 54–5, 70
Kestrel 23, 75, 85, 99
King, Clive
   Stig of the Dump 86–7, 95
Knights, *see* Brockhampton Press, Knights
Knockouts, *see* Longman, Knockouts

Lane, Allen, *see also* Penguin 74–6, 78, 91,
   115–16, 123
Le Guin, Ursula 36, 45–6
   A Wizard of Earthsea 95, 95n, 97, 99
Leeson, Robert 52, 139, 170–71, 175
   The Third-Class Genie 50
Lewis, C.S. 30–31, 35, 40–41
   The Lion, the Witch and the Wardrobe
      31
   The Voyage of the Dawn Treader 31

Lewis, Naomi 24, 42–3
Libraries and librarianship
    investment in 2–4, 51, 70, 119, 177
    sales of children's books to 22
Lilliput magazine, *see also* Webb, Kaye 76,
    80, 84, 111
literary criticism on children's literature
    growth of 15, 23–4
    in newspapers 23–4
Lively, Penelope
    The Ghost of Thomas Kempe 35
    A Stitch in Time 34
Loeff, An Rutgers van der 55
    Avalanche! 19
    Children on the Oregon Trail 19
Longman, *see also* Hogarth, Grace 75
    Knockouts 165
Lourie, Helen, *see* Storr, Catherine
Lundgren, Max
    For the Love of Liza 160
    Summer Girl 140, 160

Macdonald, Jill, *see also* *Puffin Post*,
    Odway 112
Macmillan 1
    Macmillan Children's 180
    Macmillan Education 119
        Club 75 13, 121
        Nippers 13, 22, 53–4, 119, 177
        Rockets 121
        Topliner *see* Topliner
Maddock, Reginald 181
    The Pit 140
magazines, *see Honey* Magazine, *Jackie*
    magazine
Magnet Books, *see also* Jane Nissen 23
Mann, Andrew 49
Mark, Jan 5, 16
    Thunder and Lightnings 54, 99
Mayne, William 90, 127, 177
    Earthfasts 93
McGraw Hill Guidelines 49
Meek, Margaret 16
Methuen 23
Moss, Elaine 15, 22, 49, 52, 59, 62, 67,
    112, 159, 171, 177
myth, in children's books 36–7, 63–4

National Book League 66

Nelson
    Getaways 165
Newbery Medal 20, 92
Newsom Report (1963) 126, 180, 58–9
Nippers, *see* Berg, Leila; Macmillan,
    Macmillan Education, Nippers

Opie, Peter and Iona 25, 31
Other Award 6
    winners of
        East End at Your Feet 142
        The Trouble with Donovan Croft 50
        The Turbulent Term of Tyke Tiler 49
Oxford University Press, *see also* Binding,
    Paul; Eyre, Frank; George, Mabel
    5, 22, 176

Pan Piccolo 21
paperbacks, *see also* children's publishing,
    paperback; Puffin; Topliner
    in contemporary publishing 171–2
    market for 85–6
    paperback imprints 21–3
    paperback originals 124–5
Peacock Books, *see also* Chambers, Aidan;
    Puffin; Webb, Kaye
    adult reprints in 58, 103–4
    aims of 103
    bookish quality 106
    controversial content in 107–8
    criticisms of 105
    establishment of 82, 103–4
    problem of brand identity 105
    relaunch of 106
    specialist titles for adolescents in 104–5
Pearce, Philippa, *see also* Andre Deutsch 5,
    45, 90, 183
    editorial career 13
    Tom's Midnight Garden 33, 39–40
Penguin Books, *see also* Lane, Allen;
    Webb, Kaye; Puffin Books;
    Peacock Books
    hiring policy 76
    influence on Aidan Chambers 123–4
    public service ethos 74–5
    salaries at 80–81
Peyton, Kathleen (K.M.)
    The Edge of the Cloud 61
    Flambards 62

Piaget, Jean 32
Pick, Martin, *see also* Macmillan
    Education 141–2, 144
Picture Puffins, *see* Puffin, Picture Puffins
Plowden Report (1967) 32, 52–3
Porter, Sheena
    Nordy Bank 42, 45
post-war era
    attitudes to childhood 8–9, 30–31, 56–8
    impact of war 17–18
    political and social reforms 3–4
Puffin, *see also* Carrington, Noel; Clark,
        Margaret; Graham, Eleanor; Lane,
        Allen; Penguin Books; Peacock
        Books; Puffin Club; *Puffin Post*
    brand loyalty to 84, 108, 111
    commercial challenges to 85–6
    commercial success of 81–2
    early history 73
    expansion of 81–2
    fantasy in 93–7
    literary quality in 90–93
    morality and education in 90–91, 97–9
    Picture Puffins 82
    Puffin originals 86, 95
    Puffin Plus 109
    Puffin song ('There's Nuffin Like a
        Puffin') 84
    quality ethos 74–5
    realism in 99, 101–2
    reputation for quality 86–9
    reputation for safety 88–9
    status within Penguin 77–81
    Young Puffins 82
Puffin Club, *see also Puffin Post* 109–14
    as means of making children readers 109,
        111–13
    celebrity support of 84–5
    class demographic of 113–14
    community activities of 84–5, 109–11
    community ethos of 110–11
    launch of 83–4
    membership cost 114
    Puffin Exhibition 84
    Puffineers 84
    relaunch in 2009 174
    resistance from Penguin Directors to
        109–10
Puffin Plus, *see* Puffin, Puffin Plus

Puffin Post, see also Puffin Club; Webb, Kaye
    as means of promoting Puffin 84
    children's contributions to 112
    content of 111–12
    Odway in 112
Pyramid Books, *see* Heinemann, Pyramid
        Books

race, *see also* ideology 43–4, 136, 140–43,
        145–7, 175
Ray, Sheila 15, 58, 67
realism
    criticism of excessive 56–7, 66–7
    increase in children's books 52–6, 65–7
reluctant reader, *see also* Chambers, Aidan,
        reluctant reader 59–60
Rowling, J.K 171–3

Salinger, J.D.
    The Catcher in the Rye 60, 138
Sendak, Maurice
    Where the Wild Things Are 5, 177
Serailler, Ian
    The Silver Sword 83
Signal Review of Children's Books
    (*Signal*), *see also* Chambers,
        Aidan; Chambers, Nancy 27, 121
social realism, *see* realism
Southall, Ivan
    Josh 19, 65–7
Spock, Benjamin 9, 25, 32
Stones, Rosemary, *see also* Other Award
        49, 140
Storr, Catherine
    as Helen Lourie 35
    Marianne Dreams 37
Streatfeild, Noel 21, 76, 81
    Ballet Shoes 1
Sutcliff, Rosemary 21, 129
    Knight's Fee 43
    The Lantern Bearers 19–20
    Warrior Scarlet 43
    The Witch's Brat 43

Tandem Books 22–3
Tate, Joan, *see also* Topliner 122–4, 160,
        179–80
    Clipper 145
    Sam and Me 135, 138, 158–9

Taylor, Judy, *see also* Bodley Head 1, 3, 5, 176–7, 184
television
impact on childhood 9–10
influence on children's books 5–6, 83
Thwaite, Mary 18, 27, 43–4, 93, 98
Tolkien, J.R.R 30–31, 34, 95
The Hobbit 85
Topliner, *see also* Chambers, Aidan; Macmillan
competition for 165
class in 139–40
controversial material in 143–9
criticisms of 146–9, 162–5
distribution of 124
emphasis on teenage audience 134
establishment of 119–20, 122–3
ideological and political elements 160–62
influence of teenage magazines on 130–32, 134–5
influence on teenage publishing 166–7
jacket design 135
key themes and issues in 135–6
Macmillan influence over 144–5
original titles, commissioning of 124
Pan Piccolo, involvement of 124
paperback format of 124
race in 140–43, 160–61
realism in 143
sex and sexuality in 147–8
stylistic characteristics of 137–8
successes of 125, 138, 162–5
Topliner Redstars 125
Topliner Talkback 149
community focus of 149–51
educational aspects of 151–2
Topliner Trident 125
translations in 160–61
vernacular and non-standard English in 143
writers of colour in 140–43
Townsend, John Rowe 15–16, 24–5, 52, 67, 89, 121–2
Goodnight Prof, Love 107
Gumble's Yard 51, 54–5, 65, 99
translation, works in 18–19, 121, 159–60
Trease, Geoffrey 1, 15, 21, 24–5
Bows Against the Barons 43
Tucker, Nicholas 12, 27, 56, 66

Turton and Chambers, *see also* Aidan Chambers 121, 159

USA (United States of America)
children's literature in 20–21
specialist training for children's editors in 75

vertical publishing 23
Villiers, Linda 80

Walsh, Jill Paton 15
The Emperor's Winding Sheet 65
Unleaving 64
Webb, Kaye, *see also Lilliput* Magazine; Puffin; Puffin Club; *Puffin Post*; *Young Elizabethan*
appointment at Penguin 73, 75
appointment to Penguin Board of Directors 81
creation of new Puffin lists 82
early career 76–7, 80
editorial approach 89–94, 98–9
Eleanor Farjeon Award, receipt of 7, 112–13
expansion of Puffin 81
experience as magazine editor 76–7, 80
financial success 81–6
Lilliput magazine, experiences at 76, 80, 84, 111
marriage to Ronald Searle 84
paperback publishing, view on 81–2
pay negotiations 80–81
public service publishing, view on 115–17
realism in children's books, attitude to 100–103
recognition of popular appeal 86–7
reputation 87–9, 102
significance of 73–4
social connections 84–5
status at Puffin 77–81
talent for promotion and marketing 82
teenage literature, attitude to 103–4, 108
view of women in publishing 79–80
Young Elizabethan, experiences at 76, 111
Westall, Robert 63–4, 70, 177
The Machine Gunners 54, 63, 99, 101–12 .

Whitbread Literary Award 6
    winners of
        The Emperor's Winding Sheet 65
        A Stitch in Time 34
Williams, Gladys 24
Winnicott, Donald 9, 24–5
Wood, Anne 6, 23–4
Wood, Dorothy, *see also* Peacock Books,
    Puffin 78, 106

young adult literature, *see* teenage
    literature
Young Elizabethan, see also Webb, Kaye
    76, 111
Young Puffins, *see* Puffin, Young Puffins

Zindel, Paul 5, 60, 66–7, 133–4
    I Never Loved Your Mind 155
    My Darling, My Hamburger 56, 66